Radical Acts of Love

"As exploring outer space was a pressing need of our nation last century, then equally important today is our exploration of inner space. Susan Skog, in this most inspiring and important book, calls for a revolution of the heart, imploring us to wake up and reassess where we place our values and how we look for meaning in life."

—TIAN DAYTON, PH.D.
Author, *Heartwounds* and *The Quiet Voice of the Soul*

"Susan Skog identifies our technological society as a soulless one where people have lost their compassion. In her inspired book *Radical Acts of Love*, she has perceptively recognized many individuals who are making a difference. Through hundreds of stories of individual acts of kindness, Skog's book awakens us to our own potential to live in love and to help do our part to lift society to a higher, healthier, and more caring place."

—ALEXANDRA STODDARD
Best-selling author, *Living a Beautiful Life*

"Susan Skog has a marvelous ear for love. She knows it is the only rational act. Her book, if we are paying attention, is a survival course for the heart. She opens perception."

—STEPHEN LEVINE
Author, *A Year to Live, A Gradual Awakening,*
and *Meetings at the Edge*

Radical Acts of Love

How Compassion Is Transforming Our World

SUSAN SKOG

WITH A FOREWORD BY JOAN BORYSENKO

HAZELDEN®

INFORMATION & EDUCATIONAL SERVICES

Hazelden
Center City, Minnesota 55012-0176

1-800-328-0094
1-651-213-4590 (Fax)
www.hazelden.org

Library of Congress Cataloging-in-Publication Data
Skog, Susan, 1955-
    Radical acts of love : how compassion is transforming our world /
    Susan Skog.
        p. cm
    Includes bibliographical references.
    ISBN 1-56838-730-X
        1. Caring. 2. Love. I. Title

BJ1475.S58 2001
177'.7--dc21   2001016805

05 04 03 02 01   6 5 4 3 2 1

Interior design by Stanton Publication Services, Inc.
Typesetting by Tursso Companies

I dedicate this book to Jeffrey and Evan

Contents

Foreword by Joan Borysenko   ix
Acknowledgments   xi

Introduction   1
Chapter 1: A Return to Love: The Case for Compassion   15
Chapter 2: The Hardened Heart: Extinguishing the Fire   38
Chapter 3: Heart Monitor: Examining Your Fullness of Heart   50
Chapter 4: A Change of Heart: Seeing with Love   84
Chapter 5: Compassionate Conversation: Listening from
       the Heart   114
Chapter 6: The Heart Unleashed: Speaking from the Heart   135
Chapter 7: Home Is Where the Heart Is: Creating
       Sanctuaries with Love   167
Chapter 8: Softheartedness: Nourishing Compassion
       with Small Acts   187
Chapter 9: Compassion through Suffering: Allowing the
       Heart to Break Wide Open   199
Chapter 10: The Hungry Heart: Following Your
       Heart's Desires   219
Chapter 11: Heart Activism: Reinventing Institutions
       with Love   234
Chapter 12: Conclusion: A Vision of the New World   270

Notes   274
Interviews   283
Recommended Reading   284
Resources   286
About the Author   288

Foreword

The stories of compassion that you are about to read are stunning and heartening not because they are in any way extraordinary but because they are so very ordinary. Love and caring are so basic and simple that one might wonder why we need to be reminded of them at all. But as the Dalai Lama says, love is simple, but not easy. Susan Skog's intention for this book is to make loving easier. That is a great calling, and she does it beautifully through story, research, and meditation practices that will open your heart and remind you of all that you already know, but that is so easily forgotten in our complex, fast-paced world.

I know Susan both as a friend and as a colleague. Several years ago, she interviewed me for a book she was writing about women called *Embracing Our Essence*. I felt very humble to be included among luminaries like children's rights activist Marion Wright Edelman, and former first lady and recovery expert Betty Ford. A series of inspiring conferences that took place around the country grew out of the book and gave Susan and me, as well as hundreds of women who attended, the precious opportunity to become friends.

Like many working mothers, Susan has had to balance the demands of her career as a journalist with caring for her two children. That is a challenge that is neither simple nor easy. In chapter 7, Susan tells the story about the time when Mother Teresa told a group of affluent Indian women on fire with the desire to serve, "You go home. This is where compassion comes from. You look into your husband's eyes. You look into your family's eyes." How easy it is to set our sights on becoming Mother Teresa, while ignoring the needs of our own families. I know, because I've done it more times than I'd like to admit. So, with the deadline for this book looming, Susan was put to the Mother Teresa test. One of her children got strep throat, and she had to forsake the computer for the bedside. There was no contest. Her child came first. It is Susan's own ability to choose for compassion, and to live her own message, that gives this book its authentic power.

While most people would agree that love is the most important thing in life, it is not always easy to love. When we are crazy busy, the watchword of the day, we are often unavailable to the little acts of giving and receiving that nourish our spirits. As my dear friend, the wise and compassionate author Wayne Muller, puts it, "We end up doing good badly." When we are too busy to take care of ourselves, our hearts harden, and we participate in a subtle kind of violence that is dangerous because it is so socially prized. To be busy is to be important. People tacitly understand that we have too much else on our plate to care for them. Little by little, we end up isolated and depressed. This book is a call to connection, a plea to use our common sense to return to happiness and joy.

Even the simple pleasures of life, like eating dinner with our families, are beginning to vanish in a world gone mad with want and worry. Yet in the many years I spent working with people facing life-challenging illnesses, they spoke of the simple pleasures as being most poignantly and vibrantly real. To listen with minute attention and to be heard deeply. To touch with care and to be held with love. To notice the dew on the grass and the smell of the earth and to reflect these miracles back to the Universe with a grateful heart. To give something back to the family of humankind. These are the things that give life meaning. The paradox is that these heart delights are available to us every day, but too often we take them for granted until time runs out. And as the research shows, when our hearts are closed in anger and hostility, time runs out even faster.

The most exceptional people I know are the ones who stay awake to the blessings of the human heart and, whatever their spiritual outlook may be, practice it as kindness. Like Susan, I think of these people as radical lovers. I trust that they will be there for me, and my most joyful and real spiritual practice is to be there for them. These are heroes of the heart. A therapist friend of mine, Wayne Sotile, defines a hero as a person who creates safe spaces. They are like a plowed field in which we can grow into the fullness of our gifts. To be a field of possibility is a kind of grace and a gift of its own. That is the function of compassion and love. It is the way that we co-create with the divine, and it is what this book is all about.

JOAN BORYSENKO, PH.D.

Acknowledgments

First I express my affection and gratitude to Joan Borysenko for believing in the vision of this book and supporting it with her lovely, powerful words. Stephen Levine, who believes love is the "only rational act of a lifetime," greatly supported this project, and I am grateful. I extend my warmest praise to my editor Karen Chernyaev for her editorial brilliance and personal inspiration during deep deadline days. I'm grateful to editor Kate Kjorlien for ushering the final manuscript home. To Karin Nord, Connie Carlson, M. K. Everts, Vickie Johnson, Joe Riley, and other members of the promotion team, I thank you for your wonderful efforts in elevating the message of this book. Much love to the many inspiring heart activists who took the time and energy to share their experiences for this book. Their energy and vision brought great strength to this project. I also want Annica Daum to know that this book couldn't have been done without her support of our family. Finally, my deepest love and thanks to my husband, Jim, and sons, Jeffrey and Evan, whose loyal support, devotion, enthusiasm, and willingness to eat frozen foods made this book gloriously possible.

Introduction

There is a fracture, a raw and painful fissure that runs through the heart of
each one of us. From our hospitals to our schools, our homes to our boardrooms, we have created a culture lacking in much-needed compassion,
decency, and tenderness. Despite great economic affluence, we suffer from a
form of emotional poverty. And this world we have created, this emotionally impoverished society, is breaking our hearts.

It should be no surprise to any of us that heart disease is the leading
killer in our country. No shock that depression is epidemic. Our physical
health increasingly reflects the pain we share on a spiritual level. I believe
our hearts and spirits literally ache from denying our humanity. They weep
at how disconnected we've become from one another and from the earth.
They mourn the absence of compassion throughout much of our culture.

How can we not be wounded by how we worship technology, material
stuff, science, speed, violence, our intellects and egos—when we long at
some deep, instinctive level to worship our connections as people? We've
become numbed to so many things we once knew in our hearts to be true.

If we suppress our hearts' innate impulses, how can we not be in trouble emotionally and spiritually? We can't help but feel heartsick about our disconnection from one another and the natural world. "The real epidemic in America isn't physical heart disease," says heart pioneer Dr. Dean Ornish in his book *Love and Survival.* "It's spiritual heart disease: loneliness and isolation."

A good deal of modern American culture "is an extended experiment in the effects of depriving people of what they crave most," say Drs. Thomas Lewis, Fari Amini, and Richard Lannon, authors of the groundbreaking book *A General Theory of Love.*

DEPRIVED OF COMPASSION

In many instances in our society, whether in how we try to heal patients or how we avoid healing prison inmates, we have systemically, intentionally, or unconsciously deprived ourselves of the love and compassion we need to live well. The root word of *compassion* comes from the words *cum patior,* meaning "to suffer with," "to undergo with," "to stand in solidarity with." Compassion means we care about others so deeply that we take responsibility for, and do everything in our power to ease, their suffering. Compassion is not a feeling of pity, superiority, or judgment. It's a feeling of togetherness and kinship with all life. It's knowing deep in our souls that whatever happens to one of us affects us all.

Although this sense of a common good is sorely needed throughout our culture, consider how many of our protocols and mores encourage and sanction our distance from one another. Think about how often our policies are designed with good intent, but end up suffocating our greater intentions to care for and protect one another.

About three years ago I heard the story of a preschooler in my Colorado town who wandered far from home early one morning. He followed his new dog out the door, and just kept walking. And then he vanished. As his frantic parents searched, his two sisters reluctantly got on the bus for school. Suddenly, blocks from home, the bus rolled past the little boy. "That's our brother!" the girls screamed at the bus driver. "You've got to stop! He's been lost! He can't be here. He's too little!"[1]

But the driver didn't stop—didn't feel she could stop, for some reason. She listened to her head, hardened her heart, and drove on. The little boy was missing for more than an hour. His parents later discovered he'd crossed several of the busiest streets in town before the police finally found him.

This story is one of legions that show how our seemingly logical, efficient-at-all-costs thinking, as well as policies, can become heartless in their execution. In 1998, a fifteen-year-old boy lay bleeding to death on the steps of a Chicago hospital. An institutional policy forbade emergency room personnel from going outside to help victims, so Christopher Sercye, who had been shot while playing basketball at a nearby playground, lay bleeding for twenty-five minutes as friends, neighbors, and police pleaded for help. A police officer finally brought Sercye into the hospital but he died about an hour later. A bullet had perforated his aorta.[2]

We've blindly accepted that the values of logic and swift efficiency would sustain and strengthen us. We've allowed these lesser values to blur and dehumanize our lives so much that we often barely skim the surface of our days. We need to value something of greater meaning and sustenance—and heart—to live well. It's hard to fully live out of our hearts—even with our own children—when so much of our culture is designed to keep compassion taboo.

Compassion can be "our world's richest energy source," argues Matthew Fox in *A Spirituality Named Compassion*. But we're not tapping or mining our most natural of resources. We've largely exiled it out of ignorance, forgetfulness, at times, repression, and at times because of "a conscious effort to distort it, control it, and keep it down," says Fox.

LOVE IS ESSENTIAL TO OUR SURVIVAL

And in exiling compassion, we are losing our capacity to be fully human. We've been so obsessed with creating a more prosperous, savvy world, we've bankrupted our emotional one. We can't touch or be touched by someone's heart if we're living only in our brains.

We've lost sight of something essential to our survival that our ancestors once treasured, say Gary E. R. Schwartz and Linda G. S. Russek in the foreword to *The Heart's Code: Tapping the Wisdom and Power of Our Heart Energy*: "Our ancestors knew that the heart had energy—a powerful energy—and that it conveyed deep wisdom. However, as the human species developed its brain, it began to lose sight of its heart. At this point in history as we venture into space, create global communications, and invent all sorts of technological tools and toys, we are poised to destroy ourselves, our children, and everything around us. Have we simply lost our minds, or have we lost something deeper? Have we lost our hearts?"

How connected are you to your heart? To what extent are you tapping your natural compassion? Is your heart suspended, lost in some freeze-dried holding pattern? Many people are finding their hearts are simply exhausted, along with the rest of their being, from work-in-overdrive days and technology hangovers at night. And our lifestyles have led to intense loneliness and isolation, especially for our children.

Internet chat rooms and e-mail are wonderful ways to communicate with people. But they will never have the depth and emotional potency you can have in person, seeing the flash of affection fill someone's eyes, seeing a slash of pain, or tears sliding down their cheeks. It's dangerously easy to go through life now without ever experiencing a real connection with a real person.

MACHINES ARE NO SUBSTITUTE FOR AFFECTION

Millions of kids now seek solace in machines. We're losing them, like phantom children, as they wrap their psyches around, and try to find comfort in, the phosphorescent glow of the computer screen.

A Colorado psychiatrist recently treated Erik, a teenager. At first his doctor wasn't overly concerned: Erik was full of stories about the times he spent with his mother, father, and siblings. But the stories were hollow, deceptive, troubling. Erik's "family" existed only on-line. "He described his cyber mother, his cyber father, cyber siblings, and a cyber girlfriend. He said he often spent fourteen hours a day chatting with his cyber family," said his psychiatrist. "But this constructed world wasn't that gratifying or satisfying. It was no substitute for the emotional comfort he needed from family and friends."[3]

Many of our choices, our priorities, and our philosophies have created this emotional poverty. In our schools, we've been obsessed about investing in smart kids, kids who are brilliant at math, debate, and reading so they can swell the ranks of future productive workers. It's wonderful to unleash a child's brain, but why are we not equally obsessed with unleashing their hearts? Why don't we reach their hearts as much as their minds?

Kids can be taught empathy along with algebra, compassion along with computing. Who's doing this job now? Do we care to do this job? How many heart-smart kids are we nurturing?

"It seems as if there is no particular institution that has special responsibility for taking care of the heart," the Dalai Lama observes in *Transforming the Mind*. "An education system that cultivates smart brains alone can sometimes create more problems."

We've tragically become a people who worship our intellects and our outer achievements at the expense of a real, emotional connection with other human beings. We've molded ourselves into something radically alien to our true natures. And the mold is a harsh fit. It has mutilated our hearts in the process. According to Drs. Lewis, Amini, and Lannon, in *A General Theory of Love*, "Having allied itself with the neocortical brain, our culture promotes analysis over intuition, logic above feeling. Cognition can yield riches, and human intellect has made our lives easier in ways that range from indoor plumbing to the Internet. But even as it reaps the benefits of reason, modern America plows emotions under—a costly practice that obstructs happiness and misleads people about the nature and significance of their lives."

We can't keep obstructing our own happiness—and many would say, endanger our own survival. We can't keep falling back on the rationalizations we make for closing our hearts. The illusion that our minds are more powerful than our compassion and generosity has to be shattered. We need to see the full power of being in loving solidarity with one another. We need to come home to our hearts. We can let a deeper, higher, more enduring wisdom of the heart point the way. Kindness and tenderness are the wisest approaches of all, and once we begin to live from that mind-set, we will truly achieve intellectual greatness.

COMPASSION LIBERATES THE HEART

We're suffering an epidemic of mental illness, partially because we're not being loved well or not loving well; we can't allow this epidemic to continue. We become sad, dispirited, self-centered, and heavy-hearted when love is sidelined. "It is compassion that removes the heavy bar, opens the door to freedom, makes the narrow heart as wide as the world. Compassion takes away from the heart the inert weight, the paralyzing heaviness; it gives wings to those who cling to the lowlands of the self," says Nyanaponika Thera.[4]

We also must dismantle the idea that we are separate, unconnected to others and their suffering. Thankfully, gloriously, this idea is unraveling. "The walls we're building around ourselves, around those closest to us, and ultimately around our hearts may provide a temporary feeling of security. But they can't prevent the world from affecting us," says Paul Rogat Loeb in *Soul of a Citizen*.

In this sense of union—many say sparked by our unity on the Internet—we are seeing again how connected we are in the web of life. It is here, in a renewed sense that our current culture is too damaging for our human souls, that many people are being moved to take great heart, to throw open wide the heart of the world, so something new can be born in our schools, hospitals, corporations, and other institutions.

This book is about that rapidly spreading grassroots movement of visionary, heart-centered people who fully recognize that, in many ways, our heart-starved society no longer serves us. Compassion needs to be seen as an appropriate cornerstone of our operating rooms, classrooms, meeting rooms, and legislative halls.

Throughout history, forces have risen that were so powerful they overturned and transformed every pocket of our culture. When the printing press and the height of the Renaissance simultaneously surfaced in the 1400s, both forces radically brought new light and energy to our evolution and helped turn the tide away from the heavy, oppressive energy of the Middle Ages. I think such a force is gloriously under way, as do the heart activists who share their stories in this book.

THE AWAKENING HAS BEGUN

We are awakening. As prophet Joan Borysenko saw in the early 1990s and wrote in her book *A Woman's Book of Life*, "We are awakening to a recognition of the sacred in daily life, a deep gratitude for the wonders of the world and the delicate web of interconnectedness between people, nature, and things. We are awakening to a recognition that true intimacy based on respect and love is the measure of a life well lived."

We are awakening to and, in many cases, joining what is perhaps the most sweeping movement of our time. We are birthing a new world in which our culture's toughest, most searing issues will be transformed with more humane, compassionate strategies and programs. We are ushering in a new culture in which our thorniest social, economic, and environmental problems will be solved through nonviolent, nonexploitive, cooperative choices that better serve us all. In this new world rapidly unfolding around us, many people are choosing ecology over enterprise, peace over retribution, and simple kindness and empathy over detachment.

These heart-first people—I call them heart activists—are pouring much-needed light and love into our world. They know that unconditional love is ultimately more powerful, more healing, more pragmatic, and more rational than our greatest technologies and scientific breakthroughs. "Love is the only rational act of a lifetime," heart activist Stephen Levine reminds us.[5]

This revolution of the heart is creating nothing short of a seismic, dramatic shifting in the underpinnings of our society. "Deep down, the tectonic plates that have supported the modern world are shifting. Revolutions are daily occurrences; the centers of power are moving. . . . World views are changing overnight," says author Sam Keen in *Fire in the Belly*.

As this sea change unfolds, I wanted to capture the nature and impact of this new movement. I wanted to inspire us to tap our own heart wisdom through the stories of heart activists relying on love as healer. And I wanted to hear from those who are on the front line, working within existing groups and communities, elevating our society, organization by organization, to its true magnificence.

You are likely one of them, which is why you were drawn to this book. You know of your kindred spirits in your community. You see them in action and in loving force all around you, because it's hard to find an institution, whether medicine or our prisons, not touched by compassionate visions. We're all models for one another in this heart-first movement.

HEART ACTIVISTS POINT THE WAY

To celebrate and amplify this revolution and show us all how we do this work of the heart, I gathered stories and examples from more than seventy-five heart activists in this book. They come from embassies, software companies, prisons, surgical tables, principal's offices, inner-city parks, churches, addiction treatment centers, radio shows, war zones, funeral homes, our homes—and so many other places where love is at work.

These compassionate people range from emergency room doctors to home-based mothers, who are deep into shaping a new world, based on spiritual values. Like people who used to gather at the well to advance new ideas, these heart activists are gathering a critical mass of like-hearted people and sounding the wake-up call through their actions, examples, Web sites, retreat centers, media columns. They are speaking out on behalf of our hearts through their books, television broadcasts, eulogies, town hall meetings, and the all-powerful Oz of word-of-mouth magic to fuel this revolution of the heart.

They are people like Dr. Sidney J. Winawer, one of the world's leading cancer specialists. Sadly, all his skills and dedication as a healer couldn't reverse his wife's grim prognosis when she was diagnosed with stomach cancer. After his wife, Andrea, died, he wrote the achingly beautiful *Healing Lessons*. This book is a testament to the strength of love—and of his own transformation. Even though he'd treated thousands of patients, when his wife went through treatment, he saw with new eyes both the strengths and weaknesses of our modern medical system.

During his amazing journey, Dr. Winawer discovered something we all can rediscover: "Without love there is nothing. Love for another, love for the present, for the moment, love for ourselves and our mission. The experience of love is forever. For Andrea and me, it was a feeling that came from a place of existence that is timeless. It is a feeling that will go on timelessly forever, no matter what physical and spiritual state we are in. We can only journey to other realms of existence from a place of knowing who we are and with love for each other. With love, we can never be separated."

And that is the hope and intention of this book: to stand as a testament to the power of love, to show that with compassion and love, we can come together and never be separated. We can stop suffering in ways we were never meant to. We can all commit radical acts of love and better open and live from our hearts. We, too, can become the heart activists we are meant to be.

We each can find the heart sustenance we need to fall back in love with—to adore enough to protect—the environment, the elderly, people with mental illness, or any living thing most in need of compassion. If we know we aren't alone in this heart work, that something unprecedented is building, we can connect with that contagious energy. We can go down into our hearts, call forth our own higher love, and fuel this revolution of compassion until nothing is left untouched by its alchemy.

TAKING COMPASSION TO THE STREETS

We've had lots of talk and summits, virtual and otherwise, about the power of unconditional love and spirit. It's time to push back from the table and move those conversations into the trenches, into the grassroots, into our lives. It's time to go far beyond the easy love-for-all sentiments into the harder, but so much more rewarding, compassionate work of re-creating our lives with care and concern. We need to return to love, do the bidding of our hearts, wherever we are, and become who we're meant to be.

For as much as we've tried to deny it, the powerful truth is this: From cradle to grave, our desire to love one another is still the fiercest, most unrelenting instinct of all. "It is our true nature to have an open heart, as much as it is the true nature of a flower to open in the sunlight," write Richard Carlson and Benjamin Shield in *Handbook for the Heart*.

Throughout the ages, compassion has been seen as a fire that burns away injustice and hatred, a flame that purifies and delivers us to our highest selves. We all can rekindle this radical fire in our own lives. We can align with our true natures. For at least a century, we've developed and focused on our intellectual savvy, on our cerebral brilliance—and now it's time to master our compassion if we're ever to find peace personally and as a culture. It's time to cultivate heart intelligence, or the skills involved in sensing our heart's desires; understanding and managing our feelings; showing appropriate empathy, caring, tenderness, and support for others. Heart intelligence, heeding our hearts' innate drive to connect deeply with others, is critical to becoming competent, compassionate human beings.

We can do this. We were born to do this. Compassion is a divine skill that can be learned. If we were able to master the immense skills it takes to live in the information age, we can learn the language of the heart. But we have to exert the same will, sacred intention, and choices that we did to become electron-savvy people.

We have to embrace this shift, which is swelling overnight, shifting the cultural zeitgeist, and creating epic change from our kindergartens to the

White House. We have to decide that we, not "somebody else," can be the ones to bring new hope to seemingly hopeless situations in our hospitals, lifeless workplaces, death rows, troubled schools, violent homes—or in our own conflicted, uneasy souls.

If we take the messages of this book to heart, and model the heart activists whose stories are told here, we will all become full-hearted, responsive people who fiercely create more enlightened communities that better respond to the needs of all. Isn't this what we want, after all?

In our cynical, jaded times, it's easy to dismiss compassion as weak, to see tenderness as foolish, out of touch. It's easy to be jaded and ridicule someone who "wears his heart on his sleeve." It's easy to dismiss kind words as homely homilies, sentimental slop. And, as we've learned all too well, it's easier to become more "civilized," wrestle down our wild, passionate hearts and surrender them to the will of the dispassionate intellect.

HOPE FOR HUMANITY IS FOUND IN OUR HEARTS

But it's far harder and nobler to live from the heart. To awaken from our long sleep and be startled into the recognition that compassion is a force, an energy, an alchemy that is poised to transform life as we know it. It is one of the most hopeful, positive harbingers of this new century.

"The love in our hearts, when embraced, when extended, has the miraculous power to change the course of events," said Marianne Williamson, at a Whole Life Expo conference in Denver, Colorado, in April 1999. Her talk took place the weekend following the Columbine High School shootings, the worst school shooting in U.S. history, which claimed a teacher and fourteen students, including the two gunmen.

As Columbine illustrated, we need more loving, radically compassionate, nonviolent acts to change the course of events in our schools. Teachers and principals know well the potency of love. This lesson is not lost on them. They see and model every day the difference it can make.

Lloyd Estates Elementary School is in a working-class neighborhood in southern Florida. The majority of its students live in poverty. Many also live amid violence. In 1995, two children were kidnapped on the way to school and later strangled.

Working in an environment with such stark circumstances, teachers at

Lloyd Estates—and all over the country—measure their success not only by how well their kids learn to spell and add, but also by how well they love and take care of one another. Many times, they and all of our teachers have to show kids lessons that their parents often aren't teaching: how to behave like human beings, how to share, how to care for others, how to stop calling names that hurt. How to wash your hands, avoid strangers, stay safe.

As Williamson says, love changes the course of events in these school situations. Ultimately, it is "the powers of the soul—that will heal our hearts and save the world," she says in *The Healing of America*.

When former Lloyd Estates teacher Beverly Bono heard about a fourth-grade boy who cursed at teachers and had missed about fifty school days each year since kindergarten, she responded with compassion. This act was not unusual for Bono; she ran the after-school program and took many kids under her wing. She took them to their first ball game or first movie. She helped them learn to dress themselves or prepare soup out of a can. "Many of these kids are on their own and all they have is the school. . . . School is their life. . . . This is where they play games and learn to get hugs. We have to be everything to these kids. We have to be the mommy and the daddy and social worker and nurse and teacher," she said in a *South Florida Sun-Sentinel* article.

And sometimes Bono had to be their advocate. She discovered that the recalcitrant fourth-grader lived with his mother, an alcoholic and an addict who didn't care much whether he went to school. He was known to neighborhood boys as "Six Pack" because they'd get him to sneak them his mother's beer and cigarettes when she was incoherent.

Bono appealed to the boy's grandmother to take him in. Soon, he started coming to school regularly. He seemed to really like school. He stayed as late as 6 P.M. on many evenings in Bono's after-school program. What went on there to shift this kid?

"Cuz, I got this teacher, and I love her at school," he said, trying to wrap his freckled arms around Bono's sizable shoulders. "I don't care if I'm forty minutes late or three hours late. I'm comin' to school."[6]

COMPASSION REQUIRES DEEP STRENGTH

In the midst of our often dehumanized culture, compassion is anything but weak. It calls forth the ultimate courage. In French, the word *courage* means "to be of heart." True compassion requires "the strength of a warrior," says Buddhist monk Punnadhammo Bhikkhu.[7]

"Compassion is the strength that arises out of seeing the true nature of suffering in the world," writes author Sharon Salzberg in *Heart as Wide as the World*. "Compassion allows us to bear witness to that suffering, whether it is in others, or ourselves without fear; it allows us to name injustice without hesitation, and to act strongly, with all the skill at our disposal. To develop this mind state of compassion . . . is to learn to live, as the Buddha put it, with sympathy for all living beings, without exception."

Those you'll meet in this book inspire us all to become warriors of the heart, to become courageous enough to shatter old, ignorant, misguided beliefs that acting from the heart is weak or inappropriate. To the contrary, it is the most powerful stance of all. Returning to a more tender, heart-inspired place is one of the wisest, most pragmatic, sacred ways we can walk in the world. Many, many people these days are rediscovering the power of the heart. "Love, it turns out, may be one of the most powerful physical forces in the universe," writes Diane Goldner, author of *Infinite Grace: Where the Worlds of Science and Spiritual Healing Meet*.

That the heart holds a greater intelligence the mind can only begin to grasp is now surfacing more and more in popular opinion and books. This revelation is also being heard in the words of seasoned scientists, such as Drs. Lewis, Amini, and Lannon, who practice at the University of California–San Francisco School of Medicine.

Their conclusions? "Where intellect and emotion clash, the heart often has the greater wisdom. . . . The brain's ancient emotional architecture is not a bothersome animal encumbrance. Instead, it is nothing less than the key to our lives. As individuals and as a culture, our chance for happiness depends on our ability to decipher a hidden world that revolves—invisibly, improbably, inexorably—around love."

I think we are all ready to shine a blinding, revealing light on this hidden world. We know that of all the muscles in the body, the heart has the most strength and stamina. Its magnetic field is five thousand times greater than that of our brains. That's no accident.

Our hearts are powerful for a reason. They have powerful work to do, explosive joys to be felt, sorrows to bear, and deep empathy to hold. "And we are put on earth a little space that we might learn to bear the beams of love," writes the poet William Blake in *The Songs of Innocence*.

May we learn to bear those beams of love. Our hearts aren't merely mechanical pumps that push out our blood. They can bear a lot of love. They innately hold a wisdom, an instinct, a force, a compulsion to commit radical acts of love that are key to our survival. If love loved us into existence, as Saint Augustine once said, what can it not do in our culture?

Love can deliver us to our brilliance. Love can elevate us and join us and heal us in ways our minds can scarcely imagine, much less begin to analyze and rationalize. It's time to wed our tough minds with tender hearts, as Martin Luther King Jr. wisely predicted.

"When the mind sinks into the heart, and vice versa, there is healing," Levine told me in our interview. And when we heal on this deeper, more enduring level, we will radically impact the heart of the world. We will come into godly communion with one another.

It's time to seek and enjoy that sense of union, to fall in love once again with the soulfulness of one another. I believe at this time in our evolution, we are all anxious to ignite our individual lives and our institutions, policies, and practices with greater hope and humanity. There is a preciousness about life that we've lost and desperately need to recapture. We cannot spend hours living in our brains, tied to technology, mortgages, deadlines, and schedules—and ignore our hearts' cry to be connected to flesh, bone, soil, grass, and the joy of loving one another and the earth.

No matter how sophisticated or technological we become this truth never changes. No matter how old or wise or World-Wide-Web-connected we become, we never lose our deep, basic need to connect with skin, water, bark, dirt—and the soulfulness of one another's hearts. It is time we follow the lead of people who are igniting the world by leading with love, to become people who shower everyday life with unconditional love and grace. It's time to plead the case for compassion.

"Do you recall from your childhood on, how very much this life of yours has longed for greatness?" wrote the poet Rainer Maria Rilke. The greatness we seek is within us aching to be discovered. The greatness we so long to express is our own love of self and our great love of others, of life. "The work of the eyes is done, now go do heart work," Rilke urged his students in his poem "Turning Point."

We've done our head work; now let's address our heart work. Let's commit ourselves to radical acts of love.

I

A Return to Love:
The Case for Compassion

WHEN WRITER PARKER PALMER WAS SUFFERING FROM DEPRESSION, many well-intentioned friends came to visit. They desperately wanted to rescue him, to "fix" his depression with their advice and encouragement, as I described in my book *Depression: What Your Body's Trying to Tell You*. His friends so wanted to will him well. And then came another friend.

"Every afternoon around five o'clock, he came to me, sat me in a chair, removed my shoes, and massaged my feet. He hardly said a word, but he was there, he was with me. He was a lifeline for me, a link to the human community and thus to my own humanity. He had no need to 'fix me.' He knew the meaning of compassion."

Susan was walking with her sister and her sister's ten-month-old son, Carson, through the Albuquerque airline terminal to catch a Southwest Airlines flight to San Diego. And a travel horror story unfolded. Carson was holding his bottle of formula—his in-flight meal—and dropped it. The two sisters watched in horror as his dinner spilled all over the terminal floor. How could the baby endure the flight on an empty stomach? How could they? Fortunately, someone with a full heart had witnessed the scene.

A Southwest Airlines employee came from behind the counter and offered to run to a nearby store for a replacement bottle. Thirty minutes later he returned with a brand-new bottle and nipple. He wouldn't accept any payment. To him it was no big deal; he had just gotten off his shift. For Susan, and her sister, his actions were "extraordinary kindness." From Susan's perspective, "The day and trip were saved for my sister and her baby."[1]

When Nachson Wachsman was captured by Palestinian terrorists, his family was violently thrown into the crisis now erupting all over the Middle East. A botched rescue attempt startled the terrorists who held Nachson, and they responded by shooting and killing the young man.

Nachson's father, Yehuda, was still mourning the loss of his son when the father of the man who shot Nachson called him. His son's action had convinced him that enough blood had been shed between Israeli Jews and Palestinians. Wachsman agreed, and the two men arranged to meet in Jerusalem.

"From that moment on, the father of a son killed in conflict and the father of the killer joined together to work for peace and tolerance in Israel," reported an article in *Yes: A Journal of Positive Futures*. Now, over and over, they repeat their story of coming together to promote peace through the Compassionate Listening Project. The project brings together Arab and Israeli families to share their stories, to relate their suffering, to try to find sacred, common ground.

"Through the hard work of meeting one's enemy and coming to know the human being behind the stereotype . . . of acknowledging the suffering in each other's hearts, peace walks hand-in-hand with reconciliation, forgiveness, and healing," says Leah Green, a delegation leader for the Compassionate Listening Project.[2]

COMPASSION AS A HEALING FORCE

As these three examples show, compassion is a powerful, healing force. It is the only viable way we can fully come together as people and as a world. But it won't be easy. It requires a kind of attachment, not distance. It requires the kind of attachment that causes us to keep our hearts open even when it's terrifying, even when our first impulse may be to run as fast as we can in the opposite direction.

It will be difficult, because it will require that we stay right where we are, that we stay grounded in the reality around us, that we love close-up—not at a safe distance. Living compassionately will lead us to make a pact with peace in our own hearts, inviting peace to live in us before we go to our enemies. It will be tough, but we can never be at peace in our own homes, in our daily walk, or in fractious areas like the Middle East unless we stop disassociating and running from one another. We can never be at peace until we so fully embrace and harness compassion in our own hearts that the communion we long for can begin.

We won't be able to heal the heart of humanity until we align with the power of love and see it as the most magnificent force for true healing and change. When love, not logic, becomes the rationale for how we design our programs and problem-solving, we will show our full capacity for being human.

What if we recruited and supported politicians for their strength of compassion, for their brave hearts? What a radical shift, said Swanee Hunt, former ambassador to Austria, who helped broker peace in Kosovo. And what a rational idea because "policy makers without compassion are very limited in their ability to devise the best policies, because they don't have the intuitive connection to inform their thinking, the emotional information to inform the rational," Hunt said when we spoke for this book.

LOVE AS THE ULTIMATE HEALER

Again, we need to see that acting from the heart is not a stance of weakness, but a position of the ultimate strength and wisdom. In life, we all stumble on those moments when it is gut-wrenchingly evident that love is the consummate healer and most rational choice, when it is so obvious that no words or logical arguments will touch or reach someone. At these times, a radical act of love is the only possible, glorious way.

Eight years ago Ruthanne Kastner endured breast cancer surgery. Several mornings after her surgery, she and a friend and a couple of nurses were packing up her gifts and flowers to go home. They were making silly jokes and celebrating her homecoming. "It was truly amazing the love that surrounded me those two days in the hospital," Kastner remembers. At one point, something caught her eye, and she turned toward the door.

Her surgeon, Dr. George Tutt, was standing in the doorway in full baseball uniform. It turned out he'd left his practice and his over-forties team to check up on Kastner's pathology report. Even though it wasn't due until the next day, he was anxious to get the results.

"He stood there, smiling from ear to ear, watching four silly women celebrate, and so I said, 'Come on in, George,' which is what he wanted his patients to call him. And he shuffled in and proudly announced, 'No nodes!'

"I didn't understand what he was saying, so I asked what he had just said. Dr. Tutt repeated, 'No nodes!'"

And then Kastner understood. The breast cancer had been isolated in one breast and had not spread to her lymph nodes—the best possible result!

"I started crying, my friend started crying, the nurses were cheering and clapping. The four of us were hugging and giving each other high fives. We were lost in our celebration. Dr. Tutt plopped himself down in a chair and was just smiling and laughing with joy. He came over and hugged me as tears rolled down my cheek.

"Remembering those moments still brings tears of joy to my eyes and warmth to my heart. . . . Dr. Tutt is truly a doctor with a heart. I will never forget how he sat in a baseball uniform smiling in my hospital room as we celebrated cancer-free results. Because of George Tutt, every year for five years, I celebrated a second birthday with many friends on May 8, my surgery day—the day Dr. Tutt brought his skill and compassion into a surgery room and removed my cancer, giving me a second chance at living my life with more joy and abundance than I knew was possible."

HEALTHY HEARTS / HEALTHY BODIES

Love is the truest healer—and not just in our hospital rooms. Organizations like HeartMath Institute in California are now vaulting scientific frontiers to scientifically document that radical acts of love may rival—even surpass—the brain in their significance and impact on our health. HeartMath has shown via electrocardiograms that when we feel compassionate or loving, our heart rhythms actually shift, transmitting signals that soothe the body.

Using HeartMath tools and techniques to harness and amplify these signals allows us to solve problems and overcome issues that our greatest intellectual power can't begin to touch. For instance, with one HeartMath tool called Freeze-Frame, you can begin by neutralizing your negative thoughts and anxiety surrounding and obscuring the solution to the problem.

Freeze-Frame works like this: When you feel stressed, step back from the moment. Shift your focus to the area around your heart, and imagine that you are breathing through your heart. Hold your heart focus for at least ten seconds. Now, recall a positive experience or a happy time, maybe playing on the beach or a Thanksgiving with loved ones. By calling forth feelings of love and appreciation, by shifting your attention to your heart, you neutralize your inner conflict. You remove energy from your perception of the problem. Then, you can consider more effective, transformative possibilities from a calmer, more peaceful place.

Carol McDonald, president of McDonald and Associates, a computer-memory firm in Omaha, uses HeartMath tools to help her leave the "debris" of her office workday, to allow her to shift to a more appreciative, heart-centered place. "The program immediately shifted my priorities. In the old days, I still might carry some of the stress or a less-than-perfect mood or the tensions of the day. It might have taken me a little while to realize that I was grumpy to my son or that I breezed past my husband with barely a nod."[3]

Previously, she operated from a "more head-based" perspective, so it took her longer to even become cognizant of her behavior. Now, she consults and hones in on the messages from her heart. She uses Freeze-Frame and other HeartMath tools to become more inner directed, to cut off her mind chatter from the day and instead tune in to and listen to her body to see whether it's relaxed. "If your mind chatter is still saying, 'Oh, that damn vendor' or 'Those darn employees' and you're still rehashing the day, then you are not in your heart. You won't be able to be as caring or as appreciative as you'd like."

Likewise, at day's end, if you're still in a place of fear or anger, still caught up in the pressured, stressed movie of work, you can't possibly be in your heart. If McDonald still feels fear or anger on the way home, she uses her new tools to recalibrate and "disengage from the movie." The movie can still play around her, but she takes herself out of it.

Focusing on her heart before meetings at work has also made her interactions with her employees more humane and caring, McDonald said. If she's meeting with an employee to discuss a performance problem, for instance, she prepares by first concentrating on her heart and her gratitude and appreciation for the employee. "That way, the meeting takes place in a completely different space. It doesn't mean I'm happy about why we are meeting. It doesn't mean the circumstances have changed, but it completely changes the flavor and approach of the meeting."

Compassion isn't just a Pollyannish dream of harmony and light. It is a practical, powerful, sweeping sea change for our culture. It offers solutions that even the greatest minds straining and concentrating around a round-table can't conjure up. Love manifests breakthroughs. And it makes good business sense. McDonald and Associates is a tiny giant. It is one of the top-ranking computer-memory distributors in the United States. It has more than twelve thousand clients. It thrives as Carol McDonald makes the conscious decision to weave heart-centered techniques into her intense, high-paced day.

TOUCH THAT COMES FROM THE HEART

Love may also be the way we best heal our bodies and souls. And in this touch-deprived culture, holistic medical pioneer Dr. Gladys Taylor McGarey believes that touching someone with love and respect and healing energy may be one of the supreme radical acts of love. We are already high-tech; we can become more high-touch.

Dr. McGarey remembers a Pennsylvania truck driver who came to one of her healing, mind-body programs in Scottsdale, Arizona. The man was dying of lung cancer, and he was choked with bitterness and rage. "He was mad at God, at his family, at himself for smoking. He didn't like anything about our program. He didn't like our meals. He hated the sandwiches with sprouts because he said they were like worms crawling. He was just furious."

And then on the last day of the program, massages were offered to all the participants. Amazingly, the man decided to get a massage. Dr. McGarey was in awe of what happened next: "He came back from his massage, sat down at a table, and had tears running down his cheeks, this big truck driver. He said the massage therapist had asked him to lie down on the table, and he said, 'I can't. I can't even lie down at home to sleep. What do you expect me to do?'"

The therapist replied gently, "Well, let's just try it." The man said of the experience, "When she touched my feet, it was as if light opened up above my head and began pouring through me. And when she touched my chest, those weren't her hands. Those were the hands of Jesus."

The therapist continued to massage the man for a very long time. By the time he returned for lunch, he was a changed person, Dr. McGarey said. "He did die two months later. But he died a different person. It was being touched that triggered that transformation, that opened up the hidden places within him."[4]

ANSWERING THE CALL OF COMPASSION

We are all called at this time, in medicine as throughout our world, to see and unlock the hidden pain within each of us. To respond to the pain of others with new eyes. To respond in solidarity and compassion. This is our call. And it will not be easy. Nothing of the highest possible worth ever is. It will be one of the biggest stretches our culture has ever made. The bar compassion raises is a high one—but it will finally remove the bars we've placed around our hearts. And that is a fight worth fighting.

Becoming intimate with one another's suffering will be a true signal of our spiritual evolution, says writer Sophy Burnham, author of *A Book of Angels* and other works about angels in our midst. In my book *Embracing Our Essence*, she said, "As you evolve spiritually, you also become more sensitive and possibly more touched not only by your own suffering, but by that of others and the compassion you feel for them. We feel pain and experience suffering so we can extend the cup of kindness to one another. If there was no pain, what would you do? How would you care for one another? How would you love one another? We don't love only in pain, but we find our humanity in this suffering."

If you scratch the surface of any people, in any culture, says Burnham, you will find a search for God and divine unity with one another. "Our purpose is to love one another, to love those around us, to love ourselves. Love, love, love."

Where are you called to love, to unite in love? Where in your world have you perhaps lost part of your humanity by failing to love, by ignoring others' suffering? By judging them, shunning them, keeping yourself separate and untouched by their pain? Where in your daily routine could compassion go a long way toward bringing healing or resolving a conflict or crisis?

Think of some situation you've tried to solve with reason and analytical "fixes." Is it still unraveling? Still bucking all logic? Could it be that a softer, but more powerful compassionate approach is needed? Those who work with children often remind us that tenderness really is the most rational problem-solver.

THE HEART AS PROBLEM-SOLVER

When Linton Elementary School principal Priscilla Huston is called to intervene with a disruptive student, she often responds with kindness and understanding along with logical analysis. Once a little boy came down to her office because he'd been disruptive in class. Her intuition told her that he needed something more than a lecture and to be sent back immediately. She pulled him on her lap, and he soon fell asleep.

"I think he'd gotten so frustrated, he just didn't know what to do. He just needed someone to help him feel okay, to know that it's okay to be upset. It wasn't okay to act out as he had, but it was okay to be upset. Just because he made poor choices didn't mean he was any less cared about," said Huston, a highly respected leader in education in my Fort Collins, Colorado, community.[5]

A little care goes a long way toward making the world right again and in humanizing our institutions so they become less violent, more peaceful places. The developing infant brain, when deprived of love and affection, develops into a disturbed, anxious, troubled one. The unloved baby grows into a human being who is never as happy, fulfilled, confident, safe, or capable of realizing his full potential as a loved baby becomes. When we are deprived of love, we find it very, very difficult to see the world as a loving, comforting place.

Conversely, if we and our institutions are infused with love, anything is possible. We can overcome obstacles the mind still wrestles with. "When it comes to calculating the power and reach of love, the mind is a pedestrian but the heart is a broad jumper," says Sam Keen in *To Love and Be Loved*. We can live with more joy and abundance than we ever knew was possible, as Ruthanne Kastner discovered.

Love is the force that moves the cosmos, keeps the stars on their courses, stirs us to procreate children, argues Keen. "Love is all this and more. And the nearer we get to it, the more we know we have come home. It is where we came from and return to, the before and after that we approach in our best moments. It is the source of life, the meeting place of our origin and destination. In those moments when love finds us, we lose one identity and gain another. We burst out of the dark cocoon of the ego and discover that we have grown wings."

LOVE IS NOT A LUXURY

Simply, grandly, love is not a luxury we can afford to ignore, says the Dalai Lama. Love has to become the basic, ultimate standard by which we measure our choices, ease suffering, design programs, and gauge true success. It has to be the benchmark by which schools are managed, employees are motivated, medicine is administered, profits are made, inmates are cared for, souls are ministered to from our pulpits, and wholeness of body, mind, and spirit is restored.

To not live with love and compassion distorts the heart of our culture. This may be less a metaphor than we think, as healers have discovered over the ages. In her book *Why People Don't Heal and How They Can*, medical intuitive Caroline Myss tells the story of Jeff, who was only twenty-four when his doctors diagnosed a heart condition. He was told he had a hole in his heart. Recovery, his physicians said, was rare.

After Jeff met Myss, he began a daily ritual of prayer and visualization and deepened his spirituality. He never considered feeding his spirit before, but when he did, he experienced real contentment for the first time.

In two years, Jeff's condition was fully healed, to the amazement of his doctors. At work, he says many of his co-workers now come to him for clarity and guidance: "I feel like a counselor or a therapist, which is fine, though I never expected to play that role. I believe that I'm meant to help people in just this way, quietly giving them positive thoughts and hope that tomorrow will be a better day. Symbolically, I now believe that this is the reason my illness was a heart disorder. It opened my heart."

Could it be that the rampant heart disease and spiritual and emotional pain in our culture are directly related to the holes—or lack of wholeness—in our own hearts? Isn't it possible, knowing that our psychological health and physical health are connected, that our individual and collective health depend on heeding the call to open our hearts? We are by nature a tribal species, say Myss and Dr. C. Norman Shealy in their book *The Creation of Health*. "We need each other, and we need to be needed by each other. We need to give love as well as receive love. We thrive when we are loved, and we are sapped in strength and vitality without love."

Without love, vitality and true strength are leached from our organizations, communities, neighborhoods, and entire culture. What choices do you have to make—or overturn—to follow the call of your heart? How can you invite compassion to reside in you and be the standard by which you base your decisions? How could your organization begin to take an initial step?

DWELLING IN COMPASSION RIGHT WHERE WE ARE

We can start by deciding that love and compassion are what we want. We begin to want to dwell in compassion, to make each day a divine abiding, as the Buddhists say. We become willing to commit to radically new approaches and bold choices. Getting to the heart of ourselves and our institutions demands that we step onto new ground that others may dismiss as insignificant, soft, weird.

Heart detractors are, in some ways, becoming the minority. Many, many of us are choosing to take heart instead in the growing compassion consciousness. All around us are organizations, restaurants, huge global corporations, hospital chains, prisons, schools, political arenas, neighborhoods being transformed in some unprecedented way by the intention and the momentum to dwell in compassion. Many leaders, including the following two, are awakening to the realization that caring is fundamental to good leadership.[6]

In 1986, Herbert Teerlink, the CEO of Harley-Davidson, decided to create a more meaningful workplace that cared about its employees. Part of the inspiration for his compassionate leadership came from an unlikely, chance encounter—or maybe not chance at all. Amazing how these things "just happen" when we most need them.

One morning a woman was driving her child to preschool. Her infant was also with her. She saw a dog and figured it was lost. On her car phone, the woman called the police, found out the owner had reported the dog missing, and got the owner's number.

Even though she was with her young children and the dog was muddy, she picked him up because she wanted to make him feel good. She later went out of her way and delivered the dog to his owner's office. His office was the international headquarters of Harley-Davidson. The dog's owner was Teerlink.

Because this woman acted out of her heart, Teerlink's heart was deeply touched. He resolved to reinvigorate his company with that kind of altruism and sense of service: "Wow. When this woman called and then brought the dog over, that's what life's about. How do we get people to do that? How do we get people who work here together at Harley-Davidson to feel good and feel that they make a difference?"

As the case for compassion is being made, exciting and radical new people and programs are answering the call for greater tenderness in our culture. When Tom Chappelle, CEO of Tom's of Maine, began to develop openhearted, environmentally sound approaches to business, some of his detractors thought his profits would go soft along with his heart. But Chappelle was convinced that love of others and the environment is fundamental to good leadership and good business. And good leadership, vision, and commerce can be first about caring.

"In my darkest days, I was working for aims that were too narrow for me. I was working for market share, sales growth, and profits. It was a sense of emptiness. I was to some degree depressed, undirected, unconnected to myself," said Chappelle.

After much soul-searching and studying, Chappelle decided that in his heart he was actually a "formalist"—someone who looks at the world as a series of "I-thou" relationships. If you do business as a formalist, you treat people as you'd like yourself to be treated.

What shifts in thinking, what actions do you need to make to treat others as you'd like to be treated? What could help you shift from ego about yourself and how you are viewed, to concern for others and how they are treated? Instead of asking, "What's in this for me?" what would it take to have you ask, "What's in it for everyone?"

CREATING A COMPASSIONATE WORKPLACE

Tom Chappelle decided to structure a workplace that honors the heart and spirit of his employees, his customers, and the environment. He decided to only produce, manufacture, and sell products—like natural toothpastes, soaps, and shampoos—that have a minimal impact on the natural world.

He decided to see and treat his employees like human beings. Tom's of Maine supports flexible work arrangements for its employees and offers them free financial planning and management services, stress-prevention workshops, and reimbursement for wellness classes, such as yoga or meditation. The company also has ongoing training programs in work-life issues and value-centered leadership.

Even small things make a difference at Tom's of Maine. The conference room tables are rounded and just slightly off the floor, so when people meet, they sit on the floor, relax, and see the entire group.

Chappelle simply treats people as he'd like to be treated. What about those fears about soft profits? For several years, Tom's of Maine has seen 20 to 25 percent annual growth.[7]

A higher heart-centered consciousness—and higher financial gains—are also being seen in health care when healers act out of their hearts in very visible ways. One of the most remarkable examples I've heard of is Griffin Hospital in Derby, Connecticut. More than ten years ago, its administrators decided to redesign their facility, philosophies, and programs to treat patients as human beings deserving of humane, dignified care. The spirits of patients are as nurtured at Griffin as their bodies.

For instance, there is no loud paging system for doctors, so the hospital is quieter, more soothing, as patients requested. An open-chart policy encourages patients to read their medical records whenever they'd like. Each patient has a primary nurse, who acts as an advocate and coordinates the patient's care.

Each unit is soothing and life-affirming. Pianists, flautists, guitarists, fiddlers, even magicians perform daily in the lounge. These areas contain fish tanks and artwork to lift the soul and heal pain.

LOVE AS AN INSTITUTIONAL CORNERSTONE

Volunteers from the community are trained to give patients at Griffin Hospital hand and foot rubs. Many come in and lovingly make cookies or bread in the on-unit kitchens. The kitchens may be the heart of this compassionate program, as they soothe patients and families heavy with grief and fear. "The kitchens become more than kitchens. As in our homes, they are places families gather to make difficult decisions regarding life and death," said Griffin Vice President William Powanda in our interview.

When Griffin's clinical director came to work at about 6 A.M. one morning, the night nurse mentioned that the daughter of a terminally ill woman had been in the kitchen since 4 A.M., peeling apples and crying. The clinical director went to see the woman and asked her what was wrong. She explained, "Well, I have to make some decisions about DNR [do not resuscitate], and whenever my mother and I used to have to make a tough decision, we'd sit in our kitchen and peel apples."

Another time, a young boy used the kitchen to make cookies for his father, who was dying. He knew the cookies would soothe his family.

Like the deep comfort food brings, music is also woven into Griffin to ease pain and sometimes help people make the transition as they lay dying. "Once we had an elderly man who was dying. And he asked to hear his grandson play. His grandson was about to embark on a career as a concert pianist," remembered Powanda. "So we wheeled the man in his wheelchair into the music lounge—there is one on each floor—and he got to hear his grandson play. He died three days later."

What a humane, dignified, loving way to be treated as we leave this world. And again, humanity doesn't run counter to commercial gain. We only think it does in our limited heart thinking. Like Tom's of Maine, Griffin's intention to provide more caring, humane medical care has reaped amazing commercial results.

"We've been named by *Fortune* as one of the one hundred best places to work in America," Powanda pointed out, with excitement and pride in his voice. "We have high retention and low turnover. Our turnover rate is only 4.8 percent in an industry that remains between 18 to 20 percent. Our patient satisfaction levels are at 97 percent or higher for inpatient and outpatient services."

Whenever Griffin has invested in a loving, supportive environment where people feel physically, emotionally, and spiritually cared for, the public has responded beyond the institution's wildest imaginings—against all business logic.

One of the first changes Griffin management made was in the hospital's childbirth services. Administrators knew they desperately needed to design a more patient-centered childbirth center that included everything from grandparents' classes to double beds so new dads could sleep over, to family rooms so entire families could gather. At the time, however, Griffin's board was actually considering dropping childbirth as a service altogether. Not cost-effective enough.

"But we convinced the board we should stay in this business," said Powanda, who himself was born at Griffin Hospital years ago. "So it was decided to move forward with the new childbirth center. We put everything in it the customers said they wanted. And in three years, we went from 480 births to 960."

This spike in childbirths defied all conventional wisdom that a hospital could attract only people from its primary service area, Powanda noted. "We had mothers coming from thirty miles away. In a couple of cases, we had mothers coming across the New York state line. They had all done their homework, and Griffin met their needs."

In honoring compassionate health care, Griffin knows it has created something magical that patients have been seeking for a long time. It's so magical that the word is spreading. About four hundred other health care institutions from across the United States and eleven foreign countries visit Griffin each year to see how they might also create more humane health care. "Clearly, patients are expecting more personalized, humane, spiritual care," Powanda concluded. Consumers, he pointed out, are demanding more humane treatment, and the results are unprecedented and healing.

COMPASSION IS TRANSFORMING OUR CULTURE

This can't be dismissed as touchy-feely, anecdotal, or random, according to Bill Powanda. As a leading hospital administrator who keeps his pulse on the market trends, Powanda pointed to a report from the financial consulting firm Ernst and Young that recently came to this conclusion: "The trillion-dollar American healthcare market is on the brink of the biggest transformation yet. The primary force behind this change is not technology or managed care, but the growing mass of educated and empowered consumers. 'Health care consumerism' will alter how healthcare organizations operate, how they compete, and perhaps, why they exist."

If that is what empowered, heartfelt consumers can do, never, never doubt your personal power. Directed to the right goal, aligned with the most humane intent, we can set anything in motion.

We all need more loving, responsive, compassionate medical care. We all need more tender care in all our institutions and endeavors. How can you spark a change in your health care community? As a consumer of the system, you can make your spiritual, emotional, and physical needs known. And you can honor those same needs in your nurses, staff, and doctors.

We each can speak out when compassion and humanity are sacrificed by policies driven by health maintenance organizations (HMOs). We can do this by asking that we be served with tenderness and love, by leaving dispassionate practices and seeking out more humane ones, as many practitioners and consumers alike are doing, and by setting an example and becoming a force for change as both patient and provider.

We can make a difference right where we are. As I wrote in my book *Embracing Our Essence*, "We don't have to wait for the ubiquitous 'them' to do something. We are 'them' and we are already deep into shaping a more loving and humane reality."

TUNING IN TO THE PSYCHE

Even in the absence of formalized programs, many of us have to begin to come home to our hearts and listen to the "something" in them that won't rest, something internally that screams, "This isn't the way I want to live!" or the voice that says, "I thought it would be different than this" or the nagging sense that, "If this is what I always wanted, then why am I not happy?"

We have to slow down, sit with, and be attentive to that persistent intuitive voice that tugs on our psyches until we can no longer act in such sterile, inhumane, disconnected ways. In these times of soul-searching and angst, compassion toward our own suffering and that of others is what will powerfully heal us individually and collectively.

Sit with yourself for a moment. Close your eyes, breathe in deeply, release any burdens weighing on your shoulders, arms, and neck. Breathe lightness into your being. Now focus in on your heart. Spend a few minutes concentrating purely on your heart area. Ask your heart if it needs to respond with greater tenderness in any area of your life. Where or with whom is it calling for greater compassion? Ask your heart what it would have you do in that instance.

Follow your heart's call. For when you do, it will take you to that collective place where all our hearts are swelling, softening, and coming together to take our culture to a more evolved time. The healing power of compassion is seizing center stage now, reinvigorating and humanizing organizations that touch us all. Radical acts of love are so shifting the cultural zeitgeist that some wave of this revolution of compassion is now cresting through your community.

Conferences designed to humanize and restore the spirit of the workplace are sold out. More than 140 medical schools now include courses that help future doctors care for the whole patient, physically, mentally, spiritually, and emotionally. Spiritual and emotional support is being offered to prison inmates. Elementary schools are bringing in trainers to help kids learn to show empathy, compassion, and love.

CONNECTION BEING RECOGNIZED

And the media—often the last stronghold to the fully open heart—is starting to notice. Medicine's transformation into a kinder, gentler institution was featured in a recent *USA Today* article. Reporting on the new breed of doctors, Robert Davis writes, "Being a good doctor means more than being the smartest medical person in the room. It means connecting with the patient and helping the patient get the best care he or she wants."[8]

In the same article, Dr. Carolyn Robinowitz, dean of the Georgetown University School of Medicine in Washington, D.C., says that the role of a physician is "broader and deeper than prescribing drugs and performing procedures." Medicine is "a priestly profession," says Dr. Robinowitz. "You are with your patients for life's big transitions."

Dr. Robinowitz is no anomaly. Her compassionate view of medicine is also embraced by another leader in medicine whom I interviewed, Dr. Christina Puchalski, an assistant professor at the George Washington University School of Medicine. "I try to use the best of my scientific abilities to diagnose and treat my patients. With the best technology has to offer, my patients may be cured. But in the absence of compassion, there will be no healing," said Dr. Puchalski, who is also director of the Center to Improve the Care of the Dying, in Washington, D.C.

In medicine, as in all our cultural foundations, the case for compassion must be made because love causes "a hundred veils to fall each moment," says the thirteenth-century poet Jelaluddin Rumi.[9] Love removes all the veils of denial, professional distance, fear, and judgment that keep us separate from and truly falling in love with the preciousness of one another.

Doctors have often kept their distance from patients because they've been trained to do so—and because they've been conditioned to fear getting closer to patients, especially those who are dying, Dr. Puchalski said. "So they deliver bad news, like telling a patient she has cancer, in a stern, objective way. But doctors now are saying this feels terrible. They are increasingly unhappy because they didn't go into medicine to treat patients in this way."

Where do you purposefully keep yourself distant? Where do you feel unnaturally separate from yourself and others? What walls keep you apart? The emotional pain and lack of connection among physicians—and all of us—can be eased only when we allow ourselves to be more open emotionally, to trust that this is the way to be fully professional and effective.

ALIGNING WITH THE HEALING FORCE

We can bridge the distance between ourselves and those we live with, serve, and love if we align with the power of love and see it as the most powerful, magnificent force for true healing, not just temporary, Band-Aid fixes. Dr. Puchalski discovered this with one of her first patients, a young woman named Sheila.

"She had sickle cell disease and was admitted in a pain crisis. I interviewed Sheila hoping to establish a warm rapport with my patient and help her deal with her pain. Instead, Sheila told me to 'just write a prescription for the Demerol and leave me alone.'"

In addition to easing her patient's physical pain. Dr. Puchalski struggled to help her patient on a deeper level. She saw that Sheila's only focus in life was on pain and narcotics. "At times I felt that in spite of all the education I had, all I could do was be a drug pusher and make no real difference in Sheila's life."

Then, as a physician, Dr. Puchalski decided to change her approach with Sheila. She began to accept her patient just as she was: a young woman with a serious, incurable illness who was struggling just to survive each day; a woman whose twin sister had died a few months earlier; a woman whose mother was grieving, knowing she would lose her other daughter to sickle cell disease.

Dr. Puchalski began to talk to Sheila about her life, the meaning of it, her faith in God and in her family. Dr. Puchalski recalls, "As Sheila and I talked about these issues over the years, she gradually accepted her pain and stopped struggling with the doctors about doses of medication. We found a combination of medications that worked for her and left her better able to function. She started enjoying life more and made yearly trips to Disney World with her family. She joined picnics and family gatherings. She enjoyed helping her nieces and nephews with their homework."

But Sheila's health continued to deteriorate. One day Sheila came to see Dr. Puchalski, who decided Sheila was close to death. Sheila wanted to stop all medical intervention and was at peace with her decision. But she had some specific goals she still wanted to accomplish. For the next six months, Sheila and Dr. Puchalski met regularly to explore Sheila's goals, which included helping her family come to terms with her death and exploring her love of God and the thought that she would soon be with God.

"I never once laid my stethoscope on her, nor did I order any lab tests. For those visits I held her hand and listened to her as we walked her final journey together. A few weeks before she died, she asked if I would come to her funeral. I cried as I held her hand and told her I would miss her."

The night before Sheila died, Dr. Puchalski came to visit her at home. She and Sheila's mother and niece read the Twenty-third Psalm, Sheila's favorite. When Sheila died, it brought an end to "a deep and profound relationship," Dr. Puchalski says. "Each of my patients occupies a special place in my heart. Part of their spirit is always with me. My relationships with patients are profoundly rich because we touch each other on a deep spiritual level. I try to help my patients find peace and cope with their suffering by listening to them and to their beliefs as they struggle with life's difficulties."[10]

THE REVOLUTION OF THE HEART HAS BEGUN

We can become part of this revolution and transform our own hearts, our own piece of the culture. We can each create and enjoy richer relationships with those we serve, work with, and live with. Ask yourself, How can I open my own heart and possibly bring more of myself to my hospital, my school, my soccer fields, even the hot traffic zones in my part of town where hostility and road rage reign? How can I bring a touch of civility and kindness to those I meet in my daily routine? How can I ease someone's pain?

Often it doesn't take much. Often it takes so very little, especially if we are frequently in a place where little acts of love nurture and green our hearts. I remember once finishing a workshop on balance and stress reduction at a Texas university. As I was preparing to leave, Hannah, one of the student counselors, came forward and quietly shared her story. She recalled how she came to work one day, already exhausted at the prospect of seeing the usual river of kids haunted by anorexia, anxiety, unwanted pregnancies, and other "big" stuff. But when she sat down at her desk, she saw a single, pink camellia floating in a glass bowl. One of her co-workers had brought in a camellia for each person in the office. "It was such a small thing, but it so affected me. It touched me so much, you know, that I found the energy and the ability to better respond to the students I saw that day."

LOVING BEFORE IT'S TOO LATE

We each can awaken to the realization that we can't live any longer the way we have. We can each embrace the idea that love is the only sensible, logical, efficient way to become as great as we yearn to be. But above all, it is our destiny. It is why we came here in the first place. Our destinies are so much larger than collecting more stuff, accumulating more money, career trophies, peer praise, and Martha Stewart–worthy homes. Those things are nice; we can be grateful for them if they happen. They can make life warm and affirming. But they are not the ultimate bottoms in our bottom-line-crazed culture. The bottom line, the ultimate goal, is this: We came here to love and be loved. We came to learn how to better care for one another. Many, many people don't fully see this until it's too late.

Stephen and Ondrea Levine have worked with hundreds of dying people and heard their last words, regrets, and unmet dreams. "When dying people complain," says Ondrea, "they usually regret one of three things. They wish they'd played more. They wish they'd found more fulfilling work. And they wish they'd had more loving relationships."[11]

That blinding desire to love and be loved can never be extinguished, even on our deathbeds. How many people when they are dying finally,

finally find it in their hearts to say, "I love you," to their partners, their children, even their nurses who hover like angels around them. *I love you.* Why can't we say those words more often?

In fact, why not say these words more in all areas of our living? Why don't we make them the standard by which we base all our decisions, from how we structure our company to how we educate our children? Why can't we each begin, right where we are, to rely on compassion as the doorway to a more enlightened, harmonious, and ultimately more powerful culture that meets the needs of all?

What would it take? Let's begin to dream this into existence. Let's leave the left, analytical brain aside for a while, and let's dream a bit on the right side of the brain. Let's dream what that more enlightened place would look and feel like . . .

A DOCTOR WITH HEART

The following is a dreamy story for inspiration, a story about a dream of a man who made one of the strongest cases for compassion I've ever read. It's a tale of a human being who knew the meaning of a life well lived.

Once upon a time there was a man named Paul Hamilton. Paul Hamilton was a doctor, the chief of oncology at the former Denver Presbyterian Medical Center. There were lots of things Dr. Hamilton's patients loved about him, but one thing they particularly adored was how he assured them they were never alone in their struggle against cancer and that he was fighting with them. He even brought in cancer patients who were in remission to visit with newly diagnosed patients for support. In this way, patients who might be frightened and even feeling hopeless could gain comfort from patients who'd survived and flourished.

No matter how serious their cancer diagnosis, Dr. Hamilton soothed his patients' fears and helped them find inner peace.

That's because long before it was popular, Dr. Hamilton was a passionate believer in the power of the human spirit in healing. He knew that ministering to his patients' hearts and souls was as important as attending to their physical needs. He was a brilliant physician, but many felt his greatest gift was in giving people hope in seemingly hopeless situations.

Patients always reported that Dr. Hamilton had a kind of aura around him that, even after being in his presence for only fifteen minutes, left them with a total sense of peace. Some said Dr. Hamilton's centeredness came from his regular meditations, especially before rounds. His spirit journey was heavily influenced by Buddhist tradition and thought.

Occasionally, he would even climb a tree and meditate in the branches. Once, when he was at the Denver Country Club, he saw a particularly beautiful tree, parked his bike underneath, hung some Buddhist prayer flags, shinned up—and slipped into meditation. After a few minutes, he fell sound asleep in the branches, only to be awakened by the sound of someone riding off on his bike.

Another thing that Dr. Hamilton was loved for was his willingness to venture far from the hospital to serve and love his patients. When one woman was depressed about her cancer diagnosis, Dr. Hamilton showed up at her home and took her inline skating. He left messages on patients' answering machines or popped in on their chemotherapy treatments just to say hello.

"He even accompanied me to my first two chemo treatments—as a friend, not a doctor," says a former patient. "That was his real strength—his ability to relate to his patients individually, as a friend, not a professional."[12]

Far beyond his individual efforts, Dr. Hamilton also knew the power of community would be immensely healing for cancer patients everywhere. Acting on this belief, he co-founded CanSurmount, which grew into an international network of cancer survivors. And he started QuaLife, a support community for people with life-threatening illnesses and their families.

One of Dr. Hamilton's guiding beliefs that flowed through his work was that, even as the disease progressed, someone could remain whole. Even if our physical bodies are defeated by cancer, our spirits can remain strong and vibrant.

LOVING AS WE LEAVE THIS LIFE

Many doctors spend less time with their patients once they become terminally ill. Unable to "fix the problem," they feel they can do no more. Many are simply uncomfortable with death, because physicians aren't usually trained well in easing someone's passage into life after death. But as Dr.

Hamilton's patients died, he remained at their side, spending hours, even weeks, with them and their families. "My father felt that death is one of life's transitions. He felt death was a part of life," says Skip Hamilton. "He felt that a doctor could understand his feelings about death and especially learn about and be concerned with a patient's feelings about coming face-to-face with a life-threatening illness."

A beloved, dignified way to die. Which is how Dr. Hamilton left this earth one August day. A month earlier, he had been hiking at a CanSurmount event and noticed he was short of breath. A chest X-ray revealed his own cancer—a slight tumor on one of his lungs. After surgery to remove the tumor, he experienced unexpected complications and lapsed into acute respiratory distress. During the two weeks in the hospital before he died, he had many visitors—including longtime friend Roy Romer, the former governor of Colorado—gathered at his bedside.

After his father's death, Skip Hamilton recalled a conversation they'd had: "I remember asking him how he was doing, and he said, 'Isn't it incredible that people always ask, 'How are you doing?' He said, 'It's all based upon what we're doing or how successful we are. Instead, I think we should ask, 'How are you being? I think that's much more important.'"

Paul Hamilton's story ends with an excerpt from his poem "Ode to Being":

> How are you doing?
> Is often our greeting.
> Why don't we greet with
> How are you being?
> Why are we compelled to doing and making?
> Why can't we be content with just being—not taking?
> We have been called human beings
> But we keep on pursuing
> As human doings
>
> .   .   .   .
>
> Being is loving
> The warmth of the Sun,
> The mountain summit,
> The sound of a voice,

The taste of cool water
Being is feeling
The love of the Creator
Through a friend
The warm water pouring
Over your skin
Being is singing
The music of living
Being is belonging
To one and many.
Being is moving
With the rhythm of pulsing.
Being is walking
Being is blade-ing.
Being is listening
To sound and silence
Being is hearing
The clear pure note
In the silence.
Being is hoping.
Being is praying.
Being is rebirthing.
With every new day.
Being is living.
The present moment.
Being is knowing.
To follow your blessing.

2

The Hardened Heart: Extinguishing the Fire

WHEN LEE ATWATER, former chairman of the Republican National Committee (who was widely known for his often ruthless, win-at-all-costs political maneuvering), was dying from brain cancer, he said, "Long before I was struck with cancer, I felt something stirring in American society. It was a sense among the people of the country—Republicans and Democrats alike—that something was missing from their lives, something crucial. I was trying to position the Republican party to take advantage of it, but I wasn't exactly sure what 'it' was. My illness helped me see what was missing in society was missing in me: a little heart, a lot of brotherhood."[1]

As with medicine, politics are a stark mirror of ourselves. They reflect back to us the health and state of our culture, from our openheartedness to our divisiveness and rancor. At the heart of your life, what is missing? What haunting moments have drawn a painful line in your heart? When have you chosen the ruthless path over the compassionate one? How have you broken another's heart by hardening your own?

If we hope to shape a more compassionate, kindred society, we first need to look at what we have created in our lives and in our culture and what we need to transform. We have to take a deep look at where we've hardened our hearts and suppressed our innate compassion. We need to see how we've often extinguished our natural, fiery drive to make the world a more humane place. This blazing drive appears to be our divine legacy—but how often have we celebrated this legacy?

Throughout history and across all religious and spiritual disciplines, the heart has been depicted as an inner, powerful fire, a force that purges and purifies us of all imbalance, negative influences, injustice, and corruption.

We now suffer in our world whenever we extinguish this innate fire, whenever we snuff out our longings to become connected with one another. We pay a high price whenever we smother our fiery inner impulses to reach out to another because we fear it will be inappropriate, rejected, or inadequate. Shutting down this fire weighs heavy on our hearts.

All too often, more than I am comfortable admitting, my heart is heavy, sodden with a kind of nameless grief. Other times, the sadness rises up as a sacred rage. I suspect my heart has ample company. We are the most depressed generation in history. We suffer from depression ten times more than our grandparents did, according to researchers like Martin Seligman, a leading depression expert at the University of Pennsylvania. As I discovered in researching my last book, *Depression: What Your Body's Trying to Tell You*, researcher Myrna Weissman and her colleagues examined medical records since the beginning of the century and found that each successive generation has doubled its susceptibility to depression.

What is behind this angst? Why are so many people so sad? The dozens of medical experts I interviewed conclude that many of us are feeling, and maybe even overwhelmed by, a gnawing grief rooted in the way we are living.

This grief became very personal beginning in 1999. As I lectured on my last book, which offers healing solutions for depression, I was stunned by the misery that poured out of people everywhere. These were people who on the outside seemed wildly successful—Armani-suited, luxury-home/luxury-life kind of people—but sick at heart nonetheless. Much of that grief was expressed in the aftermath of the plane crash that claimed the lives of John F. Kennedy Jr., Carolyn Bessette Kennedy, and her sister Lauren Bessette. That tragedy, as tragedy always seems to do, gave people permission to express their own unhealed pain. It was a catalyst for opening and grieving old, unhealed wounds. It forced us to see that life can be snuffed out any moment—that we are all here for a limited time. And it's often when we straddle the abyss between life and death that we can really see how desperately love and tenderness are missing.

LOSS OF LOVE EXERTS A HIGH PRICE

Much of the misery I heard pour from people was about their deep grief over not having good relationships with friends or family; about working ten hours a day in places where people don't really know them, much less care for them. They had a nagging sense that they'd lost something irreplaceable. And they often discovered that what was lost was love.

It's as if along the way to storing up more stuff, we forgot that "true intimacy based on respect and love are the measure of a life well lived," as Joan Borysenko reminds us in *A Woman's Book of Life*. Along the frenzied path to storing up more luxuries, we seem to have forgotten that "love and compassion are necessities, not luxuries," says the Dalai Lama. "Without them humanity cannot survive."[2]

It doesn't matter where you look—medicine, politics, social reform, or business. Anywhere we've shut down our instinctive compassion, we've paid a staggering price. This may be never clearer than in medicine today, which has always accurately mirrored our culture at large. An article in the St. Paul, Minnesota, *Pioneer Press* in 1996 captures how efficiently we've weaned simple compassion from medicine and how our caregivers suffer for it.

"The young man lay in intensive care paralyzed and quietly terrified. An auto accident broke his neck and a steel halo now clamped his head to the bed as if in a vice. Tears streamed down his face. The young doctor saw the tears and hesitated at the door. Her job was to change his IV catheter. A simple task. But the tears . . . what could she do? What could she say?

"'She didn't talk to him. She just focused on changing his central line and left,' said Dr. Gregory Plotnikoff, director of the Center for Spirituality and Healing at the University of Minnesota Medical School. 'She's been haunted by it ever since.'"[3]

HAUNTED WHEN THE HEART IS MASKED

We need to have compassion for our doctors and nurses who sometimes feel compelled to hide their hearts because of an often rigid system that trains them to be "professional"—meaning dispassionate, objective, and detached. We can't help but feel haunted anytime we deny our powerful hearts, and it must be extremely painful in any profession to be trained to keep emotions at bay in the most emotional moments, such as during life-and-death decisions.

What haunts you? What heartless moments when you ignored someone's suffering still free-fall in your psyche? Like that doctor, I've concluded that many of us are haunted by the lack of tenderness, the absence of life-affirming compassion in our daily lives. When Sidney Winawer's wife was treated for cancer, even though he'd treated thousands of patients as the chief of gastroenterology at Memorial Sloan-Kettering Cancer Center in New York City, he wasn't prepared for how his heart would be moved by her experience. He remembers seeing Andrea wearing the shapeless, flimsy hospital gown and being shocked. How could the hospital make someone wear something that unflattering? Dr. Winawer saw the brutal invasiveness of chemotherapy and other treatments from a raw, new perspective.

DISCONNECTION CAUSES GREAT PAIN

I believe, in many instances, we ache from denying our humanity. And our hearts are weary at how disconnected we are from each other and from a deep connection with the earth. We've even blunted the senses that weave us together. We rarely touch, see, and sense one another's souls and hearts.

This disconnection, tuning out others' needs, is all too evident in how we treat those who are dying. Recent end-of-life studies raise some disturbing facts, says Dr. Plotnikoff. "Severe pain is unacceptably common, excessive numbers of patients die in intensive care units, and physicians are either unaware of or unresponsive to their patients' care preferences."[4]

The culture of medicine "is not a nurturing process that slants people toward being sensitive and oriented toward thinking about the connection between feelings, thoughts, and physical symptoms," says Dr. Kevin Walsh, director of behavioral medicine at Kaiser Permanente.[5] "Compassion is something that's not lost, but that has taken a back seat," says Chris Ducker Jr., a respiratory therapist at St. Francis Hospital in Sacramento, California.[6]

The need for humanistic medicine may, again, be most glaring in how we treat terminally ill patients. As natural as dying is, we have a deep-seated fear of even talking about death. In ancient times, healing centers honored the cycles of life and death. Today, however, we've become fixated on curing and fixing people. Healers "fail" if someone actually dies—this scenario is played out before millions on the TV show *ER* every week.

As a result, people in the final stages of life often don't receive compassionate care, adequate pain relief, and support. They also aren't even fully seen—literally. Author and spiritual teacher Stephen Levine who, with his wife, Ondrea, has sat with hundreds of people as they die, points to research showing that it takes nursing staff longer to respond to the call-light in terminal patients' rooms than that of patients they still might "fix."

I share these stories from medicine not to blindside the profession, not to criticize it harshly, but to shine a light on it and help us have compassion for its weaknesses—weaknesses that, again, mirror our own. We can't begin to restore compassion to ourselves and our institutions until we honestly and with loving intent examine how compassion has often been exiled. Then we can see how we, along with the physicians who operate in the system, suffer because of it.

BASIC AFFECTION IS OFTEN MISSING

In our everyday lives, even normal, natural physical touch is becoming increasingly rare. In our frenetic sprint from sunrise to sunset, Americans have one of the lowest rates of casual touch in the world. French parents touch their children three times more than American parents.[7] The French and families from countless other cultures also spend more time lingering over meals to look into their children's eyes. But back to touch—or the lack thereof.

We see it in the times when kids most need to be held and embraced. We've all seen this happen. Watch how parents pick up kids from day care, kids they've been away from all day, often from long before the sun hits the horizon till after it's gone down. It's not unusual to see parents merely scoop up their kids, like grabbing milk off the grocery store shelf on the way home, without a hug or even a caress of a shoulder. At summer day-camps, it's not uncommon to see parents come for their children and not leave their cars. They just park at the curb, honk their horns, and yell, "Come on, come on! Let's go!"

Even bedtime—often the last inviolate holdout for reconnecting and cuddling—is being exiled too. "Electronic sandmen"—videos with bedtime stories—are now hotly hyped as substitutes for cuddle time. Televisions are becoming commonplace in kids' bedrooms. Knowing how violent and crass much of evening television is, sending a child to his or her dreams in this way is not a compassionate gesture. It's a nightmare of our own making.

WHAT CAN YOUR HEART HOLD?

How much do we suppress tenderness in our culture? Physical disabilities are increasingly recognized; it's the emotional disabilities that are still greatly invisible. And suppressing our hearts is the greatest disability because, from cradle to grave, our deepest impulse, our most powerful human drive, is to love one another and all living things.

Instinctively, our hearts can hold more than we can possibly imagine. What does yours hold? What would you hope it holds? By nature, we are huge-hearted, full-hearted, expansive, generous souls who need the comfort and miracle of loving well. We wither and become mean, indifferent, and weak when compassion is buried. We blaze, burn, become magnificent and strong when we are loving.

Love is undoubtedly the most vital, life-sustaining, and sought-after human emotion. Then why have we banned the expression of love from our hospitals and medical clinics where we most need life to be sustained? Why has compassion become embarrassing and inappropriate, banished from our workplaces? Why have we reduced love to the narrowest possible denominator as something we extend to our partners, children, and only a tight circle of extended family and friends—if we're lucky? These are the tough questions we have to ask if we want to return to our hearts.

Why are we afraid to "love head-on," as writer Diane Ackerman puts it in her book *A Natural History of Love?* "We think of it as a sort of traffic accident of the heart. It is an emotion that scares us more than cruelty, more than violence, more than hatred."

We have to be honest about the costs of living with such closed hearts. Physically, operating from a closed-hearted stance is a very lonely, risky, unhealthy place. Investigators such as Redford Williams, chief of psychiatry at Duke University and author of *The Trusting Heart*, have shown that chronically hostile, cynical, or distrusting attitudes contribute to heart disease.

CONNECTION IS VITAL TO OUR HEALTH

Failing to love and be loved well is depressing. And new studies confirm that those who are depressed are twice as likely to suffer heart attacks.[8] Our hearts are undermined by our lack of deep connection with one another.

We are hardwired to be in community, clans, deeply bonded with others who know and love us just as we are. When we lose this—or never develop it at all—our physical being responds.

A Duke University study tracked almost fourteen hundred men and women who underwent coronary angiograms and were found to have at least one severely blocked coronary artery. After five years, those who were unmarried and who did not have at least one close confidant were more than three times more likely to have died than people who were married, had one or more confidants, or both.[9]

The bottom line is this: Our health is compromised if we aren't intimately, lovingly connected with others—as is the health and vitality of our world.

Sure, we appear seamlessly connected with all of our technological wizardry, from our home-to-office cyber connections. But don't mistake the Internet and cellular hardware for the missing software of the heart. As much as we are connected by machines, we are sorely disconnected from tenderness, affection, human touch, and the healing balm of compassion. "It's ironic," writes R. L. Stine, author of the Goosebumps series. "Somehow our age of satellites, faxes, e-mail, cell phones, and beepers has brought people into closer contact, but not necessarily closer communication."

Consider again how many of our policies sanction this unnatural distance from one another. Doctors are trained to keep an objective distance as they fix a patient's body. Corporate managers are conditioned to leave their hearts at home and become tough, productive, efficient, competitive, and, above all, emotionless. Women in corporate environments have told me they're afraid to display pictures of their children on their desks because they fear they won't look tough enough. This is a not-tough-enough sickness that's toxic to people in our business world.

Teachers are pressured by parents, governmental "standards police," and legislators to shape intellectually gifted kids. Many work extremely hard, as well, to nurture students who are kind, empathetic, and supportive of others. But they're often criticized by parents, who value smart, productive, competitive kids. I remember how my son's first-grade teacher dedicated part of the first week of school to discussing how the kids would be expected to treat one another with respect and dignity. I overheard a parent one day confront him. "Aren't you about ready to move on?" he asked with disdain. "Isn't it about time they started learning more important stuff, you know, a little math or something?"

BANISHING OUR HEARTS IS TOO LONELY

This censorship of and disrespect for the skills that make us fully human drain our entire way of life. It makes us mean-spirited and indifferent. It makes it easier to commit heartless acts and be miserly in our affection toward one another. Again, our seemingly logical programs and professional training can become heartless in their execution. Our professional stances banish our hearts to an unnatural, lonely place.

In the moments when we should be crying out for compassion, we've too often fallen back on our professional stance and denied ourselves of a call for love. We've suffered, in our workplaces and our political arenas, by experimenting with different forms of power that don't serve us well. Much of our sense of power is based on a tough, brittle, weak, unemotional, rigid, even cutthroat stance. Yet true power comes from the tender heart.

"Clarity. Compassion. Gentleness. Love. Understanding. Comfort. Forgiveness. Faith. Security with acceptance with ourselves, and all our emotions. Trust. Commitment to loving ourselves, and to an open heart. That's the power we're seeking. That's true power, power that lasts, power that creates the life and love we want," says Melody Beattie in *Journey to the Heart*.

COMPASSION IS THE TRUE PLACE OF POWER

Wouldn't we all love to live and work in places that were shored up with such true power, strengthened by the comfort of that kind of solid foundation? Wouldn't we love to invest our talents and passions in that kind of enduring form of power? What if we really committed ourselves to remaking our institutions with such heartfelt, authentic power? How wonderful it would be to wake each morning to that kind of world.

And until we do, how can we expect to make substantial, lasting progress? Time pressures are one major obstacle we have to overcome in the creation of compassionate institutions. Unfortunately, we often let the "pressed-for-time" excuses pinch and strain our hearts. We let work stress distort our hearts so they become petty, peevish, and harsh.

In the legal profession, Janine Geske, a former Wisconsin Supreme Court justice, often hears personal stories that show the unreasonable toll professionalism exerts. "The demands on young lawyers require such incredible numbers of hours. Either you're at the office twenty-four hours a day, or you make those hours up. You either have to lie about those hours, or you can have absolutely no life," Geske said in my interview with her. "I heard about a young lawyer whose child was receiving First Communion on a Sunday who was told he couldn't go because his partner needed a brief on Sunday morning. What kind of human beings are we going to have?"

Work pressures, the desire for professional excellence, and the lust of our egos often create situations the heart finds intolerable. Julia was one of the people I met over the Internet who wanted to share her workplace experience. A college professor at an Ohio university, Julia needed to take several days off for surgery and asked one of her colleagues to cover her classes. Julia had covered for others in her department many times. Her colleague refused to help because it "was inconvenient" and "bad timing." Julia's chairman, who told others in the department he thought Julia was lying about having surgery, said if she couldn't find a substitute, she had to come in herself.

Julia did come back to work, days earlier than her doctor recommended, and she still got no compassion. "On my first day back, I was coming out of the bathroom, as white as a sheet and in pain, and a co-worker stopped me by saying, 'I know you just got back today, but I need you to do some committee work for me.'" When Julia reminded her that she was still recovering from surgery, her colleague said bluntly, "You can get it to me tomorrow."

Work pressures prune many a tender heart, if we let them. We can either create environments that allow compassion to thrive or create ones where it's not welcomed. Which kind of workplace would you rather get out of bed for each day? Does your heart sing as you're driving to work? Our hearts are meant to thunder, pound with passion, race with excitement, quicken with anticipation. These are the words we often use to describe our hearts. Does yours do so where you work or have you subdued it for the better portion of each day?

Too often we've let workplace cultures segment our hearts, and as a result, we have an epidemic of heartbroken people who've mastered the unnatural art of detaching and disassociating from their souls—like shearing off splinters of ourselves. We do all of this in the name of professional excellence, in the quest for intellectual brilliance.

COMBINE OUR MINDS WITH OUR HEARTS

Of course, it's critical that we cultivate the brilliance of our minds. Our well-being and survival depend on that too. But isn't it possible that we might be far better served if we had more people who united the brilliance and fire of their genius with the fierce fire of their hearts? Mahatma Gandhi, Jesus, Eleanor Roosevelt, Albert Einstein, the Buddha, Mother Teresa, Hildegard of Bingen, the Dalai Lama, and so many other enlightened figures in history shape our world by fusing their fluid minds with their intense love for humanity. Studies also show that those who develop human skills—and cultivate a form of emotional intelligence—are twice as successful in life compared with those who are solely intellectually gifted.

What does your heart feel about all this—not your mind, your heart? Close your eyes, take a few moments, and breathe in several deep, slow breaths. And think about your daily routine. Breathe some more, focusing in on your heart, focusing in on your chest. Breathing deeply, ask your heart what it sees and senses in your daily dawn-to-dusk routine.

Take another long, cleansing breath, and ask your heart what it feels. How does it feel at the end of the day, when the expectations are met, the phones are turned off, the faxes are still, and you're sitting alone with your soul? How does it feel as you sit here, just you and your heart? What does your heart want to tell you—that maybe your mind has denied hearing? Breathe in. Breathe out. What does your heart have to tell you?

We need to start tuning in to our hearts, seeking our heart wisdom, answering our hearts' calls. The heart is not a nuisance or something to be exiled and ashamed of so our heads can dominate. If we've dedicated the past centuries to mastering our cerebral power, it's time to master and celebrate our heart wisdom. It's time to stoke the fire of compassion in our culture so we can finally burn away toxic beliefs, negative policies, and draining fears.

WHEN LOVE BECOMES THE STANDARD

We must come home to our hearts. When we come from a full-hearted place, we will make love the standard by which we base our actions. We'll be following what we came on the earth to do. "Compassion is the fire the Lord has come to send on the Earth," Thomas Aquinas once said.[10] We each have to make sure that fire stays ablaze and lights up the heavens.

I think we are so longing to do this. "There is a huge yearning in the human heart to push out the larger self," says author Neale Donald Walsh in *Conversations with God*. Yet returning to our hearts is such a simple concept that we may feel tempted to downplay its significance, says author Sue Patton Thoele. "Choosing to bring peace and love alive within ourselves by coming from our hearts on a consistent basis is the hope of the world," she writes in *The Woman's Book of Spirit*.

CLOSING MEDITATION

Too often we've exiled compassion so far from our lives that we've become trapped in poison and pain and have become totally detached from our own hearts. We need to let go of any thoughts, beliefs, fears, and choices that keep us distanced from our hearts. The following heart-centered meditation comes from Joan Borysenko, a consummate teacher on compassion. Use this to finally let go of anything keeping you away from the power and peace of your heart.

Loving-Kindness (Metta) Meditation

Close your eyes and begin by taking a few letting-go breaths and then enter the inner sanctuary of stillness. . . . Imagine a great star of light above you, pouring a waterfall of love and light over you. . . . Let the light enter the top of your head and wash through you, revealing the purity of your own heart, which expands and extends beyond you, merging with the Divine light.

See yourself totally enclosed in the egg of light, and then repeat these loving-kindness blessings for yourself:

May I be at peace
May my heart remain open

May I awaken to the light of my own true nature
May I be healed
May I be a source of love and healing for all beings

Next, bring a loved one to mind. See this person in as much detail as possible, imagining the loving light shining down on and washing through him or her, revealing the light within his or her own heart. Imagine this light growing brighter, merging with the Divine light and enclosing this person in the egg of light. Then bless your loved one:

May you be at peace
May your heart remain open
May you awaken to the light of your own true nature
May you be healed
May you be a source of healing for all beings

Next, think of a person whom you hold in judgment or are in conflict with and to whom you are ready to extend forgiveness. Place this person in the egg of light, and see the light washing away all negativity and illusion, just as it did for you and your loved one. Bless this person:

May you be at peace
May your heart remain open
May you awaken to the light of your own true nature
May you be healed
May you be a source of love and healing for all beings

See our beautiful planet as it appears from outer space, a delicate jewel spinning slowly in the starry vastness. . . . Imagine the earth surrounded by light—the green continents, the blue waters, the white polar caps. . . . The two-leggeds and four-leggeds, the fish that swim and the birds that fly. . . . Earth is a place of opposites. . . . Day and night, good and evil, up and down, male and female. Be spacious enough to hold it all as you offer these blessings:

May there be peace on earth
May the hearts of all people be open to themselves and to each other
May all people awaken to the light of their own true nature
May all creation be blessed and be a blessing to All That Is

3

Heart Monitor:
Examining Your Fullness of Heart

WE CAN'T BEGIN TO SHAPE a more compassionate world until our hearts are pregnant, swollen with love for those around us. But the world is full of people who live from only a corner of their hearts. The world is full of those "who encounter difficulties in loving or being loved," say Drs. Thomas Lewis, Fari Amini, and Richard Lannon, the authors of *A General Theory of Love*. Leslie, whose story was featured on the *Oprah Winfrey Show* recently, is one such person.

Leslie's parents divorced more than twenty years ago. But she still carries deep in her heart many unhealed regrets. She's still sad that after the divorce, her father moved out, and she never told him how horribly much she missed him. She is sad that she kept up a good front, wore a mask, and pretended everything was okay. She's sad that she never had a father at home for perspective and humorous talks about guy stuff as she went through dating and adolescence.

Twenty years later, Leslie knows she has relationship problems because she kept her heart cautiously under wraps. "I would shut down my heart because I didn't want anyone in there to damage it," Leslie said, as she shared her story on the show.

CONNECTING WITH YOUR OWN HEART

What do you hold in your heart? Is it lush, brittle, wary, trusting? How is your heart treating you and those you are with each day? Is it responding to ease the pain it sees? A woman recently told me about an incident in which she was driving along when she glanced out the window and noticed a toddler walking by herself. The woman's inner voice told her that something wasn't right. She stopped her car and found out that the little girl was lost. She found some others to stay with the little girl, circled the area, and finally located the little girl's mother, who was running around in search of her daughter. When this woman recounted this story at work later that day, one of her co-workers looked at her and said, "I would not have done that. Today you can get in trouble for doing something like that."[1]

How would you have responded in this situation? Does your heart respond with compassion to alleviate another's suffering—even if it feels risky? Does it also open to receive awe and joy and appreciation from others? Is your heart able to accept and hold others' love for you? Does it seem lush and full? Or is it lacking in tenderness and empathy? Is it afraid? Is it atrophied? What's happened over the years to make your heart respond in these ways?

This section of the book is our bedrock, our resting place. It's our time to pull back, retrench, and reflect. This is where we go down into and make a conscious, direct hit with our hearts. What will you discover? How is yours doing? We all come into the world with good hearts. We are huge-hearted at the center of our beings. And then we are either fed by affection, unconditional support, joy, awe, and a connection with Spirit; or we become eroded by criticism, shame, slights, blame, fear, trauma, and anger turned inward, to name a few things.

What's the state of your heart these days? What is the nature of your heart? What do you know in your heart to be true? Does your heart pound with excitement or does it ache with fear and stress? These are the questions we need to be asking ourselves as we vote in a new president, as we put bowls of soup in front of our children, as we navigate rush-hour traffic. "Love is the infrastructure of everything and anything worthwhile. If someone with X-ray vision looked for love in your endeavors, what would they see? Where would they find love?" asks Laurie Beth Jones in *Jesus CEO*.

Some companies, for instance, are held together only with paychecks, and in some "the love is so strong people would pay just to be part of them," says Jones. Which is true for your company of people, whether it's in an actual business or another place you spend your day? Would love be found there? If not, how does your heart feel about that? If it's closed, what can you do about it?

SITTING WITH YOUR HEART

"We begin to open the heart by first acknowledging that it's closed," Stephen Levine reflected when we talked. "We really learn again how to love by watching how unloving we've been. It's all a process of self-reflection. If you sit quietly in a room for two to three hours, no television, no radio, no distractions, watch how agitated your mind becomes. If you constantly have to be doing something to keep down the pain, that's a sign of a closed heart."

Can you be still and just sit with your heart? Or is it too painful to "go to the personal, to go to the fiery focal point of the sun," as Levine describes merging with our core? If it is, then begin by looking at the culture at large—how huge-hearted is our culture, how closed off? Next, descend down to your city, your neighborhood, your family. Then look at your relationships and, finally, at yourself. "If you can stay with that process, it takes you to a point where you see that you need heart," Levine concluded.

As you stay with your heart, ask yourself some basic, bedrock questions. Have you made your peace with who you really are? Do you really love yourself? Have you accepted that you are both capable of giving love and deserving of being loved?

Have you really accepted that you have a heart—a powerful heart—to begin with? This might seem inane, silly, and trite, but face it: Our culture often works against us to make us ashamed of our hearts and to smother our tender impulses. As discussed earlier, our society prizes clever, witty, cynical—even conniving—minds but often overlooks the heart. To become successful at work, for instance, we've often suppressed our emotional instincts, like compassion, and ramped up our killer instincts.

We're even suspicious of people who act intentionally and lovingly from their hearts. We suspect they have some "ulterior motive." We assume they want something from us. In some cases, these suspicions have been warranted, so we learn to be suspicious of all radical acts of love—even the genuine ones.

KNOWING THE TRUTH OF OUR HEARTS

In these kinds of tough-at-all-costs environments, no wonder our hearts duck for cover. No wonder our hearts masquerade as something they're not. "A human being has so many skins inside, covering the depths of the heart. We know so many things, but we do not know ourselves," pointed out Meister Eckhart, a thirteenth-century German mystic.[2]

We can't simultaneously cultivate destructive instincts and nurture compassion. Our hearts can't simultaneously hold meanness and goodness, fear and love. Out of fear, the heart often retreats, becomes shallow, twisted. We thwart our powerful instincts to love ourselves enough to follow our passions. We stifle our drive to love one another and instead channel those natural, powerful instincts into unhealthy addictions, from violence to alcohol, drugs, shopping, sex, hyper-competitiveness, and other closed-hearted choices.

"With our free will, we have established an alien mental kingdom ruled not by love but by thoughts of fear. Love does not feel at home in the world of fear, and that is because it is not," says Marianne Williamson in *Enchanted Love.*

It's meaningful to ask yourself, Am I aware that I have this vast, miraculous heart, and do I honor it enough to act on it regularly? Do I turn to it for guidance and wisdom? Am I aware that in addition to my fabulous reasoning and problem-solving skills and my powers of induction and deduction, that I also possess an innate, even more powerful heart upon which I can rest all my choices? Does my heart know that I know? Am I losing my capacity to be fully human?

By asking yourself these questions, you're taking another initial step in connecting with your heart—you're accepting that you have one. You have heart wisdom. Just as you have intellectual talents, as a human being—a spiritual being in a human body—you are gifted with an amazing heart with an immense power for goodness. You have a wise inner talisman that can guide and protect you. How often do you heed this inner guide? How often do you let it lead and instruct your problem-solving side what to do? More important, how often do you act on it? Through the ages, many people have proclaimed that it's with the heart that we truly see. Helen Keller said, "The best and most beautiful things in the world cannot be seen, nor touched . . . but are felt in the heart."[3]

LETTING THE HEART GUIDE

The heart often knows before the mind. In making her decision to leave her position as co-host of *Live with Regis and Kathie Lee!*, Kathie Lee Gifford remembers telling a friend, "'You know, I think this is going to be my last year on the show. I feel it.' It took a few months more for my head to catch up to what my heart had already decided."⁴

One potent practice to get in touch with your heart and its longings and needs is to keep a heart diary. At the end of each day, write how your heart feels. What things happened today that struck, moved, or affected your heart? What do you regret? What are you grateful for? Who or what touched your heart? Did you allow that to flow through you and affect your entire health and being? If not, what made you shut it down? What were you afraid might happen?

As you record your day, ask yourself whether you responded to others as your heart longed to. If you did, how did that feel? Write down instances from the past that come to mind. What blocked you then from reaching out as you felt drawn to do, or what allowed you to do so?

Keep this heart diary for a month or so and see whether any tendencies or patterns emerge. At this stage of peering inward, it may be difficult to even know how much your heart comes into play in your daily life. So let's take this, again, from ground zero. Ask yourself some of the most basic questions that are crucial to an open, healthy heart—not only spiritually but also emotionally and physically.

First, how much do you accept, appreciate, respect, and love yourself, even the parts of you that aren't perfect and may never be? Does your own heart even have an inkling that you adore yourself? Or are you uncomfortable with that whole idea? Have you been so wounded or hurt at some point that you keep yourself from recognizing your true worth and essence? This self-examination and honesty is very, very hard for many of us. Being honest with yourself means looking at all the hurts and wounds that mangled your heart so much it may be indistinguishable now. It means looking at the times you protected your heart with a shield of fear. If you removed that shield, the feelings may be overwhelming, you fear. You may not be able to stop the pain from consuming you, or so we often convince ourselves.

What does your heart hold? Loving yourself and accepting whatever secrets you still harbor within is the first critical component of an open heart. You can't possibly have a loving heart if the heart of your being is based on self-loathing, shame, or lack of forgiveness.

Women, especially, have been conditioned to be martyrs, to nurture everyone else before we nurture ourselves. You can't be of heart if you've "given it away" to your husband and children, as one woman described martyrdom to me. Entirely sacrificing your own heart and what it needs is not a noble thing. It's not healthy. *Sacrifice* in *Webster's* dictionary means "to kill, destroy, or surrender." That is not what our hearts or beings are destined for. Don't go there. Don't nurture others so much that you become invisible. Don't destroy your sanity, psyche, and body to keep others afloat. You can't truly nurture others unless you regularly nurture and love yourself.

You also can't be on fire with love and compassion if you're consumed at heart by violent, hateful thoughts and actions. Are there still secrets, shadows you haven't told anyone—maybe can't even admit to yourself— that weigh on your heart? Could those shadows be taking a toll on your health in some way? "The body weeps the tears that the eyes have failed to shed," says author Jerry Jampolsky.

THE BODY-HEART CONNECTION

Doctors, especially those who honor the relationship between our emotions and our physical symptoms, see over and over how what we carry in our hearts affects our health.

Dr. Martin Rossman, co-director of the Academy of Guided Imagery in Mill Valley, California, sees daily how our physical bodies reflect our emotions, attitudes, and beliefs. Our bodies often send powerful messages that something in our physical, spiritual, and emotional beings is out of balance and needs healing. In some cases, it's often the heart that's most in need of healing, Dr. Rossman finds.

For instance, he once treated a young man with a very serious collagen disease that caused a lot of pain in his arms and legs. The man was deteriorating rapidly and was taking steroids. Dr. Rossman used imagery to try to unearth the emotional root of his patient's physical symptoms.

One symptom that flared up in the course of their sessions was burning stomach pain. Dr. Rossman guided the man to use imagery and relaxation techniques to tune directly in to his stomach pain and describe whatever image he found there. The man described a burning fire. "What represents something that might soothe or help relieve the pain?" Dr. Rossman asked. "Water," the man replied.

So the man imagined a cool stream of water running through the fire. "At first, he imagined spraying water on the fire with a hose," Dr. Rossman said. "Then, he started to imagine a cool mountain stream washing down and cooling his stomach, putting out the fire. After three to five minutes, he smiled, opened his eyes, and told me that the pain was gone. He was ecstatic."

Dr. Rossman told the man to practice the imagery frequently until his stomach healed. For several weeks, everything was fine, but soon the cooling image stopped working. No matter how much water the man poured on it, the fire in his stomach would not go out, and he became very depressed.

Dr. Rossman again guided his patient to tune in to his stomach, and this time the man found the image of a hand pinching his stomach lining. When he asked his hand why it was pinching his stomach, it turned into a fist shaking at him. "It looks like it's angry at me," he said. "Why is it angry at me?"

And then the man saw that the hand turned into a pointing finger. The finger was pointing up through his chest and heart to a bag that was all tied up. "There are all kinds of things in there, booming and bumping around," he said. "Sharp-edge objects, weird sounds, stuff like that."

Dr. Rossman told the man to watch for a while and tell him what else he noticed. His patient said, "My heart is in there, and it's getting damaged by all the things caught in there with it." So Dr. Rossman asked the man, "Would you like to open the bag and let things out?"

This brought up a tremendous amount of anxiety in his patient. But the man imagined receiving the support of an "inner advisor"—a wise, old Indian woman. The woman told him to open the bag very carefully and just let one thing out at a time. The man imagined loosening the cords on the bag, and out came the face of his stepfather. "It turned out my patient and his stepfather had a very difficult relationship. The stepfather, an alcoholic, was an angry, critical man who abused my patient physically during his teenage years," Dr. Rossman said.

Fortunately, through psychotherapy, the man learned how to ease some of his emotional pain that was linked to his physical illness. "In following up on him a couple of years later, I learned he had done quite well. His disease hadn't gone away, but it stopped progressing on a minimal dose of steroids," said Dr. Rossman.[5]

FORGIVENESS IS THE WAY TO LOVE

Our hearts—and psyches—interact with and hold so much more than we can even begin to imagine. What does your heart hold, and does it serve you well? Or does it diminish your heart? When you sit with your heart, ask yourself if there are people you still need to forgive. Are there people who still need to forgive you?

Our hearts can never be as loving and powerful as they are meant to be if they are poisoned with unresolved grief, resentments, and anger that we've stored in them. Lack of forgiveness traps us in the past. Forgiving means letting go of all that has occurred to finally live for now.

And sometimes the hardest part is forgiving ourselves. Our hearts can be swollen with grief for decades over things we've done or said and not let go of. Let go of anything that is hanging heavy in your heart. One way to do this is to use a method from author Louise Hay.

She suggests making a list of the blessings you want most in your life. Then pray for the person you hate or can't forgive to receive each of the blessings on your list. Dr. Bruno Cortis, a cardiologist who looks at how and why people heal from physical heart traumas, recommends to his heart patients wrestling with forgiveness issues that they do this once or twice a day for two weeks. "At the end of that time, the resentful feelings will be either gone or greatly diminished." Forgiveness in our culture is one of the most radical acts of love. "The pathway to love is forgiveness," says Dr. Cortis in his book *Heart and Soul*.

What about those radical acts of hate? Either those we've committed or those we've erroneously taken on? How do we even begin to forgive ourselves? Forgiveness is a huge theme for our world right now. The issue of forgiveness seized center stage when President Bill Clinton had to publicly forgive himself—and seek forgiveness from the country and his family—for his relationship with Monica Lewinsky.

The wonderfully mystical movie *The Legend of Bagger Vance* explores the issue of forgiveness from the perspective of the main character, who is consumed with inner demons. It turns out he's never forgiven himself for surviving a horrific, bloody battle in World War II in which all of his fellow soldiers died. He can't forgive himself for not being enough of a hero.

What still haunts you? What keeps you out of your heart? If it's guilt and remorse, there are ways you can finally lay them down. To live compassionately out of your heart, you have to live in the present. You have to be here, now. Guilt and remorse and a lack of forgiveness bar your heart from being fully loving because they, like an out-of-body-and-soul experience, trap you in another dimension. You can never be free emotionally if you can't remove those iron bands around your heart.

These feelings may be most intense in prisons, where both spiritual and literal bars trap inmates and their hearts. If there ever was an institution in need of compassion and humane, radical acts of love, it is our correctional facilities. The revolution of compassion is beginning to heal this segment of our world, as well.

BRINGING FORGIVENESS TO PRISONS

The visionary and compassionate National Emotional Literacy Project for Prisoners is working in twenty-five hundred correctional institutions across the country to, among other things, help inmates learn to forgive themselves and heal. The project is sponsored by the Lionheart Foundation, created by heart activist Robin Casarjian.

Again, this is where compassion is the most logical, practical, powerful choice of all. More than 94 percent of prisoners will return to our communities. "Will they leave prison as more mature, responsible adults, or will they leave more wounded, alienated, and angry than when they went in?" asks Casarjian, a therapist and an educator. She is also the author of *Forgiveness: A Bold Choice for a Peaceful Heart* and *Houses of Healing: A Prisoner's Guide to Inner Power and Freedom*.

You'll hear more about Casarjian's amazing story throughout this book, showing how all of our lives can be transformed by the type of forgiveness work that she does in prisons. "What better place is there to process the idea of forgiveness—to see the light instead of the lampshade over someone? What better place to be with people seen only as criminal and instead see them as spiritual beings with the capacity to love and heal?" she asks.

But before most of the inmates can see themselves as spiritual, loving human beings, they often have to look at the full impact of their actions, to take responsibility for them, and to forgive themselves for making choices that blew apart many people's worlds, Casarjian says.

Healing inmates may be the hardest of possible work. It requires peeling back layers and layers of actions and consequences. When we see how forgiveness works for inmates, we see how we can apply forgiveness to free and empower our own hearts. When we talked, Casarjian shared that one of the best ways to begin is to first have compassion for yourself during this process. "Write twenty-five times, 'I will be gentle with myself.' Put that on your dashboard, in your underwear drawer, on your kitchen window, in your pocket. Many people don't even know what it means to be gentle with themselves. This plants the seed of looking at yourself in a new way, without the ego's judgment."

SEEKING CLOSURE

Once you begin to look on yourself with compassion, spend time examining moments when you acted unethically, without integrity, or in ways that irreparably harmed someone else. Casarjian has inmates list how their actions affected their victims, their families, their communities, their own families. For instance, they might write, "My actions affected you in all the following ways . . . ."

Casarjian believes this exercise challenges them to ask themselves, "What do you really feel sorry for? In our culture we say, 'I'm sorry for raping your daughter,' the same way we say, 'I'm sorry I spilled that glass of milk.' This exercise really makes you look at the ramifications of your actions, not to beat yourself up, but to tell the truth. Because the truth will set you free."

Then, she guides the inmates to further challenge themselves to bring closure to their choices. "If they still carry guilt, they apologize or write a letter, whatever they feel called to communicate."

Still another step you can adopt is one Casarjian borrows from Louise Hay. It's called the Forgiveness Diet. "For seven days," said Casarjian, "you write down thirty-five times in the morning and thirty-five times in the evening, 'I forgive myself completely.' If you have a reaction that comes up to that, write it down in the right-hand column next to it. At the end of it, if you still haven't forgiven yourself completely, write down, 'What I get out of holding on to self-condemnation is . . .' And be radically honest with yourself if you think you have something to gain by continuing to feel unnecessary shame."

FORGIVENESS UNITES US ALL

Forgiveness not only brings us personal peace but also unifies our culture in ways we can only begin to imagine. "If you forgive someone, they belong to you, and you belong to them. Squatter's rights of the heart," says Garrison Keillor, writer and host of the radio show *A Prairie Home Companion*. Seek out and read or learn stories of forgiveness as inspiration in your own heartwork, stories of people like the Reverend David Kennedy, an activist preacher in South Carolina. An advocate for the impoverished, Kennedy put a homeless man and his family up in a hotel and gave them food and support daily. Compassionate sure, but he's a minister, after all, you might say. But forgiveness was at the heart of his actions. The man had been a former Ku Klux Klansman who had recently stalked Kennedy with the intent to kill him.[6]

Dr. Elizabeth Menken's sister Elaine was killed in 1993 when a drunk driver crossed into her lane and hit her car head-on. The woman had a prior drunk-driving conviction. At first, Dr. Menken wanted to "gouge out her eyes so she'd never drive again." But she learned how to release her pain and forgive through a program that brought the offender and her family together for reconciliation. They forgave the woman and, together, drew up a "restitution contract." It specifies that the woman attend Alcoholics Anonymous (AA) meetings, work to get other drunk drivers off the road, go back to school, and build her parenting skills, among other things. "Elaine would have been proud of the way we are helping a young mother and learning how to forgive the unforgivable."[7]

The alternative is carrying hatred and bitterness, which takes a toll on our bodies. Again, sometimes the hardest work of all is to forgive ourselves. But in doing so, in being tender enough with ourselves to finally forgive ourselves, we rediscover our immense compassion. We can use that dark-night-of-the-soul, sitting-in-the-wound time to develop the empathy needed to finally be present enough to turn outward and help others forgive themselves and heal. "The tenderness of a forgiven heart is a tenderness that will ultimately heal the world," says Marianne Williamson in *Enchanted Love*.

Forgiveness is really another huge way to nurture and feed ourselves. When our hearts cling to hatred and meanness, we cling to a toxic spiritual pattern. We are only human and humans screw up from time to time. But as human beings, we have an immense capacity to love deeply too.

What is still needing forgiveness in your life? How hard will it be to let go of that anger and bitterness poisoning your heart? It can be done. Work with a psychologist or other therapist to lay this poison down. There are many amazing tools with which to finally let go and free yourself of your negative feelings. Often just confiding in someone else releases the toxins, like draining an abscessed wound. This is necessary, powerful, healing work.

WHEN RECONCILIATION SEEMS IMPOSSIBLE

You might also find inspiration in the story of Aba Gayle, who told her story recently at a Findhorn Foundation's conference on forgiveness and reconciliation. She freed herself from the downward spiral of grief after her nineteen-year-old daughter, Catherine, was brutally murdered in 1980. That is when she began an eight-year "journey of darkness," Aba Gayle said. It began with a phone call from her stepson asking, "Well, what do you think about Catherine being shot?"

She hung up and called the sheriff's department and said, "This is Gayle, mother of Catherine Blount. I hear she has been shot. Where is she? How is she? I must go to her!"

The voice at the other end of the line said, "No ma'am. Your daughter hasn't been shot. Your daughter is dead."

As she waited for the sheriff to call her back, Aba Gayle remembers knowing what it was like to be insane. After three long, painful, tense hours, she finally called the sheriff's office again and said, "Someone must speak to me because I'm losing my mind."

Finally a detective came on the line and kindly and gently spoke the terrible news: "I'm sorry, but your daughter, Catherine, is dead. Your daughter was murdered. She was stabbed to death."

At that point, Aba Gayle remembers, "Something in my heart broke." She tried to remain calm and was afraid to let anyone hug her for fear she would break down. She was terrified of crying because others would hear her. But when she took a shower, with the water running full blast, she finally screamed, and screamed, and screamed.

She had no faith at the time, no support system. Her mother was just recovering from open-heart surgery and was too fragile. Her two other children had just left home to attend medical school. She had no faith and didn't believe in a God.

Aba Gayle's husband often found himself unable to share the grieving with her. "He announced that he didn't want to talk about Catherine anymore. He said he didn't intend to mourn her the rest of his life."

At work, Aba Gayle's colleagues and friends, many of whom had known Catherine well, were in denial that she had been murdered, and many could not bring themselves to talk with Aba Gayle about her trauma. Painful silence. "I had to be strong to help everyone else," Aba Gayle recalled. "I found myself more and more isolated with no one to give me the love and encouragement I needed so badly."

The district attorney sought to console Aba Gayle by reassuring her that they would find Catherine's assailant and have him sentenced to the death penalty. Aba Gayle believed him in his delusion that this would make everything all right. She then entered an eight-year period of rage and hatred, dominated by her lust for revenge. "On the surface, I carried on the false front. Had you known me at that time, you wouldn't have known about the dark, ugly cloud I carried around inside me. You would have thought I was getting along just fine. But inside of me, a deep, dark rage began to boil. There was this awful, hideous darkness, and all I wanted was revenge for the death of my beloved child."

LAYING DOWN THE HATRED

How many of us have gone into that same seething, roiling darkness? How many times have we acted as if all was well, when inside we were consumed by hatred and a lust for vengeance? Are you still in that horrifying place now? What will it take for you to finally lay it all down and let some light pierce the darkness? What will it take to forgive and heal?

Aba Gayle's recovery, her "journey into life," was sparked by a meditation class she began to attend. It was here that she learned to be still and listen within. She began a spiritual quest and acted on a longing to deepen her divinity. After joining a Unity Church in Auburn, California, she "fell in love with God" and "found her God-self." Her marriage ended because "my spiritual growth and growing love for God changed me into a different person." Her husband, whose lack of support for her grief had made her life painful, thought religion was stupid.

But Aba Gayle had the good fortune of meeting a man from the church who ran a metaphysical bookstore. He became her personal librarian and supplied her with a book every week. Her minister also began a study class based upon the teachings of *A Course in Miracles*, which attracted Aba Gayle. She was given a videotape that made a huge impression on her: "It was while watching the video that I got my first glimpse of the healing power of forgiveness."

In one interview on the video, a Jewish man, a Holocaust survivor, described how he had forgiven the German people and the guards in the camps who had murdered every member of his family. "Something in me really clicked when I heard that testimony," Aba Gayle said. For the first time, she believed that it could be possible for her to forgive Douglas Mickey, Catherine's murderer, who had been tried and sentenced to death. Through a friend, she learned that his execution was now scheduled.

She adopted what she describes as a "fragile forgiveness" based upon pride and resentment. But her desire to attend Mickey's execution helped her realize that she still had further deep work to do.

Driving home one day, Aba Gayle distinctly heard a voice say, "You must forgive him and you must let him know!" At 4 A.M. the following morning, unable to sleep, she began to write a letter to Mickey, excerpts of which follow:

> I know that Catherine is in a better place than we can ever know here on earth. I did not know that when Catherine died. All I knew is that I had been robbed of my precious child, and that she had been robbed of growing into womanhood and achieving all her potential. The violent way that she left this earth was impossible for me to understand. I was saddened beyond belief and felt that I could never be happy again. . . .
>
> I was very angry with you and wanted to see you punished to the limit of the law. You had done irreparable damage to my family and

my dreams for the future. After eight long years of grief and anger, I started my journey of life. I met wonderful teachers and slowly began to learn about my God-self. In the midst of a class studying *A Course in Miracles*, I was surprised to find that I could forgive you. This does not mean that I think you are innocent or that you are blameless for what happened. What I learned was this: You are a divine child of God. You carry the Christ Consciousness within you. You are surrounded by God's love even as you sit in your cell. The Christ in me sends blessings to the Christ in you.

THE MIRACLE OF FORGIVENESS

Aba Gayle finished the letter by writing, "I send blessings to you and to your children." Her church group gave her the support she needed to mail the letter. She described poignantly how the sound of the letter hitting the bottom of the mailbox changed her life. From the moment she heard the sound, she knew, "All the anger, all the rage, all the ugliness that I was carrying in my body for all those years—it was instantly gone. It just left. And in its place, I was just filled with a sense of joy and peace, and I was truly in a state of grace."

True forgiveness finally gave Aba Gayle the healing she needed. She didn't require anything more; she sent the letter without condition or attachment. She didn't expect an answer. Just the simple act of offering the gift of forgiveness was healing enough.

But she did receive a reply from Mickey, in which he shared his "tears of joy and sorrow" at finally having the opportunity to communicate with her. He also wrote, "The Christ in me most gratefully accepts and returns blessings of Divine Wisdom, Love and Charity to the Christ in you." He also said, "I would gladly give my life this instant if it would in any way change that terrible night."

Their contact eventually led to her visiting San Quentin State Prison in California, where Mickey is still being held on death row. As Aba Gayle arrived in the visiting room for death-row inmates, she looked around with surprise. "I did not see a single monster in the room. It was filled with ordinary-looking men. They were sitting with their grandmothers, or wives, or ministers, and/or their children. Everywhere I looked, I saw the face of God."

She and Mickey met and talked and cried together for more than three hours. "I realized the night Catherine lost her life, Douglas also lost his future," Aba Gayle said. Developing a relationship with Douglas enabled her to understand that we are all one, that we are all interconnected. Aba Gayle is now an active campaigner for the abolition of the death penalty. "I know that if the state of California ever executes Douglas Mickey, it would be killing my friend."

Aba Gayle has also established a ministry for prisoners on death row and travels internationally, sharing her story of forgiveness in the hope that it will inspire others to heal themselves. When asked by the media if any of the men on death row have committed crimes that are just too horrifying for her to treat them with compassion, she responded, "I don't deal with their crime. I don't deal with that part of them. I deal with the God-spirit within him or her. That is the truth of their being. It is the truth for every one of us."

Following are some of the universal truths—teachings expressed by Jesus, the Buddha, and other enlightened beings—that Aba Gayle shares. These teachings have guided her to a place of profound inner peace:

- You can choose to be right or you can choose to be happy.
- What you give your energy to is what you will attract into your life.
- Anger and rage are extremely detrimental to our health.
- Only the present moment exists.
- You choose to be a victim; therefore, you can choose not to be a victim.
- We are all one.

Who are the "Douglas Mickeys" in your life? Whom do you still want revenge against? Whom are you still willing to play the victim for? Now, shift it and ask, How can I begin the process of forgiveness? What steps can I take this evening before I go to sleep to take back my heart? Could I finally be ready to forgive, to lay it all down and heal? Forgiveness is the last gateway to the full heart.

CONNECTION WITH OTHERS STRENGTHENS US

Once you've worked on your healing through forgiveness, you can move to the next stage of really looking at how well you love and how well you are loved. Ask yourself, How well connected, bound up with, interwoven with others, is my heart? Is this weaving of our hearts permanent—or could it shift at any minute? Who is in my life for the long haul? Who will love me and whom will I love, in return, during thick and thin? Connection with others makes our hearts resilient, fierce, and vocal. "Our hearts can speak out and be accepted more powerfully in a large circle of friends," says Joan Borysenko. "It is often in sharing our vision and insight, hopes and fears, that we hear it for the first time ourselves. . . . Together, more powerfully than alone, we can collect the hidden jewels of our life and decide how best to use them. Together, we can more honestly and courageously face the task of composting life's garbage so that it can be used as a seedbed for words, thoughts, and deeds in which to grow more compassionate lives."[8]

It seems ironic. Illogical, even. But when we are vulnerable and share ourselves with others who accept us as we are, we become stronger, more resilient and courageous. We can survive anything. If we try to be the good soldier and stoically manage it all alone, we often crumble. We also damage our health. Without intimacy with others, our bodies are jeopardized, as countless studies now show.

A study of heart-attack survivors found that those who lived alone were more than twice as likely to die within a year. In another study, college students who reported strained, cold relationships with their parents were found to suffer extraordinary rates of hypertension and heart disease decades later. The heart always longs for connection and suffers even at the memory of not being fully loved.[9]

How is it with you? Do you feel you have enough friends and family members who love you just as you are? Are you connected to people who do more than support you at work, who do more than further your career? Are you connected to people who will come and shovel your walk or get you groceries when you strain your back? Do you have heartlines that connect you to people who are there when you've been up all night with feverish, crying kids and you need a nap?

Do those lines reach out and weave you inexorably with those who are able to celebrate your victories without feeling threatened and jealous and who can help hold your sadness without feeling endangered? Who will accept you when your hormones are surging, your hair is thinning, and your face no longer resembles the freshness of an Ally McBeal?

Wherever I traveled in discussing my book *Depression: What Your Body's Trying to Tell You*, I usually asked people this question: How many of you feel you have enough supportive family and friends? In two years and with dozens of groups, I never saw more than one-quarter of the hands raised. Today, when the average family uproots and moves to a new location every five years, social ties and a sense of community become frayed—if they were ever there at all.

Just when you've connected your souls with late-night talks as the candles burn down, just as you've commiserated with each other about kids' braces, your breast lump scares, your hilarious, embarrassing moments . . . just when you begin to rest in the knowledge that runs up your backbone that good, solid friends are close at hand, it all shifts—again.

Or worse, yet, the dearest friendships never get made. We collect only a passel of acquaintances that move interchangeably through our lives like the latest accessories. We acquire the trophy homes and cars, job kudos and pricey toys—and spend scant time collecting priceless friends.

DEEP FRIENDSHIPS ARE A RARE COMMODITY

How many of us have enough friends that we love and are, in turn, adored by? Our seize-the-day, overscheduled lives often don't have space for friendships. We're lucky if we can grab a fragment of conversation as we stuff lettuce into bags at the produce section or, over our kids' heads, dive for water bottles at the soccer games. Little time to linger over candles and food and soulful eye contact to take the relationship to a deeper level.

My good friend Susan moved away last year, and I still mourn that I'll never again find her on my doorstep at dawn, brandishing a latte and a grin. It started when we both began waking, in a premenopausal surge, at 2 A.M. It was one of the many Susan rituals that made life fuller, more satisfying.

She was one of the finest, funniest, big-hearted friends I've ever known. She also had a raucous sense of humor that I adored.

Susan was my touchstone, and I know I was one for her, as well. We had many fine afternoons, squatting in her adirondack chairs, drinking coffee, talking about how her morning glories were so blue or comparing notes on kids and husbands. Talking long about the books we loved and the people we'd love to meet in them. Sharing our spiritual hopes, discoveries, struggles, and epiphanies. I still smile when I remember that Susan, raised as a staunch Catholic, used to bury Saint Christopher statues near her lilacs for good luck—but she also sought the guidance of spiritual intuitives, for extra measure. How often do we get to know someone that intimately—and how lucky, deeply lucky, when we do.

BEING KNOWN IS A GIFT

We all long to be fully known. We all long to fully know others. How much we miss if that longing isn't satisfied. How much we miss if we conclude that our deep, hardwired need to be in relationships with others can't be satisfied in a professional work setting.

The opposite can be true, said Linton Elementary School principal Priscilla Huston. "I realize my professional needs are to be in relationship with others: relationships with my students, their parents, my staff. And what better place than in a school? Children are my passion. There is nothing else I'd rather do in terms of my life's work."

Being in relationships with others not only opens our hearts, but also stokes the passion within; it amplifies our energy. For five years, Huston worked long hours in an administrative position in her school district and was "exhausted all the time." Now, in a school setting, the same schedule builds her energy and keeps her enthusiastic and passionate about what she does instead of being grueling. It stokes her energy because she is connecting with others.

"I think every connection I make with my kids adds seconds to my life. I think kids, seeing their enthusiasm, seeing them smile, seeing their desire to share, keeps me young. It keeps me healthy," Huston said.[10]

How often our hearts never realize their full potential, how much they ache, if we never satisfy their need to see and be fully seen, to love and be fully loved. And how often we discover this, deep in our marrow, when it's too late.

Loving, ordinary moments with others can raise mere existence to a state of joy. They can raise our hearts to their true greatness.

But we also need to extend our sense of community beyond our own immediate loved ones. The concept "it takes a village to raise a child" has to become our mantra. Then we can begin to ask ourselves, How well does our village, the village we are connected to, raise our children? How well is your village doing with its kids?

In your community, how many kids are homeless, committing suicide, ignored, out in the streets unsupervised, or surfing for hours on the Internet because nobody's home? How well does your village attend to the emotional and spiritual needs of its kids? How often do you speak out when you see a child in trouble?

Too often these days, the village is obsessed with competitive sports. Many families' lives—their sacred intention—revolve around how well their kids play football or baseball or soccer. That is the chief family priority, wish, and dream. That is what the family's time together, its dinners and conversations, revolve around.

LIVING WELL MEANS CONNECTION WITH LOVED ONES

We need something more, something of greater value to live well—and to keep our entire communities well. If we put a fraction of our time into solving the needs of the homeless kids, or the kids with mental illness, or the kids who live in abusive homes, as we do in sustaining and supporting competitive sports, these problems would be resolved—or at least fully seen and addressed as they deserve to be. No question.

There's also no question that we need to extend our sense of community to include the rest of the village we are connected to and responsible for: the natural world. We have to ask ourselves, as Terry Tempest Williams, author of *Refuge*, suggests, "How do we extend our notion of community to include all life-forms—plants, animals, rocks, rivers and human beings—and step forward with a compassionate intelligence?"

We need to fall back in love with the environment and all its life enough to want to save it. Perhaps, says Williams, the most radical act we can commit is not to go searching for our cause or our mission far from home. Maybe the most radical act we can commit is to stay deeply rooted right where we are. Stay at home and speak out about the injustices, problems, environmental destruction in our own backyard. "Commit to a place. Someone must be there to chart the changes, so when the Chinook salmon no longer come up the river, we can say, 'There are no more salmon,'" says Williams, in *Embracing Our Essence*.

I think of a woman in my town, one of the fastest growing in the country, who saw a mother fox and her family threatened by a new development. She vowed each night to go out and make sure they were safe. I read that the developer eventually agreed to support the fox population too.

HONORING OUR CONNECTION WITH THE NATURAL WORLD

We need to extend that sense of community to all life-forms so we feel accountable to and conscious of how our choices affect all life around us, from salmon to coyotes to coral reefs. I find it sadly ironic during the holidays to see toy polar bears everywhere, beckoning us to pull out our credit cards, while our actions are changing global climate patterns and are steadily wiping out the polar bear habitat and threatening their population. These things have to lance our hearts enough that we can begin to be outraged and aggrieved enough to make a change.

"If we are not home, if we are not rooted deeply in place, making that commitment to dig in and stay put . . . if we don't know the names of things, if we don't know 'pronghorn antelope,' if we don't know 'blacktail jackrabbit,' if we don't know 'sage,' 'pinyon,' 'juniper,' then I think we are living a life without specificity and then our lives become abstractions. Then we enter a place of true desolation," says Terry Tempest Williams.[11]

How peaceful is your life these days? Can you do that sit-in-the-chair routine that Stephen Levine mentioned without crawling out of your skin? If you do, what comes up? What patterns can you detect? If you can't sit with your heart, why not? Are you drawn to more stimuli, distractions, unceasing motion? It's common sense that violence and chaos run counter to a loving heart. They make our hearts wither, become petrified.

And this is where we need to honestly shine a searchlight on our culture's own ingrained, condoned violence: our frenetic, nonstop lifestyles. Speed blurs life and calcifies our innate generosity. In the rallying cry for safer schools and less violent neighborhoods, we need to see that a treadmill life is a form of violence toward ourselves in the most insidious way. "To allow oneself to be carried away by a multitude of conflicting concerns, to surrender to too many demands, to commit oneself to too many good projects, to want to help everyone and everything, is itself to succumb to the violence of our time," says author and spiritual teacher Thomas Merton.[12]

FRENETIC PACE SHUTS DOWN OUR HEARTS

Survey after survey shows that we are feeling intense pressure to complete even the most basic tasks in our lives. Fifty-four percent of parents surveyed in a recent Gallup poll said they spend too little time with their children.[13] The kids won't argue with us there. In a recent survey in Colorado, nearly half of the kids surveyed said the adults in their lives don't spend enough time with them.[14]

Eighty percent of adults said they were rushed just trying to accomplish the most essential tasks of living. That's telling. It would be hard to find 80-percent agreement on many topics today.

"We live in a culture where whirl is king. . . . Ulcers, migraines, nervous tension, and a dozen other symptoms mark our psychic overload," says Richard Foster in *Freedom of Simplicity*. And that whirl often takes us away from the relationships and time for relaxation that most replenish and soothe us. Speed and stress can suck dry the most open heart. "We've so lost what it often means to nourish and nurture ourselves. Our lives are so busy that the bare necessities get tossed out the window, like the sipping of tea and watching the leaves change," observed Mariah Mannia, director of the Depression Wellness Network in Seattle.[15]

Fault lines throughout our culture show how out of balance we are. Companies are increasingly pitching "spent tents" or creating "womb rooms" so overworked, exhausted employees can crash at work. Look at some of our book titles: *Please Hold: 102 Things to Do While You Wait on the Phone* or *Eating on the Run*. We grab swigs of living, pleasure, and appreciation on the fly, like the hastily tossed back streams of bottled water that accompany us everywhere. If you sprint through life, even the barest civilities are left behind in the dust. Hard to live from a full heart when we don't slow down enough for even the most basic kindnesses.

One of the saddest places to witness this is in a mini-microcosm of our culture on a Friday afternoon after work. Watch how people drive home, road rage and all. Then narrow the lens even more and see how these same people navigate a four-way stop at a busy intersection, for instance. Invariably, on a Friday night, stressed and exhausted after the week's drains, most people can't respectfully and lovingly wait their turn.

Watch it some night. Almost every fourth or fifth person bolts through the intersection out of turn, almost causing or creating an accident. If stress and speed prevent our hearts from even staying open and respectful in these smallest of situations, how can they be expected to stay open and full for the big stuff of life when we are called to love one another? We can't be wise stewards of our hearts if we're at the brink of our emotional and spiritual breaking points by rushing through life.

EXAMINING YOUR LIFE CHOICES

How big-hearted are you toward yourself when it comes to your lifestyle, nourishing relationships and downtime to just be? How much time and energy do you place on moments that calm and build your energy and soften your heart? Do you ever sit more than ten minutes, alone and quietly, to let your dreams unspool, to remember who you really are in your heart of hearts?

Does the violence and speed of your life cause you to shut down your heart toward yourself and others? Does it cause you to conclude that you just don't have time for others? What else is there in life if we don't have time for relationships? Nothing else even comes close in comparison. If you can sit with these questions, you can connect with your heart.

It's funny that in this culture we hold our machines to higher standards than ourselves. We want our machines—our computers and microwaves and cars—to operate at full capacity, but we don't hold ourselves to achieve these same impeccable standards. We can't achieve at our highest, fullest potential or capacity if our hearts aren't part of the equation, if they've been dampened or entirely extinguished by our crazed routines.

What does your heart really feel about life as you know it? What is it holding? Does it possibly hold a sense of desperation that life is moving far too fast? How often do you feel heartsick, for instance? How often do you feel burnout? Much of the burnout today is at heart, an illness of the heart, of the soul. We long to retrieve our hearts from the wasteland they've often been banished to.

This heart-retrieval work can be grounded in nourishing, loving lifestyles. We can't be like rats on the treadmill, "running faster and faster in pursuit of cheese and yet really feeling crazed by the complexity of the maze," says Dr. Harold Bloomfield in *Depression: What Your Body's Trying to Tell You.*

More and more people are feeling called to slow down, simplify their lives, pare back to what's really important. Compassion is one way to answer that call. It's a compassion directed toward ourselves. We need to better love ourselves and stop trying to go so far, so fast, so often.

How well do you love yourself? How often do you feed yourself with the things and people you most love? The Buddha said that if we truly loved ourselves, we would never harm another. To be a truly peaceful person, we also have to stop harming ourselves. We need to find more peaceful moments, when we can just be with ourselves and breathe.

MEDITATION OPENS OUR HEARTS

One crucial way we do this is through some regular form of contemplation, whether it's meditation, yoga, or gardening. Meditation helps you open your heart and feel more compassion for yourself and those around you. It brings your heart peace in the most explosive situations. Shutting down the outer chatter and getting quiet opens the heart in the most natural, powerful way. The spiritual masters over the ages have often whispered this to us.

"Empty yourself of everything," wrote Chinese philosopher Lao-tzu. "Let the mind rest at peace. The ten thousand things rise and fall while the Self watches their return. . . . Returning to the source is stillness, which is the way of nature. The way of nature is unchanging. Knowing constancy is insight. . . . Knowing constancy, the mind is open. With an open mind, you will be openhearted. Being open hearted, you will act royally. Being royal, you will attain the divine. . . . Being divine, you will be at one with the Tao."[16] The Tao, of course, means God.

Robin Casarjian, who supports prisoners through the Lionheart Foundation, has seen over and over how meditation can bring peace to a heart torn apart by guilt: "When I first start working with prisoners, we have them align with their core center, their core self. They have to do this energetically; you can't do it intellectually, which is why meditation and other practices are so important."

By accessing their true selves through deep meditation, inmates can create a bigger space inside themselves that allows them to finally look compassionately at their darkness without self-punishment or judgment. They see that their true nature is goodness. They made some evil choice, perhaps, but they are not evil by nature. "Meditation helps us all let go of all the things that stop us from aligning with that core self. It helps us rest in the truth of who we really are," Casarjian told me.[17]

After her husband died, Sylvia began to take meditation classes at the Center for Mindfulness in Medicine, Health Care and Society at the University of Massachusetts Medical Center. She had developed such severe back pain that she had to quit her job as a nurse.

Meditation helped Sylvia find inner peace and strength—and avoid depression—even when she was pulled into a painful court case over her husband's inheritance, recalled senior instructor Elana Rosenbaum, a clinical social worker and therapist. "With meditation, you begin to feel the sweetness of life again. You can feel more gratitude and see that the glass is really half full. It gives you an inner calm you can access and take with you wherever you go. It also gives you a sense of almost being held and a knowing that everything is *okay*."[18]

COUNTERING VIOLENCE WITH PEACEFUL THOUGHTS

If you don't think meditation can shift your heart, consider what it can do in the most conflict-ridden situations. In any inner city, those who live on the edge find it extremely tough to stay calm, peaceful, and softhearted when their survival is constantly in question. It's hard to not be stressed when your environment is out of control, when bullets are whizzing by your window at night, when your family feels threatened by gangs.

Gilbert, a young Latino man, lives in a dangerous housing project in San Francisco where gangs often gather. Even when he takes his young daughter to the park, they are there and invariably taunt and harass him.

"They treat him in a disrespectful way when he's with his daughter. And in the inner city, that kind of stuff is a big deal," pointed out Kathryn Guta. "People get violent and killed in those situations."

Guta is a heart activist in San Francisco, teaching meditation, mindfulness, and stress reduction to inner-city residents. Her classes are sponsored by San Francisco General Hospital, California Pacific Medical Center, and the San Francisco jail.

Many of the people she teaches fear for their lives or are trying hard to survive every day. Meditation gives them a sense of control and inner peace.

She feels drawn to work with them because she, too, grew up in the inner city, and she knows what courage it takes to carve out a life there.

After taking Guta's classes, Gilbert has learned to pay attention to his breath as he moves through the street. He finds this helps him respond more appropriately to harassment when it crops up. "If the guys in the park treat him disrespectfully, he learns to breathe in the midst of that and just watch it pass. He enjoys his daughter more and focuses on her and not on the other people.

"In the past, Gilbert might have gotten really angry. And with men in this situation, if you mouth off, things can really escalate. In this population, it can be life-threatening."[19]

Finally, if you are seeking to reconnect with your heart, meditation also can give you an intimate understanding of your heart's desires. While our longings can often be drowned out by the noise and chaos of the day, even the faintest whisper speaks volumes in the silence of a deep meditation.

Nowhere is this more telling than in our prisons, designed to be places of emotional and physical violence, Troy Bridges wrote to me. At the time Bridges had served thirteen years of a life sentence without parole for robbing a bank in Mobile, Alabama. He is in Donaldson, Alabama's most maximum-security prison—a place with such a brutal reputation that it's nicknamed "The House of Pain."

"In prison that which is vulnerable is often taken advantage of by that which is strong," said Bridges. "The abused become the abusers, then become the abused in a never-ending cycle of pain and ignorance. . . . Participating in this game of fireball, we toss out our pain at each other until we lie smoldering in hate, then get up and burn someone else. But this doesn't relieve our pain, it only fans the flames."

Bridges practices and now teaches hundreds of other inmates how to meditate to quell the searing flames of hate and violence. His story is one of the most moving and real that I discovered while gathering stories for this book. Later, you'll learn how, through incredible serendipity, he brought Robin Casarjian's Houses of Healing program to his institution and transformed the lives of hundreds of inmates.

But first, he has a lot to say as we examine our hearts and reflect on how free they are to guide our lives: "We all have our prisons—in here or out there. Even people on the streets are imprisoned by their lifestyles, by their unhealthy addictions and prejudices. Many are imprisoned by a job they hate or a relationship that's not satisfying. Some carry their prisons around inside their heads."

ESCAPING THE PRISONS OF OUR OWN MAKING

Where are you still imprisoned in your life? What keeps you in that space? Can you tell why you've put yourself there and what it would take to get out? Meditation was one method of surrender that helped Bridges step out of his self-made prison of self-loathing and hatred. It helped him radically change his life and feel at peace, powerful, connected, and full.

But it was a long road to that place of inner fullness. Bridges recalled the following experiences, which trace his journey:

One day, five years after he was sent to "The House of Pain," Bridges was sitting on his metal locker box in his cell, drawing a pencil portrait. A guard walked up to him and said, "Stand up. This is a shakedown!"

"Man, you've got to be kiddin'," Bridges said.

"I ain't jokin'. This is a shakedown. Get up!" the guard yelled.

"I'm tired of you always messin' with me," Bridges yelled back. He threw his cardboard drawing board in the corner and wadded up his half-finished drawing into a ball and threw it too.

"You'd better chill out," the guard warned.

"I'm tired of this shit. Find somebody else to mess with. There's a hundred other men in this dormitory," Bridges responded.

The guard searched Bridges's bed and locker, confiscated his pens and pencils and a sandwich he had in a plastic bag. Bridges stood off to the side cursing him. "You happy now?"

"Just doin' my job," the guard responded.

"Yeah? What is your job? Messin' with people?"

The guard left, and later that day, Bridges was handcuffed and thrown in the hole. Have you ever been "in the hole" in your life? Are you still there? What makes up your void? Is there a hole inside you that feels like an endless chasm, perhaps? Answering these questions is like following a trail of breadcrumbs that lead back to our hearts.

When Bridges literally found himself in the bowels of prison, he sat in his heart. At first he thought, "Why does this keep happening to me? Every time I turn around I'm being hassled. I didn't do anything."

He felt as if he'd hit rock bottom. Then a few nights later, he was awakened suddenly and jumped from bed. The phrase "What goes around comes around" kept playing over and over in his head.

"If that's true," he thought, "then I keep gettin' screwed up because of what I'm doin'. If I'm having angry and frustrating experiences all the time, then it must be because I'm respondin' to the world in an angry and frustrating way."

Recalling the phrase "What goes around comes around," he saw the clear image of a large wicker basket. He realized he was placing baseball-sized rocks in this basket, one after another. When he stood on a ladder to look inside, all he saw were rocks. He thought, "If day after day I keep puttin' rocks inside this basket, what can I expect to find when I reach inside?" The answer was simple—rocks! So it is with our lives.

How is it with your life? How full is your basket with the negative rocks you've thrown in, one after another?

Bridges then recalled what he had read over the years: Christian doctrine told him that we reap what we sow. Islamic doctrine says that not one of us is a believer until we love for our brother what we love for ourselves. Native American teaching says we should not condemn a brother until we have walked a mile in his moccasins.

WE ATTRACT WHAT WE GIVE OUT

"It has taken me all these years in prison and much pain to myself and others to realize these fundamental truths," Bridges realized. "Still, why should I be concerned about my brother? Why should I care about what I do to him? Why should I love for him what I love for myself? Why should I seek to understand him?"

Because, it dawned on Bridges, "What I do to him, what I think of him, what I want for him, will either be the gold or the rock that I put into the basket of my life. What I do to him, I do to myself."

Finally, Bridges understood that if he gave hate and anger, he got hate and anger back. And then he smiled as he realized that if he gave love and respect, he would receive love and respect. It all seemed so simple. Silently, he vowed that for twenty-four hours, he would try a new experiment. He would give respect, love, and understanding to everyone he met, in every situation, no matter how difficult. He began to see the rewards of his new attitude almost immediately. Soon everyone seemed "more kind and considerate." Bridges felt so thankful for "this new revelation" that he began to pray and meditate daily.

"Daily meditation and the books on spirituality I began to read began to soften the anger inside me," he said. "I began to feel more peaceful. People and situations that would have irritated and angered me before, now only mildly bothered me."

Meditation allowed him to embrace life in a positive, rather than a negative manner, he concluded. "One of the most radical acts that a person can perform is to sit quietly and be perfectly still without moving. Try it sometime in a busy group of people and notice the attention it draws to you."

From his bed, right in the middle of the crowded prison dormitory, Bridges began to hold regular Wednesday evening meditation meetings for other inmates. He knew that even if a few people gathered and were able to hold the noise and chaos at bay with their breathing and inner calm, the consciousness of the entire prison would be changed.

"Even if only three or four of us meditate openly once a week, it will make a difference," he said to some of the other inmates.

So they began, in an area so crowded that only a foot of space separated one bed from another, and some of the beds were even double-bunked. Just being this jammed in created a lot of tension among the men.

"We also had two TV sets, and their volume was almost always at maximum. Noisy domino games were always in progress, and men were constantly yelling and horseplaying."

Twelve people from different religious and cultural backgrounds showed up for the first Wednesday evening meditation. Bridges pushed his bed against a wall so they could crowd into a four-by-ten-foot space. "We squeezed ourselves into a tight circle, face-to-face, knees touching front and sides."

Curious, suspicious eyes from the other men tracked their every move. Bridges gave a brief demonstration of a popular meditation technique and talked of the importance of learning to quiet the mind. And they began to go into silence and their meditation.

CONNECTING WITH THE DIVINE

A few minutes later, a few guys started wrestling a couple of beds away. A domino slammed a metal table, echoing with the sound of a high-powered rifle, Bridges remembers. He heard a man ask, "What the hell are they doing?" Another guy laughed, "They're doing some of that X-rated prayin'." They both laughed and moved on.

Breathing in and breathing out, Bridges visualized each man's face and position in the circle. "In and out, I saw each bathed in a golden light. Deeper and deeper, touching the silence within, I connected each with a Divine umbilical cord.

"A basketball game, blaring loudly on the television sets, faded to an unintelligible murmur. In . . . out . . . I completed the circle, then returned my attention to my breathing. Someone yelled, and it was as if the sound burst from the mouth of a tunnel miles away. Deeper and deeper, the inner silence, the inner silence comforting; the combined energy electrifying. We had created an energy link of love and peaceful calm."[20]

Having just sat with this amazing story, which continues to unfold later in the book, be with your own spirit. How calm and loving and peaceful are you right now? How are you through most of your daily breathing and living?

What are you giving out into the world—rocks or gold? What do you hope your heart gives others? If we want to have more compassion for others, we have to set the intention for that. And meditation and contemplative, quiet stillness and prayer are one way we do that. We can't just superficially say we'll go into the world and be nice people, go around flashing smiles all day, randomly saying "Have a nice day" to everyone we brush up against. We have to be willing to take it deeper.

Empty a space in our souls, in our hearts, as Troy Bridges did, to let the vastness and sacredness of life in, to begin to make room for ourselves and someone else. Let the love and good intentions for others root deeply there. We have to move into deep, compassionate action.

Set the intention for living a heart-centered life. Dedicate yourself to love. Fall with abandon into a compassionate way of living. Ask that you be used as a channel for higher purpose in the world. It helps tremendously if you can journal your thoughts and feelings. Write down the instances when you intend to be more loving. Write down, "My heart feels drawn to be more loving when I . . . "

WRITING AN INVENTORY OF THE HEART

Write down the situations in your life where you know some disharmony or animosity could be transformed by a more heartfelt approach. Describe what you hope your heart can accomplish in these situations. "If my heart could make a difference, it would be . . . " Ask to be a channel for peace in these moments.

And then speak your intentions out loud. Speak into the world what you want your heart to speak of. Many people now visualize, visualize, visualize. It's a popular deal. Some visualize in an effort to manifest their biggest commission ever, their most incredible soulmate, that fabulous summer vacation house or pricey toy. But what about visualizing a fiercely blazing heart that triumphantly takes us into the world to do good things? How often do we visualize our hearts softening, pounding, vibrating with love?

Set your intentions. Visualize how you want to act from your heart. Visualize yourself saying the compassionate things you've longed to say. Set your intention to transform your own world with more love through the things and people you surround yourself with. Visualize yourself acting on your heart throughout your life.

Spiritual teachers throughout the ages have told us that when we intend to be loving people, we spark the heavens to open. We signal our angels and divine guides and our God that we are ready to be showered with grace. We signal that we're ready to cherish others and, in turn, be cherished by the spiritual realm. Then compassion is given to us, created by our stated intention to be compassionate people.

You can take some immediate, practical, powerful steps to signal your intention to be of heart. You can write down poems or quotations that describe what you feel in your heart or remind you of how you want to be. As your heart begins to green, spend time in nature and listen to stirring music or books on tape to make it even lusher.

SETTING THE INTENTION TO BE COMPASSIONATE

Add more beauty around you. A bouquet of russet cornflowers on a weeping, gray autumn day can immediately quicken and lift your heart. Weave in whatever encourages you to be loving and heart-centered. New Jersey Superior Court Judge Sylvan Rothenberg used a gavel with a twist. Engraved on the side was the word *rachmonas*, a Yiddish word that means "compassion."[21]

Griffin Hospital in Connecticut revised its mission statement to include "Treating all people with compassion" as one of its stated values. You can also weave in your intention to be loving in your daily routines.

I know of a couple that has two heart-shaped rose quartzes. She keeps one with her at home where she works; he carries the other with him to his busy office. Periodically throughout the day, they pick up their quartzes and hold them in their hands to recall their love for the other. This signals the angels their great intention to strengthen and deepen their love.

We can weave many, many things into our lives to remind us of our desire to be openhearted people. An Irish proverb says: "Cherish these three hearts: the heart of relationship that nurtures love and family. The heart of friendship that heals all that has been lost. The heart of the soul that fuels creativity and truth."[22]

What can you mount in your heart—in your home and office—to remind you of your desire to be of good heart? What would that plaque or poster say? What is your intention to be more loving? Write it in your mind and then write it from your hand. Post it where you will see it daily, where it will get splattered with toothpaste, coffee, and tomato sauce. It will signal the angels, "This! This! This is my true intention to live from my heart." And they will respond with grace and guidance, opening your heart to fully blaze and light this world.

Many times, says heart doctor Bruno Cortis, heart attacks, like any test of our mortality, cause people to undergo radical transformations. After the initial shock, many people reclaim an inner strength. "They rediscover life, they find the joy of smelling flowers, looking at the blue sky, taking a walk, breathing the fresh air, listening to the wind. . . . Spring returns to their heart."[23]

This seems to be the time in our world when spring is returning to our hearts so we can be radically transformed ourselves. This is a time to re-discover our inner strengths and to signal and allow spring to return to our hearts.

There are many, many rituals we can do to begin to thaw our frozen hearts. I'll close this chapter with a meditation I personally love from Stephen and Ondrea Levine called "Soft-Belly Meditation." The Levines believe many of us have a lifetime of holding our compassion within us—by hardening our bellies.

"We hold our fear, grief, pain, our darkest secrets, in the pit of our stomachs," Ondrea said. "Every time our bellies tighten, our hearts harden."

The Levines share this powerful meditation as a "call to the heart that it's safe to be alive in the body once again."

Soft-Belly Meditation

Take a few deep breaths, feel the body you breathe in.
Feel the body expanding and contracting with each breath.
Focus on the rising and falling of the abdomen.
Let awareness receive the beginning, middle, and end of each inbreath,
    of each outbreath, expanding and contracting the belly.
Note the constantly changing flow of sensation.
In each inhalation, in each exhalation.
And begin to soften all around these sensations.
Let the breath breathe itself in a softening body.
Soften the belly to receive the breath, to receive the sensation, to
    experience life in the body.
Soften the muscles that have held the fear for so long.
Soften the tissue, the blood vessels, the flesh.
Letting go into soft-belly, merciful belly.
Soften the grief, the distrust, the anger
held so long in the belly.
Levels and levels of softening, levels and levels of letting go.
Moment to moment allow each breath its full expression in soft-belly.
Let go of the hardness. Let it float in something softer and kinder.
Let thoughts come and let them go.

Floating like bubbles in the spaciousness of soft-belly.
Holding to nothing, softening, softening.
Let the healing in.
Let the pain go.
Have mercy on yourself, soften the belly,
Open the passageway to the heart.
In soft-belly, there is room to be born at last,
and room to die when the moment comes.
In soft-belly is the vast spaciousness in which to heal,
in which to discover our unbounded nature.
Letting go into the softness,
fear floats in the gentle vastness we call the heart.

4

A Change of Heart:
Seeing with Love

AT TWENTY-THREE, I was pregnant with our first child. Twenty years later, it still amazes me how much, within days of knowing I was pregnant, I fell in love with the prospect of nurturing that life.

But one day at work, while I was in the middle of a business luncheon, a convulsive wave of pain slammed into my abdomen. When I called my doctor, I could barely talk both from the pain and from the panic that something was desperately wrong.

My whole body was going numb with fear as I walked into the emergency room, but I told myself everything would be *okay*. Soon my baby would get the best medical help; soon a nurse would soothe me with reassurances that all was fine. Soon my worries would be eased.

Instead, a woman was standing behind the reception wall, her back to me. Without turning around, she asked my name. When I told her, she whirled around and yelled into another room, "The miscarriage is here!" It felt like another wall of pain slammed into my whole being. I recoiled and said to her, "God, I hope that's not what's happening." She glanced up, but then went back to shuffling her paperwork. No human connection, no empathy, no tender eye-to-eye connection, even, to show that she bore witness to the pain of another person.

Years later, I can see how much in pain that woman must have been to respond as she did. How much it cost her to focus her heart on paper streams instead of another human being in crisis. How much it likely cost her over the years if she continued to clamp down her heart.

THE PAIN OF NOT BEING SEEN

This is one of my starkest, most painful memories of not being fully "seen" as a human being. We each have our own that years, even decades, later can still scald us with pain. What are yours? I'm sure our stories have more in common than we would think. We each have our own insane, inhumane moments when our hearts cry out, "What kind of world is this anyway? When did it become common, acceptable even, to respond in this way? Is life really this insignificant, this harsh?"

There is a preciousness about life we've lost and must recapture. Our sight's been dimmed, blurred, blinded. Somewhere along the way, for so many complex reasons, we've increasingly stopped seeing one another as human beings, as exquisite extensions of ourselves, as heart-of-my-heart needing decency, love, and care. We don't seem to fully see one another as human anymore, even when we need to most.

In medicine, patients are just medical conditions, referred to as "the gall bladder in 205" or the "back fusion in 426." In the workplace, employees say they often feel like disenfranchised, nameless entities with little or no connection to the common good of their organization. We used to think it was only in the congested cities, lost in crowds, that people ceased to be fully seen, but it's everywhere. Our desensitization to everything real is so ubiquitous; it has polluted even the smallest towns of middle America.

Even "the Heartland" of America is suffering.

When my family and I drove to Iowa last summer, we stopped outside a little town in Nebraska for gas. An elderly homeless man was sprawled in the hot sun near the station. He was clearly in trouble. His eyes were glazed, he was breathing heavily, and he looked close to collapsing. When we approached him to see if he needed help, he pleaded, "They're really mean here. They won't help me."

We asked the owner of the gas station if anyone was seeking help for him. She narrowed the coldest eyes I'd ever looked into and said with disgust, "I've called the sheriff on him 'cause he's hurting my businesses, scarin' the customers away."

OPENING OUR EYES REQUIRES NEW SIGHT

When did we become this inhumane? When did we fail to fully see one another and respond with tenderness? When did we siphon off the natural flow of love that runs in each of us? We can never know how much love we have—or see how much waits for us in the world—if we aren't fully present.

To open our hearts, we have to begin to see with new, fully awakened eyes. And sometimes the most important step in developing compassionate sight is to awaken to our true natures. To focus in on who we really are and accept ourselves with perfect vision. To see with our hearts the people we long to be. To see, in ways the mind can't grasp, our destiny and calling. "It is the heart that always sees, before the head can see," said nineteenth-century essayist Thomas Carlyle.[1]

David Whyte, a poet and former naturalist and wilderness guide in the Galápagos and Nepal, helps people all over the world begin to see themselves with startling clear vision. For years, Whyte has been reading his poetry and that of others to guide businesspeople deep into the wilderness of their own inner lives, into their own vast and unexplored psyches to find new direction, adaptability, strength, and creativity.

When I spoke with him, he shared how he relies on poetry—"the human heart speaking into the world"—to open hearts and souls to what's really true about one's nature and needs. Poetry is one magical thing that Whyte brings to corporations and organizations he works with to restore vision. In his resonant Yorkshire-laced voice, he shares the soulful poetry of Pablo Neruda, Rainer Maria Rilke, and Mary Oliver. He unwraps mythical images that have stark parallels to our lives, that help us examine who we really are—and what really matters.

In an executive retreat at Boeing, Whyte once gathered executives around a campfire outside CEO Phil Condit's wooded home outside Seattle. As the flames licked the darkness, images leaped to life. The Boeing managers wrote down stories about experiences in their careers they would rather forget. Those stories Whyte gathered and flung into the fire, his fingers scoring the dark. The stories they cherish were written down and saved.

Take the time to write down the stories from your own life that you want to save and share with others. Their power and intention will continue. These stories help you clearly see your visions and dreams, like the fire arching into the night helps us see what is precious and worth saving.

That night, as the flames lit his face, Whyte told the Boeing executives that in these swiftly changing times, they must become firelike and mutable too. They must be asking themselves, What is my purpose? What do I long for within my organization? Do I belong to something greater than myself? How must my identity change to support my vision—and the corporate vision?

OPENING OUR EYES TO WHAT'S BURIED INSIDE

David Whyte points out that, for years in our workplaces, we've often avoided these questions. "We spend more time in the business world than we do with our families, in our places of worship, or the natural world. And if we are not asking the real questions that are germane to our existence, then we are in a bad way. But we are now at a marvelous crossroads. We are living at an incredibly exciting time in which the very things we need to live fully and prosper and feel a participant in this incredible world are the very things we have wanted for ourselves since the beginning of time."

How often do you take the opportunity to look with clarity at your deepest needs? Do you leave the best part of yourself in the car in the parking lot, as Whyte says many people tend to do? How often do you avert your eyes from what is meaningful, as the woman in the ER did the day I came in? Are you possibly avoiding seeing even your gifts or dreams with clear vision?

When our vision is this cloudy and obscured, our hearts' deepest longings and calls are overlooked and suppressed. But through Whyte's work and that of many others, our hearts are again called to come forth, unleashed to speak of our long-ignored hopes, dreams, and passions. Our eyes are awakened to what's really buried inside each of us. We can finally feel our hearts soften and swell. We can be sure of our hearts. Then we can say, as poet John Keats did, "I can be sure of nothing but the holiness of the heart's affections and the truth of the imagination."

To spark these organizational quests, the internal questing, Whyte likes to spin tales of mythical, literary seekers, such as Beowulf, the prince who had to fight a monster. Worse still, he had to fight the monster in a dark lake where all his weapons proved useless.

One day Whyte was sharing this story with the management of a large corporation. Like Beowulf, he said, every organization must go into the dark lake. Every individual must grapple with his or her own monsters, whether that monster is a thwarted vision, a frustration about constant change, a paralyzing fear of the future, or a longing for more creativity.

"It is only by plunging into the dark waters that you will be able to seize new opportunities, adapt to change, find courage. Why not go down into the lake consciously, like Beowulf? Why not go down into the lake to confront your own shadows and those of the organization? Don't die on the shore. The stakes are very high; the stakes are your life."

When the session was over, a man who was very high up in the corporation came to Whyte with the look of someone seeing himself anew. "You know what was down in the lake for me as you spoke?" he said.

"What?" Whyte asked.

"When I was a child, I was in Japan," the man said. "My father was in the occupying forces. Society was so shattered, and there was tremendous disease everywhere. So we had to have these inoculations.

"And it seemed that we had to have these inoculations almost every week. As children, we used to have to line up in the schoolyard to get the inoculations. I was so scared of them that whoever came, I would go behind them. If three kids came behind me in the line, I would go behind them; if two more kids, behind them, until I was right at the end.

"I always had to have the inoculation, but I was always the last to have it."

The man told Whyte that as he imagined Beowulf wrestling with the monster down in the lake, he realized he was still doing the same thing. "I still do that after all these years with my people. When something comes up at work, I go back to the end of the line. I have lots of resources, energy, and persistence to convince people I'm at the front of the line. But I'm actually at the back."

But, the man told Whyte, in listening to the story of Beowulf, for the first time he had a powerful awakening. "I just realized, you know, I don't have to be at the front. I can help people who need to go to the front at that time in their lives to do their work. All I need to do is have a sense of humor, put it into perspective, and say, 'Here I go to the back of the line.'"

A GREATER ADVENTURE BECKONS

We are called at this time, all throughout our daily lives, to see and unlock a greater sense of ourselves. We are called to see how brilliantly adept we are at coming together and supporting one another, to better focus in on the hidden pain within each of us so we can respond to that suffering with new eyes. This will be an inner adventure, an interior exploration of the most far-reaching repercussions. "The real voyage of discovery consists not in seeking new landscapes, but in having new eyes," nineteenth-century novelist Marcel Proust said.[2]

Seeing with new eyes will help us respond with compassion. That is our sacred call, and it will not be easy. It will be one of the toughest things our culture has ever done.

But if our intention is to return to a more loving place, it starts with seeing, really seeing one another again for who we really are. We need to see our lives as precious and powerful enough to make a difference. The 2000 presidential election certainly underscored the raw, historical power of a single person's vote. We need to see that we are powerful beyond words when we set our intentions. We can use that power wisely. We can use that new sight to see one another as we deserve to be seen.

WE LONG TO BE SEEN

As that homeless man in Nebraska or any of the homeless show us, our deepest need is not for money, status, or fame. "Our deepest need is to be *seen*," points out Marianne Williamson in *Enchanted Love*. "Someone who has seen us through loving eyes has awakened us from the ranks of the formerly dead." We need to see with perfect vision that a homeless man is our teacher in the art of loving, even when, especially when, he impacts our revenue. The bottom-line benchmark of our lives is not how much our cash registers ring each day; it's how well we care for those around us.

Seeing someone clearly, such as when a physician clearly sees a patient, is a sacred moment. "If you understand the patient's story, then you can help him or her write the next chapter," says Dr. Gregory Plotnikoff in an article in *Minnesota Medicine*.[3] Dr. Plotnikoff helps medical students fully see the diversity and ethnicity of their patients. Minnesota has the nation's largest Tibetan population and the largest urban Native American population. It also has the second largest Hmong and Filipino populations as well as a rapidly growing population of East African immigrants and refugees and Hispanic immigrants. Seeing these patients from the lens of a white, Protestant, Midwestern background won't work.

Because each spiritual and cultural tradition has teachings, practices, and rituals that promote healing, it's necessary for physicians and their staff to see the entire patient and what matters to him or her, including what matters on a spiritual level, Dr. Plotnikoff says. Seeing the patient clearly and all that makes him or her human can be critical medical data.

Awareness of a patient's spiritual beliefs helps avoid conflict or emotional harm. It also reduces risk factors, he adds. For instance, "Medical care often is neither efficient nor effective if the patient believes illness is a punishment from God or is related to loss of soul."

So Dr. Plotnikoff specifically designed a program at the University of Minnesota's Center for Spirituality and Healing to give students and staff that chance to see deeply into and honor a patient's background, fears, motivations, and hopes. Students are shown how to ask the right questions to elicit the deepest feedback from patients. They read poetry, short stories, and fiction that explore values, human nature, motivations, dreams, and relationships. Their focus is directed so that it no longer rests exclusively in the power of technology, which can "blind us to issues of ultimate meaning," Dr. Plotnikoff says. His program, he stresses, "is not an add-on." Instead it is intended to "encourage from day one of medical school, an emphasis on the values of humane care. We want students to be sensitive to issues such as suffering and the nature of healing."

Oprah Winfrey once said, "We are here for each other." As soon as our eyes can see this, then like a baby awakening from a long, deep slumber, we will more keenly see the wonder and awe of our connections to every living thing.

Anything We Love Can Be Saved is the title of a wonderful book by Alice Walker. How do we fall back in love with everything around us so we can even want to begin to save it? How do we again see people, our environment, all of life as precious and deserving our reverence?

SET SACRED INTENTION TO SEE LIFE AS SACRED

We begin with the intention to see all life as sacred. You can start with the expressed intention, written in your heart or on paper, or spoken out loud, or offered up in your meditations and prayers, that you will view every interaction as an opportunity to bind your heart and soul with another. You will see each interaction as a chance to enrich each other's transit time on this earth, however long the ride lasts, through loving respect and care. Choose whatever method works for you to etch this intention into your consciousness and actions each day.

Think of those you interact with daily—even if only via e-mail. Are you interacting too much via e-mail when an in-the-flesh conversation is what's needed? Are you slowing down enough, stopping to really see the people you live and work with as human beings, as sacred beings?

Or do you diminish them by viewing them through a narrowed lens—like the limited, closed eyes of the Nebraska gas station owner? Do you dismiss them as merely "customers," "co-workers," "clients," "students," "consumers," "the bypass in 208," or, even worse, "derelicts," "idiots," "jerks," and so on?

Try to recall the times you failed to see the preciousness and connectedness of others—even when they were right before your eyes. That happened to Diane, a nurse at a California hospital. She recently shared her story with her colleagues at a presentation called "Revisiting the Golden Rule: The Spiritual Dimension of Customer Service." (We can have great hope because similar workshops are surfacing throughout the country. This one was conducted by Soul Purpose Associates, a Holyoke, Massachusetts, company owned by Ann C. Careau and Carole A. Schulte.)

Ann Careau recalled Diane's story. Diane said she'd recently admitted a patient, entering the waiting room with all the necessary paperwork and questions. When she was admitting him, she realized she had not yet even asked the man his name. So when he responded by giving his name, and she really recognized his voice for the first time, Diane was shocked. When she finally looked at the man, she discovered that he was her neighbor. She felt terrible and was deeply affected by this experience.

This is hope. When we feel humbled and shaken by our inhumanity, the heart can be awakened again. The painful realization is a springboard to letting our hearts break open, to again seeing with fully open and compassionate eyes.

LABELING PEOPLE BLOCKS CONNECTION

At another Soul Purpose workshop, a story surfaced about a person the hospital labeled a "frequent flier." This label refers to patients who return to the hospital over and over again, who usually don't follow the staff's advice, and who are considered a real pain. These frequent fliers are often people who are mentally ill or who are severe alcoholics. As all throughout our culture, it's easier to label and disconnect from people than it is to see them for who they really are.

During the workshop, Ann Careau initiated a discussion about seeing these frequent fliers and other more demanding patients from a compassionate perspective. She suggested seeing them not as annoyances, but as teachers. "These people come into our lives for a purpose, usually to help us with what we are here in this life to learn," Careau explained.

One nurse responded to Careau's suggestion with great anger, citing her horrible experiences with alcoholic patients. When Careau suggested the spiritual "opportunity" that existed within the encounter, the nurse again reacted very stridently and objected, "There is nothing they can teach me."

But as the discussion continued, the woman came to see, deep in her own heart, that the alcoholic patients often evoked anger from her personal experiences. She saw with fresh eyes that each encounter was an invitation to deal with her long-repressed hurt. "Even more deeply, she saw that her hurt and anger were keeping her away from deep intimacy, which made her feel more lonely and alienated from life and relationships," Careau recalled. "She decided to get some help with these issues, and I hear that she is now more open and actually advocating for better understanding of alcoholic and other patients."[4]

Compassionate sight can help us understand that we are all here to grow our souls by respecting, serving, and loving one another. This begins by first seeing that we each have a purpose, a purpose unique to each individual on the deepest human and spiritual level, Careau said. "And it teaches us that we belong to the human community and need each other, regardless of whether we meet with each other's approval."

Soul Purpose Associates works to foster and enhance the role of spirituality in the workplace. "We work to bring about a more conscious awareness of deeper values such as listening, respect, honesty, integrity, passion, and honoring the uniqueness—the personal mission and soul purpose—of each individual."

SEEING OTHERS AS OUR TEACHERS

How well do we see others with honesty, respect, and integrity? How well do we see ourselves in that light? Do we accept that we each have a soul purpose? Do you see, as the hospital nurse learned to see, that others come into your life for a reason? What would it take for you to accept that the people who pass through or inhabit your days are your teachers in the life lessons of patience, empathy, and compassion?

Do you see, as the hospital nurse learned to see, that others really do appear for a reason? I remember talking once with a woman at a mind-body-spirit conference who said she'd had the most amazing transformation. The conference was haphazardly organized with snafus around every corner. Once, this woman said, she would have been the first to complain about the disorganization.

She said she used to live in a world where everything and everyone seemed to disappoint her. The checker in the grocery store would be rude. Her boyfriend would be demanding at the end of the day. The woman who cut her hair was surly. Her kids' friends often dumped on her and were obnoxious. And then, she kept stumbling across books that explored how the world is often a mirror of our own thoughts and actions, that we attract what we give out to the world. As *Creative Visualization* author Shakti Gawain says, "My true relationship is with myself—all others are simple mirrors of it."

And this woman saw herself with new eyes. She realized how often she gave to the world a surly, demanding, rude attitude. She remembered how often she judged other people by their outer appearance, how often she cut off others in traffic or cut people down with her thoughts. She remembered the times she was too demanding and snapped at her co-workers—or cursed them inwardly—if they didn't measure up to her impossible standards. And she realized that all the rude people she kept encountering were showing her what she was offering up to the world. They were holding up her reflection. They were also her wonderful teachers in showing her that there was a better way to be in the world.

As Saint Luke says in chapter 6, verse 38 of his Gospel: "Give, and there will be gifts for you: a full measure pressed down, shaken together, and running over will be poured into your lap; because the amount you measure out is the amount you will be given back."

How do we develop more giving eyes? How do we develop the soft, tender, accepting eyes to see ourselves truthfully and with radical honesty? And then how do we turn this new vision outward? How do we see and live from the spiritual truths that we are all here for one another, that we are all here to learn from and love one another? We start with the simplest, but extremely powerful step of slowing down enough to really see well. We begin by stopping the frenzy long enough to be present and attentive to what is right in front of us, like the nurse who unknowingly registered her own neighbor.

We are sometimes so time crazed, we barely skim the surface of our days, not really seeing deeply. We all long to be fully known. Try to fully see the preciousness and beauty of those you touch day in and day out. Show others your own beauty and grace. We all have ten thousand joys and ten thousand sorrows, says Elizabeth Kim in *Ten Thousand Sorrows*. Try to see those around you as kindred souls who experience the same sorrows and joys that you do, as like you in every way that counts. Your life will never be the same.

When Margo Hunt began to see those around her as holy, a profound transformation occurred. For forty years, she worked in the visa section of a busy consulate. For a long, long time, the work was sheer drudgery. The person on the other side of the glass was just a customer, and their relationship was solely an exchange of papers with some anxiety on the part of the visa applicant.

"Then I had this whole change of attitude," Hunt says. "It was a spiritual change. I realized I wasn't talking to a customer, it was someone with a life, someone very much like myself.

"What I needed to apply was love. I needed to care about the fact that they may be afraid and I could do something to change that. I could help them by saying something as simple as, 'Let me show you what this is about.'"

Hunt ended her career with letters of praise from those she touched. "I had an interesting career, and I realized that none of it mattered except how I treated people."[5]

SEEING CLEARLY IS ELECTRIFYING

When we go about our days seeing with the eyes of love, we feel more alive, elevated. Everything about how we move through the day feels electrified. We sense something magical in the air. The air seems charged, and others are drawn to us. We recognize that something amazing, miraculous even, could happen at any moment. And it always does.

When we greet each day with the intention of being more loving, we rest in a satisfying, quiet comfort. Our senses are even heightened. The sunrise looks more vibrant, coffee smells richer, chocolate tastes deeper, our children's hugs are more precious, the sight of clouds melting into russet light at day's end moves us to tears. A return to love on a daily basis transports us to a higher state of grace and allows us to transcend much of the lower-level brooding fear and stress. Love brings forth our highest selves.

The cosmetics companies may not want us to discover this, but when we go through a day without gazing on the world with harshness and mean-spiritedness, we look dramatically different. Our eyes shine. They look joyful, relaxed, renewed. We appear softer, more radiant, years younger. The lines around our eyes are fainter. Wrinkles even disappear. We simply feel more ourselves, stronger and more comfortable in our own skin.

Scientific evidence may not support this, but there is a wealth of anecdotal evidence that living from a place of love makes us more luminous, from our skin to our eyes. You won't hear this in a Revlon ad, but love becomes us. It softens us internally—and externally.

But more important than the outer beauty, of course, will be the inner beauty, the internal knowing. Your heart will begin to know, as surely as it has known cynicism and anger, that it's all about love. It's never been anything but. As much as we've tried to find it in all the wrong places, in power coups, in shopping orgies, or through the blue-light glow of our computer screens, true peace comes only from a loving, restful heart.

Shed the scales that cloud your eyes. If you begin to know, deep in your marrow, that the way of the heart is the only way, then you will surely come home to your heart. It all begins with that knowing. "I can't explain it. I just know," you've often said. Know that love is the truest way.

Remember that your heart is not merely a mechanical pump for blood. It is a way of seeing. It is a way of seeing life and other people, so the only rational response, as Stephen Levine always says, is to respond with love.

But we all have our scales, our myths and misbeliefs, our fears and sanctioned professional distances that keep our eyes from looking on the world with compassion. What still prevents you from responding with love? What keeps your eyes separate from others and your heart hardened? What do you fear will happen if you become more openhearted, more vulnerable?

COMPASSION OVERCOMES OBSTACLES

If we allow them, if we open to them, there are always people—especially kids—around us who challenge our desire to keep our eyes clouded. There will always be people who are our teachers right where we are, helping us to respond, not with fear and judgment, but with the deepest compassionate wisdom. Five-year-old Matt was such a teacher for his preschool teacher, Laurie.

As do so many of our best instructors, Matt posed a major challenge. He wasn't simple and easy to get along with all the time. He was complex and hard to figure out. He had both behavioral difficulties and very high intelligence. Matt was a great teacher because he made those around him look deeply to better understand him. He challenged them to see who he really was at heart.

Matt's parents found a Montessori school in their Atlanta area to enroll their son. Laurie, the preschool teacher, agreed to accept Matt in her class on a trial basis. "I hope I've made the right decision," she thought.

Within twenty-four hours, she was in serious doubt. She saw the tranquillity she'd created for her students shredded by this one out-of-control child. Matt was aggressive with his classmates, grabbing toys away, yelling, pushing, and calling names. When Laurie gently pointed out to Matt that his behavior was not acceptable, hell broke loose.

"He immediately lost control and began to scream, kick, and lash out physically and verbally at anyone and anything in his path. I physically removed Matt from my classroom, and outside, he turned all his rage on me. I ended up with two deep bites on my arms, a black eye, and bruises on both my legs. It took both my assistant and me to calm him down."

For weeks, this was the pattern of Laurie's relationship with Matt. The crisis escalated when Matt fell from a tree and broke his femur. Even immobilized in a wheelchair, Matt continued to verbally terrorize the children and adults in his life.

"After weeks of this, I was frustrated, drained, and ready to give up. I wanted the calm and peaceful class I had before Matt," said Laurie.

But then Laurie tuned in to something that has dramatically changed her life. She realized she was trying to understand and reach Matt on an analytical level. And then she remembered how powerful a tool the heart can be in achieving balance.

A few years earlier, Laurie had attended a heart empowerment seminar sponsored by HeartMath. At the seminar, she discovered the research showing the heart is as important—maybe even more so—in overall health and well-being as the brain. To deal with her own stress and tension, Laurie learned to focus on her innate heart intelligence. She learned how to counteract damaging electrical impulses that raced from her heart to her brain when she was angry, afraid, or tense. Once her heart and head were in sync, she could calmly handle tension.

Like executive Carol McDonald in chapter 1, Laurie found that the HeartMath tool of Freeze-Frame helped her more than anything she'd ever experienced to achieve inner harmony. It offered Laurie the serenity of yoga or meditation—in only one minute.

Using Freeze-Frame, Laurie recognized when she felt stressed and stepped back from the moment. She shifted her focus to the area around her heart and imagined that she was breathing through her heart. She held her heart focus for at least ten seconds. Next, she recalled a positive or happy experience like a relaxing time in nature or a fun time with friends.

NEUTRALIZING STRESS AND CONFLICT

By calling forth feelings of love and appreciation when she was stressed, Laurie learned how to neutralize her negative emotions, stress, and conflict. Then she learned to ask her heart, What would be a more efficient response to this situation that would reduce my stress? She waited and listened to her heart's response.

One weekend at the height of her frustration with Matt, Laurie felt compelled to call up the Freeze-Frame and other HeartMath strategies. She sat with and listened to her heart. "It was a powerful experience, and I was surprised at the action plan that appeared. I knew clearly that my heart was telling me to try to reach Matt's heart."

On Monday morning, Laurie took Matt outside for a ride in his wheelchair. They sat under some pine trees, and Laurie told Matt about how she went home that weekend and searched her heart to find out how best to help him. And then she told him what her heart spoke and about HeartMath. "Can I try it too?" Matt asked.

The more questions Matt asked, the more Laurie realized that Matt—even at five—was painfully aware that he alienated himself from others. Laurie showed Matt how to use the Freeze-Frame tool when he was feeling out of control. From that day on, Matt tried very hard to use Freeze-Frame, and Laurie began to see some dramatic results.

"His screaming and physical abuse began to subside at school. His parents reported the same results at home. Matt told his friends about HeartMath and even taught his parents how to use Freeze-Frame," Laurie reported.

Instructing children—even the most difficult ones—in the art of compassion may be one of the highest callings of her profession, Laurie concluded. Now, the HeartMath tools of compassion are as naturally—and radically—a part of Laurie's classroom as are chalk, paint, and books. "I believe that teaching children an awareness of love is one of the keys to helping them reach new levels and dimensions of intelligence," she said.

As Laurie goes about her day in her classroom, helping other children listen to their hearts, it isn't at all unusual to hear Matt or another five-year-old say, "Oops, I think I need to Freeze-Frame and get in my heart."[6]

What a powerful shift can occur when we can all begin to see more clearly and respond from our hearts. Think how years of conflict can be erased if we only apply the innate skills of the heart to conflicts. When we see with the healing eyes of compassion, we become ourselves and help others be the human beings they were meant to be.

Ask yourself, How well do I really bring compassionate sight to my interactions with my child's teacher, my co-workers, my competitors, the other commuters on the interstate? Am I at all gazing on them through the vision of empathy and compassion?

SUSPENDING JUDGMENT AND CRITICISM

Do we see, for instance, that the doctor we're incensed at for being late might be exhausted from pulling down three days without sleep? Maybe one of his favorite patients just died of a brain hemorrhage earlier this morning. Or maybe he and his wife are having marital problems because he spends more time with his patients than with his family. His momentary well-being possibly hinges greatly on your understanding and nonjudgment. As we work to change our systems—of medicine, government, and so on— we have to be compassionate to those working within them.

Try to see and support with greater empathy and authentic compassion. Maybe the grocery store clerk, who scans our tomato soup with such a frenzy it makes our teeth rattle, is having a bad month, not just a bad day. Maybe she can't pay her rent, her kids are home sick, and she wishes life would just get better. If we see people with the eyes of empathy, our hearts can reach out and connect, with no words said, on a spiritual level. When we see people in their pain and wish and hope and pray that they will be supported and surrounded with love, a shift occurs.

Do I see and respond tenderly to the human condition that others are facing?

And that's, of course, the meaning of all of our life's work, isn't it? Whether we sell gas, serve up lattes, feed children, or litigate divorces, our call is to see all life as precious. And maybe what often blocks us from more perfect vision is our failure to see how similar we all are. We've lost a sense of the common good, of community, of what-happens-to-you-also-affects-me consciousness that most communities possessed even fifty years ago.

We've so little time to really know our neighbors' and co-workers' and patients' stories, their dreams, hopes, and tragedies, so we fail to see how alike we all are, how much we all long to be fully known and cherished. We no longer see ourselves as kindred spirits with the same joys and sorrows, the same vulnerabilities and epiphanies.

PERFECT SIGHT COMES FROM THE HEART

It's all too easy to go through life not really seeing, even if we've been blessed with vision. It strikes me how it's often those who have lost their mechanical vision who have the clearest vision. Just recently, the TV show 20/20 featured a man who was legally blind for ten years and suddenly, with no treatment, miraculously recovered his sight. Renay Poirier was working as an electrician and got caught in a high-voltage electrical explosion that caused his vision to steadily deteriorate. Over the years, after battling major depression, Poirier retrained himself by going to school to become an assistant physical therapist.

On May 23, 2000, Poirier was beginning his day at the hospital where he worked when he got an intense headache. He thought he was dying. But then he detected an intense bright light, and color and images—trees, green grass—flooded back in.

After his sight was restored, Poirier's patients at the hospital all asked, "Do I look the way you thought I would look?" His answer: "Remarkably, I don't think anyone does. You know, I learned, when I was working with patients, if you have a little trouble seeing the beauty, close your eyes for a while. See them with your heart. It sheds a different light."

Interestingly, the name of the Wisconsin hospital where Poirier works is Sacred Heart Hospital. What a story.[7]

As Poirier so achingly described, we must be able to gaze on life with our hearts, with a wiser, intuitive, inner vision. And cultivating that vision fully requires that we see the beauty in others. It calls us to stop seeing ourselves as "other than," "separate from," "better than," and unconnected to those around us. How often do you do this, even subconsciously, in your mind? How often do you rationalize that distance is really for the best? When do you most disassociate with "out-of-heart" experiences?

COMPASSIONATE SIGHT MAKES US FULLY HUMAN

I'm convinced that on some level, we all long to break out of the rigid, concrete, different-from-you stances that keep us from being grateful for one another. We long to be seen and see others as precious and wonderful and deserving of our concern. Until we develop this kind of sight, we aren't fully

human. We aren't truly alive. We miss even the simplest opportunities to
merge our hearts.

We miss the incredible chances we are given to make one another feel
safe, protected, and appreciated. The stories throughout this book are of
people who choose not to miss those chances; they capitalize on them. For
instance, Linton Elementary School principal Priscilla Huston knows that if
she doesn't see, love, and care for her students on all levels—and create an
environment that fosters that kind of care—she can never be as effective as
she strives to be. She can't reach her students' minds unless she also reaches
their hearts. "My chief role and obligation is to create an environment for
kids to feel safe, nurtured, and cared for, physically, as well as emotionally,"
she said.

Her intention "goes back to the formation of the brain," Huston continued. "When you think of how the brain develops, issues like safety and security are so important. I try to keep clear in my mind the understanding that if
we are fearful or anxious or feel threatened or are not well nourished; those
need to be dealt with first. If a child didn't receive a hug or feels unsafe or
threatened, it's very hard to focus on the events of the American Revolution
or comprehend the sound vowels make when they are short vowels."

Huston has many compassionate practices that ground her philosophies in action. For instance, one corner of her office features floor pillows
and a miniature waterfall, so if kids are having a stressful or anxious day,
they can "come down and curl up on the pillows. We dim the lights and
give them space and time to regroup."

She also is great at using simple kindness to diffuse conflicts and acting
out in class, to see all kids as worthy and special. For instance, once a sixth-
grader enrolled at Linton with an incredible chip on his shoulder. "He
would fight anyone or anything in his way," Huston said. "He was constantly trying to antagonize people. So we had a conversation about his
behavior.

"As I looked at him, it dawned on me that he didn't know how to make
a friend, so he pretended to be a tough guy. He wanted to show he didn't
need friends because he just didn't know how to make them. This was his
defense system."

So as a "consequence" for his inappropriate choices at school, Huston
again used a novel tactic. His consequence was that he needed to invite

another student to go on an outing with the two of them. "I provided the transportation and the money, but he was required to invite another student on his own. So he did. And this outing didn't fix the entire problem. But it did give him the opportunity to engage in a friendship and have enough of a sense of success to see that people could like him. The incidents he was involved in went way down. He is now a ninth-grader—and he still drops in periodically to say, 'Hi.'"

To make all their kids feel accepted and safe, Huston and her staff set the intention that they will see and respond to their students as they would want their own children to be seen and treated. "We ask ourselves, Do I want my child to be lambasted, ostracized, made fun of, or put down? We treat kids as we would want our kids to be treated. That is truly the secret of it," Huston concluded.

HEART WORK REQUIRES GREAT SKILL

The Linton Elementary secret makes for a truly magical educational experience. And it reaches the hearts and minds of kids who otherwise might be overlooked. "This is not 'soft' stuff at all. I would call it intuitive. It takes great skill to peer into the hearts and minds of kids, to read between the lines and understand what they are really saying. To look beyond a specific incident to the deeper understanding of the roots of their behavior. To read facial expression and body language. To offer comfort that the child is ready to accept. These are not soft skills at all. These skills take real ability, which I see in my staff every day," Huston explained.[8]

Think of how often we miss these critical insights if we operate more from our heads than our hearts. It's all too easy to dismiss kids as troublemakers, patients as cranky, clients as irritating, customers as a pain in the neck, if we don't engage the heart on some level of the interaction.

To see with compassion takes great skill and intention. Think of the times you didn't fully see others as human, as one with you. Think back on the moments when others failed to see you with affection or even basic respect. Is that what you want to put out in the world by keeping your eyes clouded—by averting your eyes or keeping them narrowed and blinded by judgment, indifference, or ignorance?

Slow down enough to be awed by what is right before your eyes. A study at the National Zoo in Washington, D.C., found that visitors spent an average of seven seconds viewing any one animal or exhibit.[9] Time sickness is rampant. When was the last time your heart was in awe, in rapture, over something beautiful? In the next week, spend at least five minutes watching the sunset unfold or watching the branches sway with new leaves. Feel your heart soften with the sheer awe of being alive.

TRANSPORTED BY AWE

Our hearts also open when we read book passages that invoke feelings of awe and wonder. Our hearts are so responsive, they soften at others' heart-felt moments just as they harden when they are exposed to meanness. I love reading over and over passages from Diane Ackerman's *The Moon by Whale Light*.

In it, she writes how nature transports us to an ecstasy, a state of "being flung out of your usual self" by the wonders around you. She describes her awe of swimming in the otherworldly world of the whales where "their songs are set by the rhythm of swells in the oceans. If you listen to whales when you are being borne on the sea, you can feel that the rate at which they're producing a given phrase is about the same as the rate between the swells that are coming by. What an extraordinary experience that is!"

Ackerman describes swimming with the whales' songs floating around her, "floating in what may be a whale's epic poem. . . . Each time I dove a few feet under the surface, I heard and felt the radiant booming again, and wished I could hold my breath for hours, stay down and listen with the whole ocean cupped to my ear like a single hand."

Awe. The pounding, potent sense of awe. It can fling wide the most closed doorways to our hearts. Anything of beauty that makes your breath catch is a good thing. It's making your heart catch too. It is shifting the rhythm of your heart. It's also lowering your blood pressure and making feel-good chemicals flood your being.

Spend time being in awe, even if it's just to watch for ten minutes— without moving, without flicking your eyes to check e-mail—the sky melt from turquoise to crimson, night after night. Make that the awe ritual that feeds your heart.

Spend more time, as well, being in awe of those around you. The next time someone stops by your desk, when your child calls your name, when you look at your reflection in the mirror, slow down, stop, and breathe. Take a minimum of five minutes to look in the eyes of the person interrupting your work. Let your soul meet his or hers and ask, "How are you—really?" And be willing to listen. Look into your own eyes in the mirror and ask yourself, "How am I—really? How goes it with me? What do I long for right now, not tomorrow?" The answers aren't far away.

What more can you do right where you are to develop new, compassionate sight? Just as there are practices you can use to sharpen your mind, intuition, or vocabulary, there are powerful practices you can tap to see with an open heart. Tools to rediscover the depths of your humanity.

One ritual you can enter into and practice is becoming aware of the sense that we are all connected. We are one. Practice seeing everyone and everything around you as literally, powerfully, divinely connected. Practice seeing them as they really are.

I don't mean figuratively, like some sentimental love-makes-the-world-go-round Hallmark card. I mean recognizing your literal connection to all living things. We are one. We are one with the Divine, with Spirit, with God. We are one with the One—so perfectly one that what is done to one of us is done to us all. We don't throw thousands of people in prison each year without suffering too. We don't mistreat a colleague or a clerk in the store without affecting the entire universe. We can't wipe out hundreds of species from the face of the earth and not feel a part of us die too.

THE WEB OF LIFE

Any loving act sends out loving reverberations in the world, just as our hateful actions, words, and thoughts spread a mean-spirited malignancy.

This message of unity with all life and with the Divine is found in all great religions and traditions since the beginning of time. Zen Buddhism teaches, "One Nature, perfect and pervading, circulates in all natures."[10] Saint Paul in the New Testament speaks of our union with God, saying, "Let this mind be in you, which was also in Christ Jesus: Who, being in the form of God, thought it not robbery to be equal with God."[11]

The Oneida Indians say, "Everything is alive, everything is related, everything is connected, and everything affects everything else." Native

American Black Elk said, "The first peace, which is most important, is that which comes within the souls of people when they realize their relationship, their oneness, with the universe and all its powers, and when they realize that at the center of the universe dwells the Great Spirit, and that this center is really everywhere, it is within each of us."[12]

Lao-tzu further says, "Being divine, you will be at one with the Tao."

We are one with one another and with God. It's just that in our great arrogance, we often don't want to believe it's true. Yet this idea of mystical fusion is as truly enduring a message as any words that echo through time. If you merely scratch the surface of our literary archives, there it is, everywhere. Frances Thompson writes:

> All things by immortal power
> near or far
> Hiddenly to each other linked are.
> Thou canst not stir a flower
> Without troubling a star.[13]

A growing number of physicists talk about the "butterfly effect"—the idea that we are so connected in some unseen physical way that if a butterfly flew into a home and somehow got hurt, the entire universe would feel it. We are so incredibly composed of and connected by a divine, loving force, energy, light—however you wish to view it—that our every atom, cell, and thought are connected to all others.

Sink into a meditation; sit in silence to remember we are part of the One, "a feather on the breath of God," says the great mystic Hildegard of Bingen as she is quoted in Matthew Fox's *A Spirituality Named Compassion.* If we are of God, "You may call God love; you may call God goodness; but the best name for God is Compassion," says Hildegard's fellow German mystic Meister Eckhart.[14]

WIDENING THE CIRCLE OF COMPASSION

Scientist Albert Einstein also observed how we human beings suffer when we experience ourselves as separate from the rest of life. A "kind of optical delusion of his consciousness," he described it. Believing this way "is a kind of prison for us, restricting us to our personal desires and to affection for a few persons nearest to us. Our task must be to free ourselves from this prison by widening our circle of compassion to embrace all living creatures and the whole of nature in its beauty."[15]

To see with more loving eyes, then, means you can start to see yourself as part of the whole, as lovingly connected to life around you. Now this is where our compassion's mettle is really tested, isn't it? It's easy to have a heartfelt moment with someone you like, but it gets really prickly when you try to feel expansive to the "jerk" next door who won't turn down his music at midnight, or to the "a-hole" who leaps in front of you at the four-way stop—and then laughs.

It's easy to fall in love with humanity. It's easy to feel expansive to the universe at large. It's the people we meet and live with every day that we often find hard to love.

That's why daily life is a perfect way to consciously fortify our hearts. When you go about your daily flow, picking up bread and milk at the grocery store, e-mailing colleagues, or standing in line at the post office, consciously see yourself connected to all your surroundings. Visualize streams of light linking you, and imagine your hearts and spirits reaching out and touching each other. Feel your heart open and swell with empathy and affection to all around you, even the strangers right in front of you.

Take a deep, cleansing breath and see how precious they all really are. Today, 250,000 people will die and leave the planet. They won't smell today's breeze or see tonight's sunset. Gone. But we're all still here, alive and together. And we're so incredibly lucky to still be here, together, with the opportunity to be kinder, gentler people, to feel our connection with one another.

For me, traveling is one of the best ways to feel this connected-to-all sense, like when I am forced to cool my heels in crowded airports during holiday travel. There we all are, tossed in together, a mass of tightly packed, highly stressed humanity waiting at the gate for a plane that's often hours late and seriously overbooked.

As you know, such times bring out our tense, whining, weary, and self-centered selves. "Why is that jerk taking up two chairs? Does his briefcase really need its own chair? *My* holiday plans have been made for months. Why did this have to happen to spoil *my* life?"

A great time to beckon the heart. A perfect moment to look around and try to invoke a sense of the preciousness of those wedged in and sprawling all around us. When I practice this, I try to see us all not as strangers thrown together, forced to share some cramped space, but as kindred, connected human beings, privileged to have this spiritual breathing space to stop, bring down the blood pressure, and recognize what really matters. I try to see that we are actually united in all our neuroses, headaches, anxiety attacks, sweaty palms, and all.

I look around and see light radiating off us all. I close my eyes and imagine us all becoming aware of our connections, wishing the best for one another, and finally being at peace, whether we make our connections or not.

The last time I did this, I was flying on standby, praying to make it back to Colorado from San Francisco a day early because I had a major upper respiratory infection. Another night in a cramped hotel room with hot, dry air blasting my sinuses was unthinkable. I got to my gate and the reservationist blurted out that my flight was two hours late and way overbooked. She didn't hold out much hope for my getting on. "You'll be biting your nails before this day is over," she said sarcastically. So much for a heartwarming exchange there. We've a long way to go in learning the art of comfort, haven't we?

Well, there were no seats open near the boarding gate either, so I found a warm patch of sun near the windows, sat down on the floor, and began to breathe. I closed my eyes and did a short meditation, imagining the sun's warmth wrapping around me and enveloping us all. I saw paths of light drawing everyone onto the plane and safely home.

Ten minutes later, my name was called. I went to the counter and the attendant told me that I had been cleared to fly. Yes! I couldn't believe it. I would sleep in my own bed that night and see my family. I could take a long, hot bath and steam my sinuses open. And when I got on the plane, it got better. Not only did I have a seat, but also that precious seat I collapsed into, Sudafed bulging from my pockets, turned out to be in first class. There was a white tablecloth, crystal glasses, comfortable seats—and a kind flight attendant. A wonderful man sat next to me and described how much he loved his work. He talked with the same affection about his wife and teenage son. When you think more lovingly, you attract more loving, first-class-type experiences—literally.

A STATE OF DEEP PEACE

But more important, when you start to see people for who they really are—divine, lovable, loving, connected to you—you reach a peaceful, restful place that often eludes us in our coarser, stressed, competitive moments. It's easier then to respond gracefully to those we meet, instead of adding more hostility into the world.

We can all use a little grace, a lot of empathy. Life throws a lot at us: cancer biopsies, kids' health scares, job losses, aborted dreams. It also blesses us with new discoveries: amazing serendipity, births, celebrations, promotions, lush spring leaves, loving caresses, and glittering snowfalls. We're all in it together, literally. "It is this awareness of togetherness that urges us to rejoice at another's joy and to grieve another's sorrow," says Matthew Fox in *A Spirituality Named Compassion*.

We can begin to diffuse indifference with empathy. When we begin to cultivate more empathetic eyes—eyes that see someone else's pain and respond appropriately—we can melt away much of the indifference, hostility, and numbness in our culture. As with loving acts, we can learn the skill of empathy.

This is also a valuable skill we can pass on to our children. Children may never learn this lesson well if we don't model it for them. Psychologist Myrna Shure found in writing her best-selling *Raising a Thinking Preteen* that empathy—the ability to understand and be sensitive to another person's experiences, feelings, and thoughts—is a learned behavior, one that too few children are learning. None of the eight- to twelve-year-olds that she interviewed and studied for her book even knew the word *empathy*, but when she explained the feeling first, they nodded in recognition.

Let's relearn the art of empathy. Let's model how we learn and show empathy for others' experiences and how empathy can enrich our lives. We can relearn this. We can cultivate the ability to understand another's feelings and respond appropriately. We can, again, learn much about empathy from Griffin Hospital in Derby, Connecticut, where compassion and empathy are cornerstones.

CHANGING THE CULTURE

When Griffin management decided to humanize its organization, it knew that the outer, structural changes to the building would be much, much easier to make than the interior, cultural changes in its people. So it took extraordinary measures to instill a sense of caring and empathetic sight among its 1,100 employees

For instance, at the start of its redirection, Griffin surveyed and took the pulse of its volunteers, staff, management, and board and found that, lo and behold, everyone wanted the hospital to be more human. "Everyone wanted a place where they were treated as an individual, not a machine," said Griffin Vice President Bill Powanda.

"From our housekeepers to our nurses, everyone wanted to be treated like human beings. They saw the current system, such as the restricted visiting hours, as rigid and designed more for the provider than our customers."

So Griffin decided to bring the patient experience closer to the staff, to help employees see through the eyes of those they serve. One of the most effective strategies Griffin uses to cultivate patient empathy is employee retreats at an austere convent along Long Island Sound. The intention is to create an experience in which employees feel what it's like for a patient in a hospital, in a new environment, without the usual comforts and touchstones.

"You spent the night in a room with someone else you don't know. The rooms have just bunkbeds—no TVs or telephones," Powanda said. There's no private bath—and no room service. "At one point, you have to feed and be fed by someone else. That was really challenging for me. At one point, in a blind trust exercise, you are led around blindfolded, which I also found difficult. Some people were very firm and others almost push you down the stairs!" Through this experience Griffin employees learn empathy, understanding what it must feel like for patients to have to trust in caregivers they don't know, when they are feeling most vulnerable, isolated, and often alone.

Staff members at Griffin aren't allowed to remain detached from patients' suffering. They are trained, from the custodians to the surgeons, to see their patients as human beings. "It makes you think twice when you're doing things with patients, about what they must be going through," said nurse Cathy Higgins. "You understand what it's like to lose control of your life."

Griffin management and staff continuously do reality checks to make sure they are staying patient-focused. Some repeat the off-site Long Island Sound retreats to become further sensitized. Sometimes management needs to reinforce and reinstill, over and over again, the sense that Griffin is designed, above all, to support and care for patients and their families.

HUMANIZING HOSPITAL EXPERIENCES

For instance, when the hospital's new childbirth center was created, the intent was for families to use the new family room as they would a family room in their own homes. The goal was to really make the hospital family room a gathering place for the entire family as it awaits the birth of its new member.

So one night, not long after the new childbirth center had opened, the nursing staff went ballistic. They were upset because a large Italian family, waiting during a very long labor, had come in with pizza, wine, and beer to the family room, settled in for the long birth, and started playing cards. "How could they do this? It's a hospital!" the nurses complained.

"And that's when management said, 'Look, they live two to three streets away from the hospital. If they were at home, waiting for this new baby, that's what this family would be doing. That's what Griffin wants them to be comfortable doing here," Powanda laughed as he recalled this and other inaugurations of the birthing center.

Griffin also puts its money where its philosophies lie. Each month four employees who model the best in patient-centered empathy and care are honored and given a $250 check. They then become eligible for the annual employee-of-the-year, $1,000 award and recognition. Empathy and seeing with love are amply rewarded.[16]

Do you feel as if these qualities are in your life? Is this a form of sight you'd like to cultivate more deeply? The next time you feel like judging or ridiculing or distancing yourself from others near you, try to understand their pain. Begin to empathize with how they must be feeling. Ask them how they are feeling and whether there's anything you can do to help. If they say they're afraid, for instance, ask them what their greatest fear is.

Often by just saying it out loud, you can help them release that fear. Empathize by describing the times you felt this lost and scared. Tell them you can relate. Simple gestures powerfully open the heart.

Even if you don't know someone well, if you extend yourself in mutual goodwill, the sensation that will flood you and pour out into the world is incredible. "To feel the intimacy of brothers is a marvelous thing in life," writes Chilean poet Pablo Neruda. "To feel the love of people whom we love is a fire that feeds our life. But to feel that affection that comes from those whom we do not know, from those unknown to us, who are watching over our sleep and solitude over our dangers and our weaknesses—that is something still greater and more beautiful because it widens out the boundaries of our being and unites all living things."[17]

SEPARATED NO MORE

We need to cultivate this ability to see all things united. We need to learn to use compassionate sight and empathy so all the veils of illusion and judgment that separate us fall away. When we do this, we can finally see the true nature of others and then really know, as author Thomas Merton did when he said, "It was as if I suddenly saw the secret beauty of their hearts, the depths of their hearts where neither sin nor knowledge can reach the core of their reality, the person that each one is in God's eyes. If only they could see themselves as they really are. If only we could see each other that way, there would be no more need for war or hatred, no more need for cruelty or greed. I suppose the big problem would be that we would fall down and worship each other."[18]

What an absolutely glorious "problem" to have. That we could all be overcome not by grief, violence, or stress but by our compassion and love for one another. A paradise worth imagining. A utopia that would bring out the very best in us.

Once again, we all long to be fully known, to be understood. We all yearn for the comfort of being seen and cherished for who we are. How else can we say we have fully lived? How else can we experience the joy of being alive?

We all long to be fully seen for our preciousness, power, and beauty— no matter what our situation. We never lose this yearning. One day David

Martin, a hospice volunteer, bent down and gave ninety-two-year-old Verla Fernau a hug. She burst into tears. "Verla, why are you crying?" Martin asked. "I haven't had a hug in thirty years," she replied.

I find immense inspiration in Martin's story. He has developed the kind of sight we need more of—and can foster—in our culture. He has helped between forty and fifty people die a dignified and peaceful death through Compassion in Action, a volunteer organization that provides companionship for people in the last months of life.

A successful architect who scaled back his work to focus more on hospice work, Martin said his friends don't understand why he doesn't hang out at the country club more. "I've never been more fulfilled in my entire life," Martin responded. His sight is way beyond twenty-twenty.

"A person's body may have been ravaged by disease, but I see a perfect person. I call them perfect souls," Martin said. "The odors, the bed sores, none of that matters. It's all about unconditional love."[19]

That's the kind of sight we all can cultivate.

CLOSING PRAYER

Our time on earth is so limited, and we waste so much of it not seeing clearly. We narrow the loving vision we were born with and begin to see falsely with judgment, fear, and hatred. I share the following prayer I wrote to help us all see with loving, blindingly clear eyes:

A Prayer for New Sight

Dear God (substitute how you refer to your Higher Power), my guide of love and light and all that is holy, I have spent too much time seeing through darkened eyes, eyes that are mean, eyes that are judgmental, eyes that keep me apart from others. I no longer want to stay in this lonely, cold, harsh place. Give me new eyes to fully see the preciousness around me.

Every day, I have the opportunity to see what's really true, to see what really matters. Let me see as I've never seen before the true, divine essence of all. Give me new sight so I can fall in love with the beauty and tenderness and connectedness of all.

Please let me open my eyes wide to see the gift I have within to be love.

Saint Francis of Assisi once said, "The one you have been looking for is the one who is looking." The love we have been seeking is inside us. Please give me new eyes so I can recognize and delight in and be the love inside myself. Please give me new eyes so I can recognize and delight in and truly see the love inside others.

Let me fall into love with all that is. Let me see all as holy. Let me see with a loving heart. Let me see that God is in all things.

When Saint Francis walked the hills of Assisi, he stopped in front of a cherry tree, and he said, "Oh, little tree, speak to me of God." And the little tree burst into bloom. Soften my eyes so I can see that we all are blossoms of God. Make my eyes so tender that whenever I look on someone else, or whenever I watch the crescent of the moon in the night, or whenever I see and hear the geese winging overhead, or whenever I look on those right before me, I see God looking back at me.

5

Compassionate Conversation: Listening from the Heart

IN ANCIENT TIMES—and still in some countries today—spiritual healers and shamans spent hours with their patients, listening to their dreams, their fears, their diets, habits, premonitions, hunches, and intuitive nudges. They found out what kept them awake at night as they watched the stars hang in the heavens. They discovered how sturdy their relationships were and with whom they were locked in conflict.

And today, when we see our modern-day shamans, our HMO-bound healers, we get an average of eight to fifteen minutes to uncover our symptoms and their source. With increasing pressure from insurance companies and the sheer frenetic pace of life, doctors find themselves racing more and more to fulfill their patients' most basic needs. Time to listen and focus in on patients' needs gets sorely jeopardized. Medical care, as with the rest of our culture, gets compressed and truncated when we fail to spend the time to listen deeply to one another.

LISTENING IS CRITICAL IN HEALING

Trained as both a chaplain and physician, Dr. Gregory Plotnikoff says medical training doesn't teach doctors how to just "be" with patients and listen. "In two minutes of uninterrupted speech, a patient can tell you quite a lot. But most doctors interrupt after 18 seconds."[1] Medical students are trained to be active, doers, and problem-solvers, which puts them at risk of missing what patients need to share about their illnesses.

The art of listening is not a lost skill only in medicine, but it is in medicine that it may be the most visible—and maybe the most life threatening. The Roman statesman and philosopher Seneca once said, "Who is there in all the world who listens to us? Here I am—this is me in my nakedness, with my wounds, my secret grief, my despair, my betrayal, my pain, which I can't express, my terror, my abandonment. Oh, listen to me for a day, an hour, a moment, lest I expire in my terrible wilderness, my lonely silence. Oh God, is there no one to listen?"[2]

A poem used at the University of Minnesota School of Medicine speaks into that space where we often feel unheard:

> When I asked you to listen to me and you start giving advice
> you have not done what I asked.
>
> When I ask you to listen to me and you begin to tell me
> Why I shouldn't feel that way,
> You are trampling on my feelings.
>
> When I asked you to listen to me and you feel
> You have to do something to solve my problems,
> You have failed me, strange as that may seem.
>
> Perhaps that is why prayer works for some people, because God is
>   mute and God does not offer advice or try to fix things.
>
> So please, just listen and hear me. And if you want to talk, wait a
>   few minutes for your turn, and I promise I'll listen to you.[3]

How well can you sit with someone and just listen? Deeply listen without peeling out in your brain, treadmarks laid down among your neurons, out into the distance where you can stay detached? When was the last time you just listened to someone without scurrying off to the fix-it shop for a ready solution? How well do you listen without putting your funny or erudite spin on something someone shares with you? Tamala Edwards, a writer at *Time*, decided she wanted to spend more time listening instead of just "shooting off words like buckshot."

DEEPENING FRIENDSHIPS

She'd always prided herself on being the first with a bon mot and the quickest with the witty aside. But becoming a conscious listener, like sitting with a friend "as she told me about a newly train-wrecked relationship," made her feel like a better friend. It also made her discover her own personal inner power. One night, Edwards attended a reception and met a fierce, beautiful, witty woman who scared her. But instead of trying to interject her own arguments or jokes, Edwards just listened "as if she were speaking in Dolby sound."

Listening so deeply made Edwards feel "masterful because I was able to give more to her and to myself. . . . I was now able to draw her out with my questions and silences. I allowed myself to let her in."

The result of allowing this woman to share her worries and insecurities was that "by the time we parted on a drizzle-dampened street, she had moved into the category of likely friend."[4]

How well do you open your ears to let others in? Who returns the gift of silence? Who listens to you—in your dark night of the soul? Who listens to your worries and anxieties? Who hears you in your own home, in your office, in your medical visits, in your interactions at restaurants, grocery stores, and drugstore visits? How well are your needs heard? How well are you doing at offering that amazing gift to others?

Dr. Plotnikoff and his staff at the University of Minnesota Center for Spirituality and Healing have a visionary program to ensure that medical students will become compassionate listeners. Physicians who know how to listen and respond to patients' imbalances on a body, mind, and spiritual spectrum.

In a recent guest opinion in *Postgraduate Medicine* magazine, Dr. Plotnikoff advocates that patients be listened to and heard at a meaningful level and not just at a disease level. "Symptoms are interpreted in ways that can reflect the patient's most meaningful beliefs, and being heard at a meaning level can itself be profoundly therapeutic."[5]

HEARING WHAT'S REALLY IMPORTANT

If a doctor's listening is focused only on a patient's symptoms, chills, fever, and bowel functions, for instance, what is most meaningful to the patient can be overlooked. Here's an example: In our interview, Dr. Plotnikoff remembered a medical student who was doing an internal medicine rotation in her senior year where she met an elderly patient who was hospitalized with pneumonia. The patient was also in the advanced stages of Parkinson's disease and had limited ability to swallow, write, or speak. Dr. Plotnikoff recalled, "This medical student said that she noticed that each day a team of doctors would go in and 'talk at' this woman. It was quite the monologue, which made her very uncomfortable, the student said."

So one day the student went in to see her patient, leaned over, and put her ear right next to the woman's mouth. And she heard the woman distinctly say, "I want to die."

It so freaked the student out that she talked with her attending doctor, and it was agreed that psychiatry would consult with the patient. But when the psychiatrist came into the room, the woman slowly and deliberately folded her arms to convey that in no way would she talk to him.

So the medical student was left wondering, "Why did she say that to me? What is behind her desire to die?"

And she went back and asked the patient, "Ma'am, what is most important to you?" And she listened as the woman opened up and told her that all she wanted to do was to go home and feed her cats. And so that became a goal, a source of meaning, a point of hope, that the woman and the medical student could explore together. "And then the woman no longer wanted to die. Someone was there with the intention to listen to what needed to be heard and then could respond," Dr. Plotnikoff said. "I think those are incredible skills and that is what our program is all about."[6]

The lack of respect for compassionate listening plagues our culture in all our institutions, including, and many would say especially in, our homes. Survey after survey shows that kids don't feel their parents really listen to them, especially when they are in their teenage, and less adorable, years.

We just don't take the time to listen deeply and well. We're constantly making snap judgments, racing ahead to what we want to say, or often just tuning out. If we don't listen well, we lose the opportunity to connect deeply and well at a soul level. And, as doctors often find, they overlook critical information that could dramatically influence a patient's diagnosis and healing. They also may prescribe drugs that may not even be needed.

For instance, in treating elderly patients' depression, "what too often happens is that because the family doctor doesn't have time to talk, he prescribes medication. It's the easiest thing to do. What people need are human connections," says Rose Dobrof, a professor of gerontology at Hunter College's Brookdale Center on Aging.[7]

ULTIMATE PRODUCTIVITY AND EFFICIENCY

In our solutions-at-all-costs culture, we strive to be "efficient," "smart," "right," "productive." Yet, it's only by blending the heart skills, such as compassionate listening, with our intellects that we will ever be any of those qualities we revere. We can't be as productive or as smart or efficient as we yearn to be unless we bring our hearts into every interaction. Take medicine, again, as an example. Mayo Clinic studies found that history taking—when you tell the doctor what's bothering you—identifies ten times as many problems as urinalysis, and five times as many as a complete blood count.[8]

Listening with a heart blown wide open to discovery can make all the difference in diagnosing a problem—and delivering humane health care, according to Dr. James Gordon, founder and director of the Center for Mind-Body Medicine in Washington, D.C. Dr. Gordon is also a clinical professor in the departments of psychiatry and family medicine at the Georgetown University School of Medicine.[9]

He sees the power of compassion vividly in his work when he chooses to go to Kosovo. He goes there to counsel people traumatized by the war and often finds that deep listening is one of the best and first ways to unlock others' suffering. Therefore he views listening and conversation as "going inside the patient"—not only to humanize, but also to greatly improve medical treatment.

"Sometimes I just sit in the cafes or places people gather and wait for people to come and talk," he said in our interview. "I especially remember one man, a dentist, who wondered if he was depressed. He said, 'I get so angry, especially with my patients. My colleagues all think I should take antidepressants and tranquilizers, but I don't want to. Maybe you can help me.'"

Dr. Gordon tried to better understand the source of the dentist's pain, so he asked, "When do you get angry? Is it when you are filling your patients' teeth, for instance?"

"No, no," the man said "It's when my patients first come in, and we make small talk. Then they say, 'I offer my condolences for your brother.' See, my brother was very popular, and he was killed in the war. It makes me angry, and I don't want to think about it. The war is over. I just want to practice dentistry."

The man wondered whether he needed to be taking antidepressants, as many of his acquaintances had suggested. And in that moment of listening to the man's untold story, Dr Gordon realized what this man really needed was to finally express his feelings about the insanity of war that took the life of his brother—and about the grief he still harbored over his brother's absence. Instead of prescribing medication, Dr. Gordon prescribed a way the man could finally release and be free of the angst he'd buried inside himself: "I recommended that he spend fifteen minutes each morning in the countryside, yelling, screaming, and jumping up and down to get his anger out. He said, 'That's a great idea. Maybe if I let it out, I won't be depressed and angry anymore.'"

OFFERING THE GIFT OF BEING HEARD

When someone offers us compassionate listening—really listening until we are empty, sated, and free of whatever we've kept inside for far too long—we receive a gift. Too often, Dr. Gordon said, we're told or we feel that our depression, insomnia, anxiety, or other conditions are something beyond our control and should be treated with medications. "Instead, we need to go inside and see what is happening. What is disturbing, agitating, and overwhelming you? For most people, the answers aren't such a terrible mystery after all," stated Dr. Gordon.

Medical schools are rapidly adding effective communication, caring, and empathy courses to their curriculums. With grueling routines and bombarded by endless medical data, even the most openhearted students can forget to see and listen to their patients as human beings. So training, the profession knows, is critical. Twenty years ago, only 35 percent of medical schools had explicit communications skills classes, according to Dr. Mack Lipkin, professor of medicine and director of the division of primary care at the New York University School of Medicine in Manhattan. Today, all schools do, says the Association of American Medical Colleges (AAMC).[10]

This is again being partially driven by enlightened consumers. AAMC public opinion research shows patients rate communication as the most important factor in choosing a new doctor.[11] Never negate the power you hold to shape a more humane world.

With or without formal training, we can all learn how to listen deeply and with compassion. We can all learn how to become comfortable with the silence needed for secrets to be shared, confidences to be extended, bridges to be spanned.

As Dr. Gordon's story shows, sometimes just emptying ourselves enough so others have room to share provides the key they've searched for forever to unlock themselves from their spiritual hell. That is the ultimate expression of love—to take someone that deeply into your heart.

Stephen Levine has sat with and emptied part of his heart to make room for the stories, hopes, regrets, and needs of thousands of people when they are ill and dying. Levine has worked with Ram Dass and Dr. Elisabeth Kübler-Ross, both pioneers in helping terminally ill people die a compassionate, loving death. Levine remembers sitting with a catatonic woman in a hospital. One person after another tried to get the woman to speak and come out of her comalike state. But she would only come out when Levine was with her, listening or talking.

"One day I asked her, 'Why do you come out for me?' The woman answered, 'Only love is safe enough to come out to.' She speaks for our whole culture."[12]

Only love is safe enough to come out to. That is so incredibly thought-provoking when you consider that we have an unprecedented number of kids who are trapped in autism. These are kids who can't fully connect and bond through communication and touch. Autism is up nationwide, and California has witnessed a 273 percent increase in children with autism seeking support services, according to the *L.A. Times*.[13] What is behind this? No one fully knows. Some suspect it's our unprecedented use of childhood vaccines. Others think it's linked to chemical exposure via our foods and environment. Could it possibly be that these kids sense that it's not safe to come out, that there isn't an abundance of love in our culture to make it safe enough to leave their protective safehold behind?

WHO HOLDS YOUR SECRETS?

Who loves and listens to you so well that you feel it's safe to come out and reveal yourself? Do you bury yourself in a self-made cocoon, whose strands cover your heart? When will you be willing to come out? Whom can you find to sit with you and hold your secrets—a therapist or minister or friend—so you can finally leave your silken-webbed prison behind? Just as we need air to breathe, we all need someone we trust enough to reveal our true selves, from our shortcomings to our epiphanies until a real heart-to-heart bonfire blazes between us.

"What a delicious irony," says Lynn Brallier, a professor at George Washington University School of Medicine and Health Care Sciences, that in the midst of profit-driven medical care where "time is measured in nanoseconds . . . one of the most powerful ways to survive and even thrive in daily life as a caregiver is to embrace the ancient wisdom of keeping one's soul accessible at all times. Doing so not only improves our own lives, but allows us to function as a deep well from which patients can draw the healing benefits of loving-kindness."

In less poetic terms, a more spiritual approach to medicine "not only serves as a personal coping resource, but as a noteworthy element of clinical competence," concludes Brallier, also director of the Stress and Health Management Center of Metropolitan Washington.[14]

Compassionate people often are competent in the best possible way. But listening well is really hard. Our tendency may be to recoil, to run away, to keep things on a more superficial level. "Sometimes I care for people with whom it is difficult to connect or who are disheveled or rude. Yet, I know they need my attention as much, if not more than those who are personable and polite. Compassion does not discriminate," says Dr. Christina Puchalski, director of education at the National Institute for Healthcare Research. She is also an assistant professor at George Washington's Center to Improve the Care of the Dying.

When Dr. Puchalski starts to lose compassion, or is tired, or is focused on her own difficulties, she finds sustenance by remembering the Dalai Lama's talking about keeping compassion as a mental attitude. He faced the danger of losing his compassion to the Chinese when they imprisoned him for years, but instead he kept a compassionate attitude.

By taking the risk of sharing patients' joys, pain, and suffering, "I also am more at peace with myself," says Dr. Puchalski.[15]

LISTENING UNLEASHES INNER POWER

Listening well with all of our being is simply good, solid medicine. But it extends far beyond medicine, of course. We need to extend compassionate listening even to those we have most judged and banished in our culture. Author Wally Lamb has compassionately gone into a maximum-security women's prison in Connecticut to help support an inmates' writing group. Instead of merely dispensing writing tips, Lamb found that he could make the most powerful offering of all just by sitting and being attentive with his heart and mind.

Diane, one member of the writing group, eyed him suspiciously and only wrote under a pseudonym. She said she never, never wanted her work to be read aloud. But by session three, she couldn't hold back. "In a shaky, tentative voice, she voluntarily read to the group a disjointed chronicle of her life story: savage abuse, spousal homicide, lawyerly indifference and parallel battles against breast cancer and the hopelessness that accompanies long-term incarceration. When she stopped, there was silence. Then, applause. The dam of distrust had been sledge-hammered. The women's writing began to flow."

And Lamb was allowed to see the women not merely as drug abusers, gang members, thieves, and killers, "but as the complex, creative works in progress they are. Each discovered the intertwined power of the written word and the power that resides within."[16]

Letting others into our hearts, making way for their presence, can be such a soothing balm when we are in deep crisis, when we're still drifting from shore. That's when compassionate listening—not necessarily solving the problem—is so blissful.

We don't want anyone to fix "it" because "it" may not be broken. We don't want anyone to give us the spiritual lecture of the day. When my life is unraveling—even if it only feels that way—I loathe when someone tells me that I should *instantly* honor it as a personal growth experience. "You're not in crisis, you are in the middle of an opportunity to be cherished," someone once scolded me.

Sorry. We're not talking about nursing a hangnail. When you're in deep pain, even lifting your head off the pillow can feel impossible. Why bother when just a gray numbness awaits, even if the sun is white-hot outside?

Sometimes things happen that are so jarring, so explosive to the soul, that it seems to retreat into a self-protective zone. Here we move in slow motion, have dulled senses so the pain of the knife's edge can only be felt a bit at a time. And in that numb and lonely place, we don't want a lecture on honoring and cherishing our pain. We feel that we'll be lucky to survive the experience.

And that's when a kind, nonjudgmental listener offers the grace, the bridge we need to cross the abyss without falling in. Such a listener can help us to return to feeling, and sensation, and acceptance, slowly and lovingly, to allow us to find balance again so, if we are blessed, we can see the blessing in the pain.

That is the gift of grace that Swanee Hunt, former ambassador to Austria, offered people throughout Bosnia. Because thousands of men were slaughtered in the war in Koscvo, many times Hunt found herself connecting most with the women, women who were widowed and displaced, women who had lost many of their children and had siblings missing in action.

Once when about six thousand women gathered for a memorial service, Hunt told the women that the world would not forget them. One way she made sure the world would remember was to listen to their stories and then to bring in journalists so they could hear and record the stories as well.

At the memorial service, one woman told her story. She said she knew nothing of the fate of her brother and two nephews. "I dream about them every night. I dream about how they're tortured," she said, her words coming out in sobs. "It is impossible to forget."

OFFERING HUMAN EMPATHY

Swanee Hunt assured her that the U.S. State Department would not let the matter rest. But the old woman seemed to want more. Hunt put her arms around the woman, and for several minutes, they just held each other in a tight embrace. No quick-fix diplomatic solutions from the embassy were offered. No shallow, "official" response. Just human, deep empathy and listening in the silence.[17]

"I have been told, over and over, that I am one of the most trusted people in the Balkans in terms of working with women," Hunt told me. "I don't know why that would be if not for the fact that when I have been with the women there, I didn't immediately come up with answers. But I just listened. I would listen, and then come back and listen some more. Certainly, I would plead their case to President Clinton. In fact, that's how he came to create the Bosnian Women's Initiative. But my hunch is I'm trusted because the word has gone out that I care and there is this connection through listening that is very much a soul connection."[18]

If listening can ease the pain in a country assaulted by war, think of how it can soothe the assaults our lives regularly endure. When someone listens to how brutal our deadlines are, how mean-spirited our colleagues were, how jarring it feels to function after rocking a sleepless baby all night, we release what we've stored inside. It's as if emotional debris hits the floor. And then a new lightness and grace and vitality rush in to fill the void.

Where can you spend more time just being with someone, listening and absorbing what he or she needs to share? How often do you listen well? How often are you distracted, bored, prone to refocus the conversation to yourself and your own story? How often do you split your head and already start to spin off toward something "more important"? Or something that happened to you that surely has higher priority? We listen with the heart, never the ego.

How regularly do you listen to others reveal something they haven't shared with anyone—and then you judge them harshly? Or betray their confidence and gossip about it to a mutual acquaintance? We listen with the heart, never with malicious intent.

LISTENING TO OUR OWN HEARTS

And maybe the most important question of all: How well do you listen to your own heart? Many religious traditions refer to the heart as the seat of the soul. How connected to your soul are you—via your heart path? We so long to be adept and productive in our solutions-at-all-costs culture. Yet it's important not to overlook that "intelligence and intuition are heightened when we learn to listen more deeply to our own heart," say Doc Lew Childre, Howard Martin, and Donna Beech in *The HeartMath Solution*.

Know that these questions aren't intended to make us feel ashamed, unworthy, less-than. They are intended to shine a light on what compassionate listening is—and what it is not. They are intended to help us prepare to start really listening with the heart so we can become as compassionate as we long to be. Remember, when we are ready to listen with our hearts, we are transformed.

Just as we can't develop an open heart until we fully acknowledge ours is closed, we can't develop keen listening skills unless we accept responsibility for the times we've fallen down in the art of listening. These deaf-eared moments are what help us hone the ability to listen with acceptance, love, and power, Lutheran pastor Don Marxhausen came to realize.

Almost forty years ago, in his earlier training as a social worker in inner-city Chicago, Marxhausen listened with the limited, judgmental ears of an "Anglo-Saxon, white Protestant, German." In his work, he regularly met people whose story "would just tear your heart out."

He encountered a man who was down on his luck, unemployed, and suffering from ulcerative colitis. One day Marxhausen couldn't stand the situation any longer and confronted the man: "Why don't you just get a job?" That night the man almost bled to death. His doctor told Marxhausen that his lack of support and compassion had so affected his patient that he began to bleed internally.

Another time Marxhausen met an African American teenage girl who was finally getting out of school, and he arrogantly asked her, "What took you so long?" She patiently explained that growing up in Alabama, black kids weren't even given schoolbooks.

"I crawled out of there," Marxhausen told me, "and began to move from my judgment position to my 'walk with' position. It's like the biblical reference in Galatians, 'Bear ye one another's burdens.' You have to go with people right where they are. I finally discovered I have the gift of imagination to walk with the suffering of other people."[19]

Swanee Hunt believes strongly that wherever we are we can develop the ability to listen from the heart. In her current position as a distinguished fellow at Harvard's John F. Kennedy School of Government, she still purposefully hones the ability to attend to her staff and listen to them on a personal level, as well as a professional level.

"Even if I've only had a three-minute conversation with someone, they will say, 'There is something about you. There is this presence that is so calming.' They describe this presence as 'peaceful,' 'connecting,' and 'loving,'" said Hunt. "At some point, some physicist will win the Nobel Prize for figuring out what this 'presence' is." Hunt suspects she shaped her listening skills through her accumulated life's work and study.

One way she uses her skills is by bringing together groups of people who most need to listen and learn from one another. For instance, she once set up a meeting of New York politicians and people with mental illness, so the lawmakers could listen and learn about the needs of those who struggle with psychological and emotional issues.

Mental illness is too often considered a deep, dark zone of our culture that we'd rather sidestep at all costs. We would rather sanitize and whitewash and minimize conditions like depression and call them "funks" or "blues." But to be truly compassionate, to truly listen with the heart of a warrior, we sometimes have to go deep into the darkness to help others out of theirs.

SUPPORTING IN CRISIS

Don Marxhausen's listening heart took him into the deepest, darkest woods of all. On April 19, 1999, he was driving past Columbine High School in Littleton, Colorado. He was planning on meeting someone for lunch, but as he was driving by the school, he noticed a squad car in his mirror. He assumed he was being pulled over for speeding. But then the police officer peeled off to the school, and Marxhausen looked to his right and saw kids jumping over the fence.

Marxhausen was dressed in black, and as he approached the school, a running student told him, "A kid dressed like you is shooting people." He tried to persuade the police to let him into the school. Someone needed to be with the bodies, he reasoned. But they refused to let him in. So after counseling some of the parents who had gathered at a nearby elementary school, he returned to his church, which is just miles from the high school.

He knew the people would start coming, and they did. They didn't stop coming for months. "We had forty-six kids in our congregation who were in the line of fire," he said. "We had one boy who was in the library, between Isaiah Shoels and Cassie Bernall when they were shot. He couldn't figure out why he was still alive.

"Another young man ran out of the cafeteria, right past the killers. He's not slept for sixteen months. Something as traumatic as Columbine isn't like a death in the family that you can understand. Trauma scrambles your brain. Reality is so changed that, even months later, nothing makes any sense."

Through the community grapevine, Marxhausen let it be known that he would be willing to meet with and support Tom and Susan Klebold, the parents of Dylan Klebold, one of the two shooters. Serendipitously, two days later, without receiving Marxhausen's message, Tom Klebold called on his own and asked, "Would you help us out?"

Marxhausen agreed not only to listen to them and walk with their suffering, but also to conduct Dylan's memorial service. A police escort secretly took him to the church where he met the Klebolds and their relatives for the service. Marxhausen thought he was used to being in the presence of grief, but he was rocked by what he saw that day. Dylan's mother, he remembers, "just vibrated with her grief." So instead of immediately beginning the service, he gave those present a chance to talk. And he just listened as Dylan's family members emptied themselves of their feelings of grief, disbelief, and inconsolable pain.

OFFERING A RECEPTIVE HEART

After that day, Don Marxhausen spent many others just sitting with, being with, and listening to the Klebolds. So did some of their neighbors. "One family visited them or checked in with them or took a walk with them every day for a year after Columbine. That is deep compassion." So are the more than four thousand letters of support the Klebolds received.

Being with others as they suffer, listening with a receptive heart, making space inside yourself for their emotions may be the most compassionate gesture of all, Marxhausen believes. "The greatest gift you can give someone is to let them affect you."

Marxhausen's decision to go into the darkness with the Klebolds and other families was not only compassionate, it was courageous. The toll exacted on him has been incalculable. He lost his job, partially because of pressure from parishioners who disagreed with his decision to support the Klebolds. He got a hate letter that said, "Scum runs with scum."

He also got heat after speaking out when he felt too many Christian ministers were counseling people with a heavy-handed "only-Jesus-can-save-us" judgment that likely offended many of the non-Christian families who were also grieving. When he spoke out about that religious intolerance, more pressure came.

"After a Columbine happens, people don't know where to go with that kind of anxiety and fear. They need a scapegoat," said Marxhausen.

He now has relocated and is the senior pastor at a Lutheran church near Chicago. Would he listen with such compassion again, knowing the price he would pay? "Without a blink. It was the right thing to do," he said.

Marxhausen wasn't the only one who concluded that. During the darkest year following the Columbine shootings, he received an amazing letter from a Texas minister. "He was the minister at the church in Dallas that Lee Harvey Oswald's mother asked to please bury her son after he assassinated John F. Kennedy. By a vote of the church committee at that time, they refused to bury her son. The minister's note that he sent me said, 'Thank you for what you did.'"

How well do you go into the darkness with your friends and colleagues, family and children? How well are you willing to release any semblance of control and just sit with them, listening to whatever their hearts harbor? How willing are you to empty yourself enough of your own life to let someone else's story reside within? How well do we, as Don Marxhausen said, give others the gift of letting them affect us?

JUST BEING PRESENT IS ENOUGH

"It's not always about 'doing something,'" pointed out corporate ombudsman Kenny Moore. "Often it's more about 'being with someone.'"[20] Compassionate listening is more about a "quality of presence," said Soul Purposes consultant Ann Careau. Compassionate leaders "know when to speak and when to be quiet. They are comfortable with other points of view and recognize the essence of their role as humble leaders. They see themselves as supporting their staff and enabling them to be and do their best."[21]

How comfortable are you with just being with someone, empty of judgment and suggestions, empty and open enough to allow them to empty themselves of hurts and wonderings they may have back-burnered for years, even decades?

As Kenny Moore has long seen, hostility and bitterness can smolder forever unless someone is willing to listen to our feelings. For the past fifteen years, Moore has been a human resources manager for KeySpan Energy, assisting with organizational change, leadership development, and executive development. Before that, he spent fifteen years in a monastic community as a Catholic priest.

When he joined his company, Moore discovered that the very nature of corporate life—where large numbers of people come together, some in charge and others not—is ripe for hurts, misunderstandings, and personal violations. As he shared, "If you add to this fallout from downsizing, re-engineering, mergers and acquisitions, and rapidly changing business requirements, there's going to be employees who're hurt, offended, threatened, and alienated. And if that's how I feel at the end of the day, it's difficult for me to care, trust, or believe in you or what you're trying to do."[22]

Moore discovered that "fixing" these spiritual problems was far more difficult than fixing his company's operational ones. But knowing that much of his company's discontent was rooted in the need for healing—healing of people who felt they hadn't been heard or responded to appropriately—Moore came up with a radical-acts-of-love kind of solution that involved his company president.

"Most of our employees are union workers, and our president wanted to make sure he wasn't losing touch with the concerns and issues of our rank-and-file people. He asked my help in running a program that would allow him to meet informally with them to get their input and feedback about company happenings. I designed a simple program where he would meet twice a month with about fifteen union employees for about three to four hours over lunch."

Employees were given opportunities to focus on the "positives" of their company—what was going well, what they liked, and what they wanted the company to continue doing. And then they focused on the negatives—what they didn't like, what wasn't going well, what policies, practices, behaviors needed to be changed. The president asked each individual employee his or her thoughts or feelings and summarized what he heard. Each sharing session of the "positives" and the "negatives" often lasted up to ninety minutes.

LISTENING WITHOUT DEFENSES OR SOLUTIONS

And here was the compassionate twist: Instead of hearing the employees' feedback, concerns, compliments, and grievances, and responding with his own defenses, solutions, or comments, the president, as coached by Moore, was to merely listen.

"He wasn't allowed to disagree, correct, or judge any of the comments made. His role was to be there in service of them—what they thought and felt was far more important than anything he had to say. He went around the room asking each individual their thoughts and feelings, allowing each person as much time as they needed to surface their concerns and criticism, again, without passing judgment on their comments. He had to let go of his 'executive' need to disagree or correct what was being shared," said Moore.

After experiencing this program, month after month, several things began to surface for Moore. First, he saw how difficult it was for executives to listen—not solve, correct, or judge what is being spoken in these candid, heart-baring sessions. "In a corporate environment, whoever speaks the most and the loudest wins the discussion. Silence is not seen as a virtue.

"My experience was, though, that only after individuals have said all they wanted to say—emptied themselves—were they free to hear anything that you or the others had to say. All too frequently, executives ask employees for their opinions, but senior management's discomfort with silence doesn't give anyone a real chance to speak. Very often, when no one responds immediately, the officer quickly moves on to his or her canned speech—often losing the group and leaving them with the feeling that the officer really wasn't interested in what employees had to say."

Something else really struck Moore about the conversations the company president was having with his employees. He began to see more clearly the "deep hurt" some employees had experienced while working for the company. Insensitivity, discrimination, unfair treatment, and many other issues surfaced in their sharings.

"One employee spoke with bitterness about how his opinions were asked for and then nothing was ever done with his input," Moore said. "No action was ever taken. As the conversation continued, the resentment was so raw that it sounded like this had happened last week. In reality, it happened ten years ago. But for him the wound was real and present, and he had vowed since then never to offer another piece of advice to the company."

LISTENING LANCES OLD WOUNDS

Another woman spoke of her experience after her sister died. She'd had to leave work for a few days to help her family. She'd been a long-term supporter of the company's "food for the poor" volunteer program, and the corporate supervisor running the program wasn't told of her sister's death. When she came back to work, she was discharged from her volunteer work and publicly criticized. She explained that she'd had a death in the family, but the supervisor still refused to allow her to volunteer her services any longer, the woman said.

"In some regards, there were hurts that were long-standing and deep," Moore said. "And while ongoing efforts can be put in place to develop supervision, reduce discrimination, and so on, it would not undo the hurt inflicted on these people."

It was seeing this need for healing in the organization that compelled Moore to work further with his president. As they continued with their regular meetings, the president now began to listen to his employees' pain from an even deeper perspective. And he finally said what they'd longed to hear for years: "I'm sorry to hear that was done to you. That's not in line with our values nor the type of environment we're trying to create in this company. While I know that wrong which was done to you can't be reversed, on behalf of the company, I would like to apologize to you and ask your forgiveness."

Can you imagine how potent and healing those words would be if we could hear them when we most need to? Doesn't just hearing them now make your heart stir?

The impact within the company stirred amazing shifts too, Moore said. "It was startling! Employees all at once felt heard and affirmed. They felt an injustice had been rectified and were now free to let go of a 'corporate' hurt and move on with their lives. They began to understand that the organization isn't perfect, that it's similar to them, and worthy of compassion and forgiveness. Two qualities that were probably always available for them, but nobody ever asked for them."

As he continues his work, Moore finds inspiration in Henri Nouwen's book *The Wounded Healer*. Nouwen talks extensively about the need for healing that's always present with any community of people joined together for a common purpose. Moore explained, "Henri also points out that the people doing the healing within the community are not those who are whole and have their act together, but rather those who are struggling with their own brokenness, and while ministering to themselves, are also more available to heal the woundedness of others."

COMING TOGETHER IN HEART AND SOUL

Whether we work in a large corporation or are joined with others in another form of community, we examine the original meaning of the word *company* and carry that in our hearts.

The word *company* comes from the Latin "com," meaning with, and "apen," meaning bread. In other words, company means "the coming together over bread."[23] In the early Christian community—and in ancient communities since the beginning of time—the sharing of bread is a central, critical ritual for union and healing. If we want this depth of healing to continue in all our communities, corporate and noncorporate, we'll need leaders who can create the compassionate environments where employees can come together "in community"—in service of business success. "We'll need to engage not only the hands of our employees, but also their heads and hearts. In many regards, this is a spiritual undertaking," Kenny Moore pointed out.

How well does your workplace, your home, your community allow you to engage your head and heart? Where could you find that kind of outlet? Maybe it's already out there, waiting for you to show up. For instance, Chicago is home to a center called the Wellstreams Center. It is a place where people can go over their lunch hour and, in small groups, share their stories and explore their spirit, their passions, and their purpose. "We're all here to pay a little closer attention to our life paths. We come here to challenge our hearts a little. The sharing helps give me courage to keep on moving," says Jane Mueller Ungari, a Wellstreams participant and faculty member at Robert Morris College.[24]

Are there similar gatherings in your community where you could freely share your thoughts and feelings—and where hearts are ready to listen to them? Or could you begin one where you are? Do others around you yearn for that? As the stories in this chapter illustrate, listening with the heart, inviting someone into your heart, is the consummate gift. It is also life-affirming. "The ear is the most powerful part of the body. People are healed by the laying on of ears," says Doug Manning in *Don't Take My Grief Away*.

Gathering with others to listen to what is said and unsaid, what is shared and still unspoken, is a spiritual, sensitive ritual of the highest kind, says Wayne Teasdale in *The Mystic Heart*. "It is a generosity and magnanimity of heart, a willingness to sacrifice for those in need, who suffer, who need us in some essential way. . . . Sensitivity puts others first; it never considers self, but setting self aside, reaches out in a healing, appropriate way to all those who need us. Sensitivity is never rude or unkind; it always seeks the good of others. It never imposes on them, but patiently waits until an opening occurs. . . . It is love transformed by divine union or enlightenment."

May such light shine down on all our conversations, on all our ears.

CLOSING MEDITATION

In our culture, for centuries, the head has ruled the heart. "I think therefore I am" has been the credo of our left-brain-dominated world. No wonder we feel out of balance. "Individually and universally, we need to return to the balance and harmony that can only be achieved by training our heads to surrender to the wisdom and compassion of our hearts," says Sue Patton Thoele in *The Woman's Book of Spirit*.

Whenever you feel the need to bring greater balance between your head and heart, rely on the following meditation from Thoele.

Surrendering Head to Heart Meditation

With your eyes closed, breathe deeply into your heart area and feel it accepting and absorbing the life-giving infusion. Imagine that your heart is expanding and that loving energy is flowing from its center like circles on the surface of a pond. With reverence, physically bow your head toward your heart. Even if it feels awkward, silently tell your heart that your head wishes to cooperate with it, surrender to it, and serve it. Ask your heart's inherent wisdom and love to guide you.

6

The Heart Unleashed: Speaking from the Heart

WE OFTEN RETREAT INTO OUR HEADS when it becomes too scary to talk from our hearts. We freely share what we rationally know, but run from what we know to be true in our hearts. We wall off the heart behind dams of distrust the minute our heels hit the office. We mask our hearts even in casual encounters with family and friends. Why risk being vulnerable again when we've often been hurt in the past?

We intimately know how devastating harsh words can be to our psyches. Although a whiplash to the soul may mend and heal over time, it often leaves a lingering ache. But what if it's the words that aren't said that leave the most indelible, enduring pain? What if our hearts are scalded more from words left unspoken than words lashed out in anger and cruelty? What if we're wounded more by the moments when life brought us to our knees, and no one lifted us up with kind words? Those we believed would offer comfort instead pulled the hard-hearted routine and wordlessly walked away.

"The things we're not saying are the things that most need to be heard," says Marianne Williamson, author of *A Return to Love*. "It's not that hate is so loud, it's that love is so quiet."

SAYING WHAT NEEDS TO BE SAID

As children, we all longed to hear we were precious, that we were appreciated and brought delight to our parents' lives. We were fed by their words of comfort when we fell off our bikes or were chased on the playground by the class bully. We hung on to words of encouragement from teachers when spelling words started moving beyond *boy* and *cat* and math began to scramble our brains. As kids, we all needed to be "affirmed"—that sanitized, pop-psycho buzzword we're comfortable with today. In other words, we all needed to be loved and appreciated.

And we still do. We don't lose this need to hear words of comfort, support, and appreciation just because we're walking around in bigger bodies, weighed down by swollen mortgages and seemingly bloated problems. To live well, we still need to hear kind, healing, supportive words that lighten our hearts and shore them up to go back out in the world. If those words never come, the world's a very hard place. "It is the history of our kindnesses that alone makes this world tolerable," writes Robert Louis Stevenson. "If it were not for that, for the effect of kind words, kind looks, kind letters . . . I should be inclined to think our life a practical jest in the worst possible spirit."[1]

"Our lives are fed by kind words and gracious behavior," says writer Ed Hays. "We are nourished by expressions like 'excuse me,' and other such simple courtesies. . . . Rudeness, the absence of the sacrament of consideration, is but another mark that our time-is-money society is lacking in spirituality, if not also in its enjoyment of life."[2]

Words of compassion are simply—and powerfully—one way we know we are loved and are loving others, in turn. So if our intention is to create a more powerful, effective, compassionate society, we need to ground ourselves in compassionate conversation. We need to cultivate and muster up the words, expressions, skills, and courage it takes to express from our hearts what must be said, what makes life worth living.

How comfortable are you with expressing from your heart? How well have others offered the succor of words when you needed them? How often have you used compassionate self-talk as a balm for your own broken heart? This heartfelt communication is often the hallmark of true intimacy. But when it comes to talking straight as an arrow from our hearts, my guess is that we too often struggle with a form of emotional muteness and illiteracy.

THE TIMES WE WERE MUTE

Think back to times you were unable to offer words of comfort or support to someone else. When was the last time you really wanted to say how you felt and couldn't bring yourself to do it? How did it make you feel? What did you wish you'd said? What did you yearn to hear in return?

Remember the story of the medical student discussed earlier who went in to change the catheter of the man who was crying? She didn't know what to say, so she didn't say anything at all. Again, as part of the University of Minnesota's effort to humanize medicine, Dr. Gregory Plotnikoff, trained as both a chaplain and a physician, has designed a groundbreaking program that helps medical students communicate and connect with their patients in a meaningful, respectful way. As a student, Dr. Plotnikoff intentionally postponed medical school to attend divinity school, where he studied social and political philosophies, medical ethics, pastoral care, world religions, and other subjects. "Then I started medical school and found that the medical curriculum and the practice of medicine was completely restricted to biomedical science. And I thought, 'Boy, there are some incredibly profound truths missing here,' and so for the past fifteen years I've been working on weaving those into the medical curriculum."

And his weaving goes against the tide of the sanctioned dehumanization of medicine that has been occurring for years. Dr. Plotnikoff said, "When students started medical school in the eighties, one of their biggest fears was losing their humanity. And lo and behold, those fears came true. There was no recognition of human values and compassion and that connection with others. Right now, what we stress in medical school is that you cultivate what you honor. If you only honor memory and regurgitation, you won't cultivate the doctors you want to cultivate. And you won't meet patient expectations."

CULTIVATING COMPASSIONATE CONVERSATION

What is cultivated with the greatest care at the Center for Spirituality and Healing is the art of speaking from the heart. This is the skill of responding to patients who often get admitted along with their grief, isolation, alienation, brokenness, and loss of meaning. In this visionary program, students are trained and guided to approach patients with simple invitations and open-ended questions such as "You seem to be feeling sad. Tell me about it" and "What do you fear most about your illness?" and "How else do you hurt?"

Then the students are guided to ask even more complex questions in their service of patients, questions such as "How has this illness affected your relationship with your family and friends? Your financial situation?" and "What do you miss most as a result of your illness?" and "Has your illness made you think of religious or spiritual issues?"

CAN WE HEAL A TROUBLED SOUL?

"We can transplant a heart, but can we heal a troubled soul?" asks Dr. George Simms, a professor at Penn State University Medical School.[3] Speaking from the heart can be the balm a soul most needs.

Dr. Plotnikoff is even learning Vietnamese and Hmong so he can better communicate with the rising number of patients from those cultures. A humbling experience, considering that he is tone deaf—and both are tonal languages. He admitted he sometimes asks patients if their "rice" rather than their "pain" is better.[4]

"My patients often find my attempts to communicate in their language quite amusing, and they respond with great humor. But I think it also tends to break down barriers, so it's quite well received."

Even if it's embarrassing, or uncomfortable, or a huge leap of faith, Dr. Plotnikoff and his students are trying to learn how to speak from their hearts. It can push our level of comfort far beyond our comfort zone, but we need to learn how to express what needs to be said if we are intent on becoming people of heart. If we are to become heart activists in our own right, we have to master the basic foundation skills of speaking with love and tenderness and mutual empathy. These are prerequisites to becoming heart warriors.

When Bailey Stenson's oldest son, Toby, committed suicide while away at college, she was struck by how many people just didn't know what to say. So they didn't say anything, which can be even more painful. Some people avoided her glance or looked or walked away because they were just unable to express themselves.

When she returned to her job at a local school, instead of expressing how she felt, one of her colleagues handed Stenson a pamphlet that offered a philosophical treatise on suicide. Cold comfort when your child is gone.

Another woman, with whom she had enjoyed many intimate conversations before Toby died, became more distant, couldn't bring herself to discuss this topic. Even looking at Stenson, she said, made her leave school one day to sit in her car in the parking lot and weep.[5]

Stenson wrote the following poem to express how those moments felt to her:

Uncomfortable to Be Around

It's uncomfortable
for other people
to be intimate
with me
I remind them of
their hidden pain
and unspoken words
of comfort

I am the red flag
that there are
no guarantees
to life's journey
and sometimes
it seems
a dead end
with no rewards

Avoid me
turn away
your eyes
protect yourself
from feeling
the pain and
agony too

Be safe
and numb
so that
nothing
can
"hurt"
you.

Often because of family or societal conditioning, we don't know or want to "deal" with the issues of death, and loss, and change, and grief, said Stenson. "It's like you've got the plague or leprosy. Our society wants to push these issues away and focus only on the young, the beautiful, the healthy."

AVOIDING TENDER EXPRESSIONS

A co-worker has a miscarriage, a friend's father dies, a teacher is diagnosed with terminal cancer, and we find ourselves at a loss for words. We panic, grope, feel uncomfortable, foolish, or inadequate. I think we also feel very, very scared. Or, worse yet, we feel unconnected: "That's none of my business. I've got enough of my own to worry about."

Click. . . . Connection broken.

And, for whatever reasons, we can't speak from our hearts. From our workplaces to our neighborhoods, incalculable suffering and pain occurs because we hold back from binding our hearts with another. Even the simple expression of shared pain, "I'm so very sorry," has become tough to say in our culture. Our society has a "taboo on tenderness," observes Carol Schultz, who works as an extension agent at Colorado State University. "Simple, open affection and honest compliments embarrass some of us."[6]

Many people will argue it's not embarrassment at all. They will argue that it's simply not appropriate to give issues of the heart and soul any berth in our boardrooms, oncology offices, schools, or other "professional" pockets of our culture. Quarantine the heart to the appropriate zones of church and home.

"I don't dare show any weakness or vulnerability at work or it will be used against me," a businesswoman e-mailed me recently. Others have shared that, for fear of reprisal and many other reasons, they have kept secret from their managers and co-workers their children's disabilities, divorces, deaths in the family, and any chronic illness, physical or emotional. Some said they were afraid they would be viewed as a weak link, not "pulling their weight," a millstone around the organizational neck—as less than productive, efficient, competent.

COMPASSION IS APPROPRIATE

They were also afraid, even if they wanted to tell their stories, that it just wasn't appropriate to give such a glimpse into their personal lives. Do you want to know what's truly not appropriate? It's not appropriate to pretend we can survive without compassionate conversation in some of the most critical parts of our lives. It's not appropriate to deny ourselves life-sustaining empathy, appreciation, and concern no matter where we spend our days in the world.

It's not appropriate that far too many of us at far too young ages suffer from unprecedented depression, cancer, ulcers, migraines, heart disease, high blood pressure, and panic attacks. How much of this is related to the unhealthy, heart-starved atmospheres in which we work and live? Remember William Blake's words, that we are here "to bear the beams of love"—as we jockey in the marketplace, as we race to catch that bus, as we stand before a class and look out at a crowded room of college students. The "bring-your-daughter-to-work" movement has caught on in our country right now. How about a "bring-your-heart-to-work" revolution? That's something to model for our daughters and sons.

If each of us would model how to apply heart to our work life, for instance, the next generation would see it as normal and noble to do so. Can we begin to show the younger people around us how that's done—and inspire them to do likewise?

Heather Meyer, a recent psychology graduate of Colorado State University, will always be grateful that one of her professors wasn't intimidated about bringing his heart to work. In all the hundreds of hours she spent working toward her degree, the most valuable lessons she learned took place in just a matter of minutes on the second-to-last day of a summer school class she took her senior year.

Meyer described the experience: "I was in a class called Child Exceptionality and Psychopathology taught by Dr. Lee Rosen. This day he wasn't lecturing, it turned out. He decided instead to tell us a story of what it would be like to work with children.

"So Dr. Rosen took his class on a journey back in time to over thirty years ago when he was working at a residential treatment facility for behaviorally disturbed kids, right before his graduate school training."

The story Dr. Rosen told Meyer and his other students was about a time when he was in charge of the older, ten- to thirteen-year-old boys at the facility. And then there was nine-year-old Andy, who was too young to be in Dr. Rosen's group.

Andy, however, tried as hard as he could to tag along all the time. He'd been at the center the longest, and the staff generally agreed that he was the most emotionally disturbed child there, as far as his behavior went.

Dr. Rosen was quite popular with the kids because he'd devised a system that rewarded the kids with "pop cards" when they did something good. They could trade in the cards for sodas whenever they felt like it. So with that in mind, "Dr. Rosen told us how one day he decided to try to get his group to clean up the grounds of the center."

His group was reluctant. "What's in it for us?" they asked. Dr. Rosen answered them sarcastically, "You'll get a big hug from me," which was greeted with moans and groans from the boys, as he expected. And they went about doing just what they wanted to do.

But Andy shyly approached Dr. Rosen and told him that he would pick up the yard. Dr. Rosen said, "But Andy, I'm not giving any pop cards for it."

Andy replied, "I know, but you said you'd give us a hug," and he started cleaning the grounds. When Andy was finished, he timidly approached Dr. Rosen with an expectant look on his face.

Slightly annoyed, Dr. Rosen said, "Andy, I told you I wasn't going to give you anything. Thanks for doing the work, though."

CONNECTING AGAINST ALL ODDS

Andy quietly stood his ground and answered, "You said you'd give me a hug." Shocked that Andy really wanted a hug and humbled because he'd forgotten all about it, Dr. Rosen obliged and leaned down and gave him a hug. After that, Andy seemed to follow Dr. Rosen and his group around even more.

Soon it was time for the holiday. Most of the kids had relatives and got to go home for a break, but not all of the boys did. Andy didn't have anyone and stayed at the center. Dr. Rosen, being low man on the totem pole, had to work the holiday break there. So it turned out that he and Andy spent lots of time together, and they became very close. One night, Andy had a nightmare and came to the kitchen seeking solace from Dr. Rosen.

After the other staff left them alone, Andy told Dr. Rosen that he wanted to tell him his story. Dr. Rosen was amazed—and honored. Andy had always, always remained silent and stoic about his past. So Dr. Rosen listened.

Andy told Dr. Rosen about an abusive home life. When he was only six, he saw his father murder his baby brother. His father had been drunk and scalded his brother in the bathtub because of something he'd done. Because Andy was the only one who had witnessed his brother's murder, his father threatened if he ever told anyone, he'd kill him too.

As the only witness, Andy was required to testify against his father in court. His father was found guilty and sent to prison, all the time vowing that he would eventually find and kill Andy. None of Andy's family would bring him into theirs because they were all afraid that his father would eventually retaliate against them. What a story. No wonder Andy went through a string of foster homes and had behavioral problems. "Andy cried himself to sleep that night in my arms," Dr. Rosen told his class. "My heart broke for him that evening."

But, Dr. Rosen went on to say, the next morning Andy was a terror toward him. And the next day, and the next. Dr. Rosen was bewildered; hadn't they finally gained some headway? But then he realized what was happening. "Suddenly it was like the lightbulb went on. You'd think anyone with a psychology background would have picked it up. Andy had told me all his terrible secrets, and now he was testing me to see if I'd still love him with that knowledge."

So Dr. Rosen approached Andy and told him he knew what Andy was doing. He told the boy he was not to blame and that he would be there for him no matter what.

From then things improved in a hurry. When the other kids came back from their holiday break, Andy was made an official part of Dr. Rosen's group. "It turned out that Andy was very intelligent, and with some work, he began to go to school out of the center a little bit at a time," Dr. Rosen told his class.

Eventually a foster family was found for Andy. He was leaving the center at last. The night before Andy was to leave, Dr. Rosen got a phone call. Andy was on the line. He was very upset.

"Andy was crying," Dr. Rosen remembered with his students. "He told me he was afraid that his family wouldn't love him, how he was afraid that he would ruin it. I tried to reassure him, saying what a great kid he was, how far he'd come, and of course, he'd be loved."

And as Dr. Rosen shared the conclusion of Andy's story with his class, he looked out at his students with tears in his eyes. He got choked up and said, "But I don't know if I told the truth. I never did find out how Andy's case finished because the next day I was off to graduate school in New York."

"By this time," Meyer recalled, "there were some teary eyes in our class, including mine."

And Dr. Rosen continued, "I never did find Andy, never knew what happened or how he turned out. That's what it's like to work with kids; very rarely do you get to see the ending. And if you can handle that, then you've got it made."

THE MOST VALUABLE LESSON

Heather Meyer is still in awe of how moved she was by her professor's story that day: "This man and all his compassion that he brings to child psychology left a lasting impression on me. You don't get that kind of education or training from a textbook. You don't even get it from professors, because they often are so swept up in their careers that compassion seems to get left behind. But Dr. Rosen was true to compassion and shared it with his whole class, giving all of us the most valuable lesson we could learn that day: a true glimpse of the future."

The heart speaks volumes. Textbook-derived lectures pale in comparison to the magical spell of the heart. When we fail to bring this magic to our classes, our meetings, our surgeries, business deals, institutions, the cost is unimaginable. Look how drastically we change and touch the lives of those around us by showing our more vulnerable side, by revealing our passions, doubts, fears, and dreams. And what we lose if we don't. Think of speaking from the heart, wherever you are, to transform your environment with the magic of the heart.

As you do so, keep reminding yourself that speaking from the heart is one way you honor those you are with. Who doesn't yearn for that? Even the most seemingly heart-hostile people yearn for that, and something within them still recognizes and reaches out to connect with the simple language of kindness and compassion. Stephen Levine told me about a moment years ago when he and his wife, Ondrea, went to speak to kids in a tough junior high school class.

One of their classmates had been killed in a car accident, and the kids complained at school that when they wanted to talk about how they felt, their parents didn't want to. When Stephen and Ondrea visited with the kids, they realized they'd walked into one tough class. "There were some thirteen-year-olds carrying knives. So we started talking about compassion, but these kids couldn't hear it."

Compassion was not an idea they'd been exposed to in their lives. But when the Levines started talking about simple kindness and the value of it, a light went on. "This was a language they understood. The toughest people in the room were the most to share. Those who were the most unkind were the most to appreciate kindness."[7]

Many, many times we are unkind and dispassionate with others because we've been hurt so much that all we can do, we conclude, is wall off our hearts so no one can ever mutilate them again. We're all here to learn lessons and to love one another in the process of doing so. A little kindness frees us to do both.

BREAKING OLD PATTERNS

Speaking with love is so powerful because it breaks down the illusion that we are separate and disconnected from the people we meet each day. It shatters the belief that it's *okay* to remain indifferent or callous, even to the suffering that walks into our lives. Recognize that maybe we build calluses around our hearts because we're afraid of feeling, afraid to get wounded again. We're like the Grinch, said actor Jim Carrey, who plays the character in the holiday movie. "He's a callus. Like a lot of us. You get hurt a few times and build up calluses against the world."[8]

Is it time to lance our wounds so they can finally heal? Could it be time to break the pattern of separateness in your life? Are you ready to have deeper conversations that your heart is longing for? Can you begin to speak from the limitless heart rather than from the smaller, fearful, isolated place you've come from before? "Then the day came when the risk to remain tight in a bud was more painful than the risk it took to blossom," says writer Anaïs Nin.[9]

Have you reached that day? Then start slowly; begin by taking the time to speak with concern. Take enough time to really be present with others and see them with greater depth and caring. Show them they matter to you, as former Wisconsin Supreme Court Justice Janine Geske models. Instead, too often, "We are so busy running, we don't connect, and we miss that opportunity to be compassionate and receive compassion from others," she remarked.[10]

Taking the time, or finding the courage, or overcoming the tenderness taboo—whatever blocks us from saying what needs to be said—can be done. We can do this. There are many people leading the way, showing us how, people who felt the pain around them and knew the toll was too high to continue with "business as usual."

COMFORTING WITHOUT WORDS

What are some ways you can begin speaking from the heart? How can you start showing those around you that you feel and are willing to support their pain, that you simply care? Sometimes the best words are no words at all. "One of our good friends came to Toby's memorial service," remembered Bailey Stenson. "And he walked up to me and just put his arms around me, and there was such comfort there. It was so loving and went to a place beyond words."

That's because sometimes the most healing, compassionate response involves going to an energy field "far more fine than words," according to psychotherapist and author Sue Patton Thoele. "Words are among our densest energy expressions. So if our hearts can actually move into a field or intention toward compassion, the energy that emanates from it will be healing and magnetic. . . . With people who are grieving, it is enough to be present because when we are in the midst of crisis, the thought of even lifting our toe is overwhelming let alone having to hear people say, 'Oh, time heals everything' or 'Soon, you'll put this all behind you and be thankful.' That is bullshit when someone is in deep crisis."

Instead of talking, we can start with the "tiniest little openings" for connection, including just sitting silently with someone; this is so powerful, said Thoele, also a hospice chaplain.[11]

After Toby was gone, Stenson and her husband, Dennis, spent a lot of healing time in that wordless place. "When a death or suicide happens, it's like you go beyond the sense of the physical. You are blown out of your body, and the places you can meet with someone lovingly, to honor your pain, are often in silence, prayer, meditation, and devotion," she said.

"Once we went on a walk with friends and it was so beautiful. The leaves on the trees were so full of color; none of us needed to say anything. It was enough to unite in a place where our hearts could connect."

Stenson wrote the following poem after one of those moments among the trees.

Beauty

The beauty of nature
fills my dark, sad places

I am filled
with the flaming colors
of fall

Reds, oranges
yellow and brown
burn inside to keep
my soul warm
and comforted

The endless blue sky
so vast and deep
helps me feel
my loving connection
with him

The crashing of waves
and their magnetic jewel colors
help me remember my power
even when I feel empty

If it's the silence and solace of nature's stillness that is most comforting at times, the same is true for the small admissions, the tiniest human expressions we make to those around us. Never negate how important it is to show even a glimpse of yourself, your needs and hopes. That then opens a space for the other person to show his or her humanity, as well. A few words from a real, authentic place can speak volumes. Revealing yourself, just a story at a time, opens the window for others to see you in a new light—and to tell a little more of their stories too.

EXPRESSING OUR NEEDS

A few years ago, Dave Potter was the CEO of a small software company. He was working with Intel on a project they would jointly introduce. A planning meeting, critical to the success of the products, was scheduled at Intel's headquarters.

Only a week before the meeting, Potter discovered that it conflicted with his daughter's birthday party. His Intel contact, Paul, was a "take-no-prisoners/get-the-job-done-even-if-means-no-sleep-or-food" kind of guy, and he knew a phone call telling him he couldn't make it would be a bust. Potter knew he'd get no sympathy or understanding.

Taking a big gulp, he called Paul. "Something has come up. I can't make the meeting on Tuesday."

Almost before Potter finished the sentence, Paul blurted, "*What!* What do you mean you can't make it!??!! It took us months to find a date that worked for everybody. I've got people from Phoenix flying in on Tuesday just to meet with you, and you want me to reschedule it? What could possibly be so important?"

With Paul's voice ringing in his ears, Potter toyed briefly with the idea of fabricating something. Maybe he could say he had a multimillion-dollar deal he would lose if he left town. "I could almost even convince myself of it because I did have a big deal that was pending and I was feeling a time crunch," he recalled.

But he knew Paul had a samurai-like quality about him. He knew he lived by the ironclad maxim "There is never a good enough reason for breaking your word."

Knowing there would be no acceptable response, Potter took a breath and told Paul the truth: "Tuesday night is my daughter's birthday dinner, and I promised her I would be there. It's not a kids' party, but a small group of family and friends who will be taking this entire evening to honor Tracy."

There, he'd said it. He'd bared his heart—at work. How many of us have tried to unmask our hearts in similar circumstances and been met with cold-eyed silence, a sarcastic grunt? It's not hard to imagine how Potter felt waiting for Paul's response. In our culture, there's often a big, uncrossed chasm from one heart to another.

But to Potter's surprise, suddenly Paul's whole tone changed, and his pace slowed. He actually said, "Oh . . . how old is your daughter?"

"Eight."

"Eight. My son is nine. If I promised him I'd be at his party and didn't show . . ."

There was a noticeable pause on the line; he softened even further, and with a tone of understanding and acceptance, he volunteered, "You can't miss her party. We'll reschedule the meeting."

And that was it. The meeting was rescheduled for the following month. It was successful and well-received, and Potter's backing out of the original meeting was never mentioned again.

By being honest about his own truth, Dave Potter realized that a crack in the normal "business-is-business" veneer was created. And he was able to touch a part of his colleague Paul that those around him almost never saw. Plus, had he fabricated a purely business reason for missing the meeting, the conversation would likely have ended very differently and could have even jeopardized his relationship with Intel.

"Even worse, had I decided to go to the Intel meeting, I would have missed an evening with my daughter that is still, five years later, a high point in our family. Sometimes by being about who you are, you *can* have your cake and eat it too."

It's not enough for our hearts to lie quietly in wait of our return at the end of the day. It's not good enough for us to assume we can wait for simple decency and compassion until we're safely in a more "appropriate setting." Our bodies and spirits can't wait that long. We have to bring our hearts to our everyday routines, our fears and our longings, and have the heart-to-heart conversations we long for.

FINDING OPPORTUNITIES TO SHARE

And, yes, honesty and openness are "appropriate," whether you spend your days formulating public policy, nurturing children, working on an assembly line, cooking in a restaurant, or planning a corporate takeover. We all have too much at stake to shield our hearts and assume the stoic, separate, professional stance. The heart's got to enter into the equation.

Are there already opportunities in your life to speak and share from your heart? Do you already see some openings? How comfortable are you with speaking from your heart at work, for instance? Can you choose at least one person with whom it's safe to bring your whole self to work? Or do you still feel you have to leave the deepest, most enduring parts of you at home? Or do you even feel compelled to keep them hidden at home too?

Maybe things would unfold if you felt the fear and did it anyway, as psychologist and author Susan Jeffers suggests in her book *Feel the Fear and Do It Anyway*. If it's scary, bring that into your language. When you approach someone with whom you want to speak from your heart, feel free to say, "I'm really afraid to say this, but I need to tell you that . . ." or "I don't quite know how to tell you what I'm feeling, but . . ." Acknowledging your vulnerability may soften their heart resistance and allow them to meet you in kindred space. And then the words will begin to flow. The silence will be broken.

Former World Bank leader Richard Barrett now works to help companies and organizations around the world bring and share their whole selves. We can weave variations of his ideas into our own workplaces, homes, and relationships to coax and give voice to our hearts.

Sometimes the simplest sharing yields the deepest information. Barrett often conducts workshops focused on exploring what's often left unsaid. "Once we were gathering in Houston, and I asked everyone to introduce themselves. They shared their names, interests, why they were there. Then we went around the room again, and I said, 'This time, let's do something different. Share something you normally don't in the workplace with your colleagues.'"

And the energy shifted palpably in the room. A young man in his late twenties spoke up, "I have something to share. I'm going to be divorced tomorrow." And again, the energy in the room shifted even more as people let their hearts breathe. One woman turned to him and responded, "Well, I have to tell you. I have been through it, and it gets better."

From then on, the group had a real sense of connectedness and compassion, Barrett said. People were able to open up on a deeper level. Often the smallest admission is all it takes because we so want to do this sharing. "This is the kind of work we need to do. It gives us the opportunity to have the conversations we've not had before, to get deeper feedback," said Barrett.

DEEPENING THE CONVERSATION

Another exercise Richard Barrett uses to break the ice surrounding our hearts is to have people write down why they come to work each day, why they stay in their jobs. Then they share their responses with a partner, and the partner has the opportunity to ask questions about the response. Some people are guided to go deeper than ever before into understanding what motivates them, to excavate some real "soul stuff," according to Barrett.

In our interview, Barrett described how the exercise works: "One person might share, 'Well, I come to work to make $5 million.' And his partner will probe deeper, 'Why? Why is that important to you?'

"'Well, you know, I want to give my kids a good education.'

"'Why? Why do you want that so much?'

"Silence as he thinks. 'I want them to have a chance at making a difference in the world.'"

And then, with that kind of shared self-reflection and speaking out loud, said Barrett, we get to our greatest level of motivation, which has to do with meaning and service. And often has little or nothing to do with making millions of dollars.

"When people read out loud their deepest level of motivation, again, we get a real energy shift in the room," noted Barrett. "People share things they've never shared before. They then write down their common themes about what motivates them, and these often tend to be around making a difference in the world, becoming all they can, helping others become all they can. These motivations all have to do with higher levels of consciousness and nothing to do with making money and productivity. This realization in a group can create a real sense of community and compassion."[12]

Other companies are ramping up the emotional intelligence of their organizations by creating scheduled times and spaces for employees to speak from the heart. Employees of Show Business Software Ltd., a British organization, meet every Monday morning to check in with their spiritual, emotional, mental, and physical needs. "We look at our physical health. We examine whether we have any emotional upsets, if we're feeling happy, acknowledged, satisfied. Mentally, are there any problems, distractions, resentments, niggles—do we have a clear head with which to think?" said Jon Wheeler, Show Business product specialist. Spiritually, members of the group examine whether they feel used by a "mighty purpose."

The Monday morning group originated because company president Morel Fourman was finding it difficult to manage Show Business operations when emotional issues and resistance got in the way. (Fourman is also the author of *Managing in the New Economy: Performance Management Habits to Renew Organizations in the New Millennium*.) Employees of Show Business were committed to their company, but they were finding it hard to be productive, as they were struggling with other issues. So the group was created to help people manage their emotional and spiritual issues in a constructive way.

Members raise issues not only from their work lives, but also from their home lives and relationships. "By sharing in this way, we create a team, an environment that supports and nurtures the individual and encourages authenticity.

"We no longer feel we have to have it all 'handled.' We can declare 'breakdown,' 'procrastination,' upsets, or anything that occurs as 'being in the way' for us to perform at our optimum."

People at Show Business have the freedom to be, Wheeler told me. They can become open, real, related to each other, experience a sense of family, and support each other. "There is nothing to hide, so authenticity becomes the norm. This provides a solid foundation on which to create and build. We have the freedom to say what works and what doesn't work for us. Conflicts are resolved with speed, with certainty, with peace, and are then declared complete."

Wheeler said it's an amazing feeling to work at a place with such integrity. To talk straight to one another and their customers too. To go to work and feel at home. "Home from home. This makes such a difference," concluded Wheeler.

FINDING SUPPORT AT THE WORKPLACE

Once, Wheeler came to one of the Monday morning sessions feeling low emotionally and mentally. When others asked if he wanted to share what was going on, he told the group that he'd been thinking about breaking up with his fiancée, but at the same time thought he was "mad" for having such thoughts. After all, he and his fiancée had been together for three very happy years. They enjoyed and loved one another and hardly ever argued. But Wheeler realized he wasn't prepared to commit himself to her and say that he wanted to be with her the rest of his life.

As soon as he told the group what was going on, "This made a difference straight away, as I was no longer trying to do it all on my own. People who cared about me were willing to listen. Just saying what was going on in a safe space allowed me to 'clear' myself of some of the confusion that was going on in my head."

Once he felt less stressed and clearer, some in the group offered advice if he wanted to hear it. Their thoughts were "straight and at the same time compassionate. They did not make me wrong for having these thoughts. They seemed to understand how this could affect me at work and in general how it would play on my mind."

Wheeler's co-workers also helped him see that he did need to listen to his heart and trust his instincts about getting married. They helped him realize that he needed to share his reservations with his fiancée. When he did, they were able to go through the upsetting and difficult end of their relationship together without getting angry and closing down their hearts.

"We are now close friends. We still love each other and speak and write regularly. This whole process was started by me having the freedom to share what was going on in my home life at work. I know that having a compassionate environment at work allowed me to not try to 'do it all myself.' Sharing what was going on cleared the confusion and self-blame I was having," said Wheeler.

Can you imagine your work group or workplace welcoming this kind of sharing? Are you fortunate to have found it already? If not, what attitudes or policies stand in the way? Would you want this kind of environment, this depth of conversation about what really matters in your life?

ASSUMING RESPONSIBILITY FOR ONE ANOTHER

Jon Wheeler revealed that previous cultures he worked in would have regarded such sharing as "time wasting" or "moaning" or "stupid, silly, and not appropriate to the workplace." But he knows that this kind of openness, integrity, and honesty at work "produces a strong team who genuinely love and care for each other." He knows how empowering it can be to reside in a community where "we are not alone and do not need to suffer in silence. As a committed team, we are all responsible for our own well-being and the well-being of the other members of the team."

When a problem or imbalance arises, such as low productivity or a conflict, within an organization that has a sense of union and connection, then—as in the interdependence of the natural world—the community openly works to support, heal, and restore balance. "There is a focused power from the team in resolving a dispute, coming from a place of possibility rather than blame," Wheeler said.

If only we all felt that sense of responsibility for one another, what a shift we would feel and see in our culture. And how healthy for businesses to be based on such integrity and consciousness. Show Business—which develops performance management, knowledge management, and business intelligence computer software, products, and services—thrives on this kind of consciousness. Its partners include Lotus/IBM, Arthur Anderson, Lucent, Hallmark, and many other major heavyweights. Its customers range from United Kingdom (UK) governmental departments to AT&T.

Show Business thrives while operating from the higher spiritual principle that "to deliver the required returns, we must begin with the creation of organizational cultures and practices that harness the power and passion of people first. . . . The personality or even the soul of the organization is essential in achieving organizational effectiveness," Wheeler emphasized.[13]

What principles are you operating from? Are they what sustains and supports and heals you and those around you? If you now rewrote them, what might they say? What would those principles look and feel like if they guided your choices each day?

We all can find a sense of purpose and passion from helping others find their own purpose and passion, from wanting to support others. If only we could feel so connected, so sure that our well-being was dependent on the well-being of others in our community, and that their angst was our angst. Then when others were restless or out of balance, we would proactively step in and help them find firm ground once again. Think how easily and blissfully and confidently your heart could rest in and be inspired by that atmosphere. What keeps you from finding that bliss?

Keep remembering that we are all in company together, whether in an actual corporation or some other organization or group. There are ways we can show others we want to listen and speak from the heart. What works best for you? It helps to maintain eye contact, as much as possible. You can give others an entree, "How is it with you?" If they just shrug and say, "Oh, you know" or "You don't *want* to know," then you can follow up with, "Well, actually I do. Tell me about it."

And then listen without interrupting, solving, or judging. Listen more than you talk. When you do, you open up a space for others to speak from their hearts. That's why so many of us tell our biggest secrets to our pets and hairstylists—they listen and listen and listen. Tilt their furry heads, massage our scalps, and listen, listen, listen until we are full and sated with well-being, like after a great feast.

Again, as with listening from the heart, this all involves time. It takes time to let others find the courage to tell you something they need to release from their chests, remarked Janine Geske. Early in her career, when she was still a felony court judge, Geske presided over a horrible case involving the sexual assault and homicide of an eighteen-month-old boy.

"And as I was heading into court, I was praying and saying, 'Let me see some good in this god-awful day.' When I arrived, there were lots of TV cameras and a large pool of potential jurors waiting."

Because of the nature of the case, in screening the jurors Geske had to ask them one key question: Have any of you ever been the victim of sexual assault? And one young woman in the sea of people raised her hand.

"We wanted to make this process as comfortable as possible, so we took her into chambers," explained Geske. "But we still had to have the court reporters, lawyers, and bailiff around the table, so it was still a large crowd."

BREAKING THE SILENCE

Trying to be sensitive to the woman's feelings, Geske gently asked her, "Why did you raise your hand? Have you been the victim of a sexual assault?" And the woman hesitated, and said, "No. I really haven't. It's okay."

But Geske sensed the conversation needed to go deeper. "I said, 'It's okay. It's really okay. Tell me why you raised your hand.' And then the woman finally told me that she wasn't really a sexual assault victim, but that for five years her father had molested her. Because there had been no intercourse, she didn't think she had been sexually assaulted. You could just feel the compassion in the room for this woman. The lawyers quickly said, 'Judge, you can excuse her.'"

But in slowing down enough to listen to the woman's story, Geske's heart intelligence kicked in. "Something told me to wait. My heart said I should stay with her for a few minutes," Geske said. She told everyone else to leave the room. And then she asked the woman, "Have you told anyone else this story before?" And the woman said, "No."

Geske told the woman that right in the building they were sitting in were professional counselors who could help her, counselors who spent their lives helping people who'd been victimized and harmed by their mothers and fathers. And the woman agreed to see them.

"This was just such a lesson to me," Geske said in our interview. "It showed the importance of always being attuned to those around you, taking those grace moments so something good can come out of something so bad. How easy it could have been to miss that moment."

How often have we missed many such grace moments? If people continually come into our lives as our teachers, how often we must be missing the lesson.

POWER FROM THE HEART

Love's a potent, potent thing. Janine Geske had an outward position of power and status, but perhaps what made her most powerful was her heart. She spoke from her heart with acceptance and compassion, so the woman felt free and safe enough to speak from hers. That's when true healing begins. That's when miracles are in our midst.

And just as Geske modeled for the woman that day, we can model for our kids how compassionate words counter loneliness, separateness, and violence. We can show that taking the time to connect on a deeper level is something valuable and meaningful to us. As parents, we are spending less and less time in real conversation with our kids about the things that really matter. Many families report the only time they have to talk is during front-to-backseat car exchanges while dashing to the next function. Once I spoke to a high school class in my community, and many kids said they had no one they could trust enough to confide in. They said they often exchanged just e-mails or cell phone voice-mail messages with their parents.

Know that while we may be missing these opportunities to deepen our love via conversation with our kids, advertisers aren't as lax. They seize and capitalize on every available opportunity to talk directly and loudly with our children. They bombard them with crude, materialistic, violent, less-affirming conversation. So when we finally do find time to really connect over the dinner table, we often find we can't break through this tough, commercially honed shell our kids have around them.

Some kids are so immersed in the sea of violence around them, both at home and in the culture, they don't even realize there is another way to be in the world. They assume that's the way all families relate and move through life. And again, isn't that often the way families relate on TV?

But the revolution of the heart is at work here too. We can join efforts to talk with our kids about what really matters to them and to us. Countering the more harmful tide of words kids get hurled at them are exciting programs, such as Project Pave, a Colorado program. Project Pave educators come into schools in Denver to sensitize kids to the violent words they use that can harm others. The average middle school student knows at least forty-seven harmful words, the project has found. Verbal abuse is so insidious, many kids no longer even realize how traumatic it is, say Project Pave representatives.

DIFFUSING VIOLENT TALK

The thousands of kids who've gone through the Colorado program learn how to heal hostility and indifference through humane, cooperative ways to stand up for themselves and disagree with one another. They learn anger-management and relaxation skills so they don't react impulsively in rages. They learn how to support, not tear down, one another. They learn how to counter gang influence, peer taunting, and domestic violence. They learn how to stay safe.

"We focus on diffusing emotional violence, name-calling, harassment, and sarcasm. These are the seeds of physical violence," explained Nicole Tembrock, Project Pave director of education.[14]

How easy it is to lapse into emotional violence. We drive down the road, some guy pulls out in front of us, and we crunch the brakes, yelling, "You _____!!," while our kids listen and watch from their car seats, absorbing our example.

How can we each curb our own sarcasm, harassment, and name-calling—done either wittingly or unwittingly? How can we purge ourselves of the language of violence that we perpetuate by our own choice of words? Project Pave uses a wonderful sensitization model for name-calling we can all try. "It's really important that kids develop empathy for one another's feelings, and one of the ways we do this with Project Pave is to have them list every name they call each other. This lesson is so powerful," said Carla Frenzel, a former Project Pave educator and eighth-grade teacher at Grant Middle School, who uses the program exercises with her students.[15]

"They list the horrible names they hear in the hallways, in the streets, and then we talk about who these words are targeted to, whether it's women or homosexuals," explained Frenzel. "Then we talk about how these names have been used to dehumanize groups, such as Jews during the Holocaust, or through time. At first the kids get kind of rowdy as we do this lesson, but then all of a sudden they sit back. When they see how name-calling really hurts, they are immediately silenced."

ONE WORD HOLDS POWER

This is yet another example that our true nature is to be compassionate, not mean-spirited. The kids then talk about how historically people of various religious and ethnic backgrounds and disabilities have been singled out and persecuted. They see how we all suffer, individually and culturally, when we use words or labels to treat each other as less than human, said Frenzel.

"We talk about how in our culture people often say things without thinking about them. Many times a word holds a lot of malice, even if we don't intend it to. But we show them that when you take a word and look at it historically, those words often hold a lot of hurt. They see that a lot of deaths surrounded that word. And if we use those words over and over, their power is escalated even more."

Frenzel believes Project Pave and similar school programs are so important because many kids don't have safe havens and supportive families that teach them compassionate ways of expression. She also has high hopes that such exercises and discussions in our schools can counter the negative influence of TV where it's "so acceptable to put someone down, laugh about it, and move on without looking at the fact that we are fellow brothers and sisters. We are human beings who look out for each other, but you see that modeled in very few places in our society or in the media."

When have you been on the receiving end of racial or other slurs? What names were you called years ago, and how do they still bring back a sense of shame and unworthiness, maybe decades later? When have you taunted or ridiculed someone and injected more violence into our culture? Do you take care of your fellow human beings by speaking without meanness and judgment? Are your conversations inspiring and uplifting to those around you? What words are you burning into your children's hearts?

We can all follow the example of our kids and learn greater empathy so we better speak with intention, integrity, and compassion. This may be an area in which our children will lead the way. Since Project Pave opened its doors in 1986, about 61,000 students and 14,000 adults have learned how to use more compassionate language and other emotional intelligence skills through the organization's violence-prevention education programs. The skills are taught in grades K–12. By raising kids' understanding of the roots of violence, the goal is that they will break the cycle of violence that many of them come from or that many kids feel they are steeped in each day, even in their schools.

SOLVING CONFLICT PEACEFULLY

A *USA Today Weekend* survey, for instance, found that 43 percent of public school students avoid school restrooms because of fear. According to junior and senior high students across the nation, the top reason for engaging in physical fights is that "someone insulted someone else or treated them disrespectfully," according to a study done by the Harvard School of Public Health in 1998.[16]

"A lot of kids learn that violence is the only way to solve problems. That's been modeled for them by parents, the media, video games, and so on. The violence is so pervasive in our culture, it's hard to go through a day and not consume some part of it," noted Frenzel.

The compassionate seeds to counter emotional and physical violence in our youth have to be laid early. In an exercise for younger students, a Project Pave educator tells the story of a little boy whose heart gets broken repeatedly throughout the day. The little boy wakes up late for school, and his mom yells at him. He falls in a mud puddle, and all the kids at school laugh at him. Each time his heart is broken, a piece is torn out of a paper heart. The students then talk about how they would feel if they had such a brokenhearted day. Empathy, empathy, empathy. Then they talk about what they could do to stand up for the little boy, to love him and ease his pain. As they come up with heartfelt solutions, the Project Pave educator bandages the boy's paper heart back together.

If we'd had some of this emotional intelligence training when we were kids, maybe we wouldn't have so much road rage and so many hockey dads hurting each other. Maybe we'd be better equipped to model for our kids how to disagree with people without resorting to knee-jerk explosions. Maybe our own broken hearts would be mended as soon as they were hurt instead of bleeding for years, leading us to unhealthy addictions, choices, and relationships to try to numb the pain.

Empathy can be learned, according to Nicole Tembrock. We can still learn it. "These skills come naturally to us. I believe we are born with loving hearts, and our environments either sustain or change them," she said. The next time you feel like judging, labeling, ridiculing, or distancing yourself from someone, try to understand that person's pain. Quell your violent put-downs or judgments and try to empathize with what that person has gone through.

We so want to be powerful people, a powerful nation, and a powerful world. But some of our most reputed institutions, from Congress to newspaper chains, are among the most insensitive and emotionally bereft places of all. They often shred people in these institutions for showing compassion, for displaying emotion. This does not make us great; it tragically diminishes us. It's only by empathy and love for what others experience and feel that we truly become powerful. It is indifference, hate, and closed-hearted expressions that drain us and make us weak.

Gannett newspaper columnist Dinah Eng knows more than most the power of words to open hearts or clamp them shut. She writes the award-winning column "Bridges" because "I wanted to write things that could create bridges between people. These bridges can be generational, cultural, and economic. There are all different ways people separate themselves easily from others. We need to find ways to find our commonalities and to express the things that make us One."

Eng explores issues in her column, such as violence in the entertainment industry, or racial and spiritual issues, from that vantage point. "I look at the place where we can agree on something," she explained. "Where is the place where our feelings or emotions meet? Once we get to the heart of the matter, the mind can find a way to solve our problems."

Eng has found from her readership response that people want to talk about deeper issues. They want to find reconciliation and common ground. Whether it be in discussing abortion or diversity, "more people are realizing they have to expand their view of the world and their understanding of each other. The more we talk about these things, the more comfortable we are. But in ordinary commentary in newspapers, very seldom do you read the kinds of stuff that you want to connect to on the level of the heart."

Her cultural "background and baggage" as an Asian American woman lend her a certain understanding of and perspective about human nature, Eng told me. Plus, when she was a teenager, she was gravely injured in a car accident and had a near-death experience. "Coming out of my body and being told that it's not time to die yet, that there are still things I need to do, that changed my view of what life is all about. In some ways, that set me on my spiritual journey to look at spiritual issues."

It also led her to write about spiritual issues so her readers could better understand and empathize with the pain as well as the joys in her life—and theirs. So they could better explore via her columns how to best solve conflict with compassionate conversations, how to live out of their hearts, how to ease the heart of the world by finding common ground—and bridges.

In solving any conflict, said Eng, compassionate, respectful conversation comes into play. "We have to acknowledge who we are as individuals and then acknowledge the other person as equally respectful. From that kind of respect and love of another human being, the goal shifts. It doesn't become, 'How do I get my point across?' but it becomes, 'How do we solve that issue together?'"[17]

LOVING WELL IS HISTORIC

Love elevates us to the highest position of power and effectiveness. When we share a tender thought, a touch, or a tear with readers—or colleagues, students, constituents, co-workers—we connect with and caress the deepest part of ourselves. And those are truly the honorable, venerable, and historic moments.

Isn't it true that in those moments when our world is unraveling around our feet and someone puts his or her arms around us and says, "I'm so sorry," that's when we know we're in the presence of true greatness? That's when we know how heroic real compassion can be.

And passionate conversation, such as that found in Dinah Eng's columns, is the key to reinvigorating our communities, no matter where we are joined together with others. "Everything is bearable when there is love," observes Dr. Elisabeth Kübler-Ross in *The Wheel of Life*.

Speaking from the heart with anger, a kind of "sacred rage," is also a high form of compassionate conversation. Expressing our outrage at what is no longer tolerable is one way we show heroic compassion. It's one potent way we reseed and reinvigorate our lives and our communities. When Mildred Lee looked around at her crime-ridden neighborhood in Omaha in 1991, she almost gave up and moved away. The home she loved and had lived in for ten years was surrounded by drug dealers. They were outside her doorstep, across the street, and down the block. They were there when she went to work and there when she came home.

But Lee, now sixty-seven, decided to speak up. She called together neighbors and city officials, and an aggressive plan was kicked off with a "take-back-the-community" parade. Neighbors poured out to march past drug dealers' hangouts, chanting and carrying signs, handing out flyers, and pulling caskets on flatbed trucks. After a month of vocal, compassionate, fierce conversation, after a month of constant police presence and drug raids, most of the criminal element was driven out.

More, much more of Mildred Lee's story later. "It takes more than just police to change a community. Someone has to act," Lee believes.[18] Speaking from the heart . . . this may be the scariest territory of all. But someone has to do it. Someone has to speak into the stubborn, taciturn silence that surrounds many of us. Someone needs to start the conversation, hoping that his or her words will fall on soft, receptive hearts. Can you be one of the someones?

BLOSSOMING LIKE FLOWERS

Keep remembering that, by nature, we are loving, openhearted people—and that someone has to spark these deeper conversations. We can't close down our hearts forever. Keep remembering, "It is our true nature to have an open heart, as much as it is the true nature of a flower to open in the sunlight," as Richard Carlson and Benjamin Shield say in *Handbook for the Heart*.

Just as a flower can't stay dormant forever, we can't stay stuck forever in a place of isolation, discouragement, and longing for connection with others. Finally opening wide and courageously becomes the only choice, we often find. And often for the first time, we discover what being alive, what being truly human is. We can finally see with clarity the power within.

When people are eulogized, no one says, "Man, he could crank out a report faster than anyone I knew." As someone is laid to rest and we all gather to honor that person, no one says, "This I want you to know. She got top ranking on every one of her performance reviews." Instead, we usually praise and celebrate people's brave hearts, their depth of love for their spouse and children, their kindness, caring, and compassion for others. Their support of the underdog, the most in need.

Contrary to popular belief, compassion isn't weak. Compassion requires the strength of a hero. We each have that kind of strength within.

It's so ironic that we say love and compassion aren't appropriate displays, for instance, in our public arenas. Yet, when we lose someone of public stature, it's those raw, emotional displays of the heart that we most raise high and find comfort in. We don't celebrate someone's ability to be productive and efficient and produce bottom-line results. Instead we reflect on how the individual touched those around him or her. How well the person loved and was loved.

Colorado legislator Gary McPherson died in 2000 when a plane he was piloting crashed in British Columbia. Only thirty-seven, he left behind a wife and three daughters. Governor Bill Owens eulogized his colleague and close friend by remembering how McPherson followed his heart, despite the risks. To McPherson's daughters he said, "Girls, your father was honest and kind. In a professional atmosphere that is sometimes contentious and at times even breeds disdain, Gary was someone who could always look for the positive in a situation. . . . He was always armed with a smile and a kind word for his friends, his acquaintances, and even those he had never met."[19]

Mother Teresa once said, "Kind words can be short and easy to speak, but their echoes are truly endless."[20] So endless that they still echo long after we've slipped into the arms of angels.

Speaking from the heart allows the best and wisest parts of ourselves to break our bonds of flesh and bone and reach out and touch something ineffable in someone else. There is no higher calling. As you go out and use your words to touch other people's hearts and to create what you want in your life, may you find much sustenance from the words of Caterina Giglio Digison, a minister at the Gathering, a New Thought church in Fort Collins, Colorado. This is from her recent talk "Keeping Our Word."

Keeping Our Word

We are an amazing group of people, aren't we? We know: Our power comes from the knowledge that our word is our treasure. It is our creativity. In the gospel of Saint John, it says that, "In the beginning there was the word and the word was God." From Genesis, we have, "And God said let there be light and there was light."

Through our word, we express our divine creative power. Since Spirit is in, of, and through us, we know that we have the same ability as our Creator, to manifest anything we are wanting, through the power of our word.

The word is not just a sound.

Although there is power in the sound, it is not just a symbol, though there is power in a symbol. Our word is our force. It is our spiritual will. Our word is a magical tool, and the most powerful tool that we have. Your word is big *juju.*

Some people don't understand that, and they misuse their power. Like a sword, it can cut and create or cut and destroy. They chatter mindlessly, afraid of silence. They gossip, spreading stories and half-truths, feeling inadequate.

They carelessly use words that carry energy loaded with pain, just to stir things up. Or they dismiss the word by claiming it's all just semantics. But words and thoughts thicken into things!

Many years ago, a man in Germany, a single man manipulated a whole country of intelligent people with the power of his word. Just words! . . .

He led them into a world war. He convinced some to commit atrocious acts of torture, imprisonment, and killings. He used the juju, or the power of his word, to create fear. This is the power we all share.

Our mind is fertile ground. The seeds of word are planted there. It is universal soil. A seed of fear or doubt planted when we are young can live with us full time, inhibiting our life and even changing the course of our life. We always have to choose to create with love or hook others with pain and by the law of attraction, whatever we give will come back to us.

Keeping our word is a way of saying that we are being impeccable with our word. Impeccable means "without sin," with "pectus" meaning sin. A sin is anything we do against ourselves, against spirit—which is who we are.

When we are impeccable with our word, we take personal responsibility to tell our truth. We accept others. We think before we speak. We do no harm and we love unconditionally. . . .

When we pray, we use five affirmative steps to create the ultimate power word, linking words like pearls on a cosmic strand. In the release stage, we often use our word to acknowledge that the prayer is already manifested. It was so before we spoke our prayer. Our word is our affirmation and prayer.

There is a story about prayer that comes from Africa. It's the story of a woman who had worked hard all night to assist a mother in the labor ward. But in spite of all they could do, the woman died leaving a newborn girl and a screaming two-year-old. With no incubator and no special feeding facility, the child would probably die.

In Africa, the nights are often chilly, so the student midwife went to fetch the box they had for such babies. She got the cotton wool the baby would be wrapped in. Another went to stoke the fire and fill the hot water bottle, which would incubate the baby since her mother was gone.

But the woman came back and said that the hot water bottle had burst. It was the very last one.

"All right, put the baby near the fire and sleep near the door to ward off the drafts," the doctor said. The next day, the doctor went to the orphanage to pray with the children. She explained the problem of the tiny baby and the hot water bottle. One ten-year-old, Ruth, prayed with the usual blunt consciousness of the African children:

"Dear God, send us a water bottle. It will do no good tomorrow as the baby will be dead. So bring it now and bring a baby doll so the little girl will know that she is loved."

The doctor was put on the spot. Could she really say "Amen" after such an audacious prayer? Yet she knew that God could do anything—absolutely anything. She had been in Africa for almost four years, and she had never received a package from home. If anyone did send a parcel, who would think to send a hot water bottle—to Africa of all places?

Halfway through the afternoon, a package arrived and everyone crowded around. After pulling out some raisins and nuts and T-shirts—there was a brand-new hot water bottle. The doctor cried. She had not asked God to send it because she had not really believed. But the child had believed and as she reached into the bottom of the box, she pulled out a beautiful doll.

The parcel, it turned out, had been on its way for five months.

As the gods and goddesses we are, we can choose to use our word, knowing that it was done before we asked, knowing that aligned as we are with our Creator, there is no end to the good that we can do. By keeping our word.

Namaste.

7

Home Is Where the Heart Is: Creating Sanctuaries with Love

ONCE MOTHER TERESA WAS VISITED by a large group of prominent, wealthy women from India. They were wearing lots of gold and visibly displaying their affluence. They were also on fire with Mother Teresa's message of service and wanted to know what they should do. "Can we give money to prisons, to drug rehabilitation centers, or to the hospitals?" they wondered. "No," Mother Teresa said. "You go home. This is where compassion comes from. You look into your husband's eyes. You look into your family's eyes. People want to serve outside because they don't know how to serve their family."

I first heard this story about Mother Teresa from Stephen Levine about two months before I was to complete this book. But ironically—serendipitously? divinely?—I stumbled across it when I was in deep, deep deadline. Surfacing only for basic bodily functions—and occasional hits of chocolate. I knew how many thousands of words I had to lay down in three weeks, and it seemed staggering. But, I knew, barring any messy complications, that I could do this.

And then my son got sick. Really limp, feverish, sore-throat sick. All of a sudden, I was forced to pry my fingers from the keyboard and instead use them to stroke his back, shake Tylenol from the bottle, carry him to bed, and stir chicken soup with a wooden spoon, the Mother Teresa story really sunk in.

We can't go outward with great compassion—or even write about it for that matter—unless compassion resides deeply and lovingly right where we nest. We won't be present or authentic enough to see and respond to the pain of our co-worker, or see the need to protect a wetland from a bull-dozer, if we fail to focus on those around us with loving intent.

INTIMATE LOVE IS HARDEST OF ALL

Again, it's easy to talk about love of humanity; it's damn tough to love and stay connected to the human beings we share our lives with on a daily basis. But if we "want to go to God. If we want to be one of the cells in the universal body, we have to go where it's closest to our pain," says Stephen Levine. And it's right among our families that we often learn how to be most godlike.

"Intimate love is spiritual training for everything in life. It is not meant to be an exclusive sanctuary from the pain of the world, but rather an inclusive balm for the sorrows of the world. In learning to show up more fully for one person, we learn to show up more fully for life," says Marianne Williamson in *Enchanted Love*.

Being in relationship with others also allows us to do our greatest heart work. It allows us to see our true natures—and our petty ones—mirrored in those we sip coffee with, fight for the shower with, snuggle with, clean with, make love with, and argue with. Living with others is the best training ground for living compassionately. It calls us to muster up all the heart skills discussed up to this point, from seeing with love, listening with love, and speaking with love. It puts all those theoretical ideas for opening the heart to the ultimate, most grueling, but potentially rewarding, test.

To learn more about the state of the heart of your home, do an assessment as you did in chapter 3 to monitor your own heart. Begin by asking yourself these questions: Do the people in your home see with love? Does your family listen and speak with affection and support? Do you make the small gestures, like running a hot bath for your partner, to show you are precious to each other? Do you bring your teenager a cup of herbal tea when he's up late, cruising the Internet for a paper due the next morning? Do you give each other the space and safety to speak honestly from your hearts, even when it's not what you want to hear? Is your home a loving sanctuary, a place of solace and comfort?

How well would you do in this self-reflection? How would you grade yourself? The purpose of this exercise, as always, is not to beat yourself up or to feel shame, but to honestly look at how well you love. How loudly do compassion and respect speak in your home?

This, sadly, is getting harder and harder in our culture that prizes material success more than emotional achievement. In pursuit of riches and status, more and more people have less and less time to really look into one another's eyes, to listen to what their children or partner has to say, to speak with affection. And relationships thrive on time. Kids blossom and feel sated and full and become affectionate people if they are given our loving attention.

TRUE INTIMACY TAKES TIME

Intimacy devours time. Intimacy is built on secrets, information people share about their history and experiences. My kids love the stories we tell them about our most embarrassing high school moments—which will never make it into any of my books. But to share these secrets that bind us together takes time. Time to retrieve them from our memory banks—the older we get, the longer the retrieval time. Time to unwrap the tale and remember even more in the telling.

Such sharing binds us irrevocably to our family members, yet we have less and less time to offer our stories up as gifts to one another. Instead, we are increasingly becoming the "dot-com culture," says pediatrician and author Dr. Barry Brazelton. "These poor young people are working 12 to 16 hours a day, never see their children except on the weekend. By then, they don't know their children, and the children don't know them, so it's a nightmarish weekend they spend together, and there's no real communication."[1]

Dr. Rudolph Virchow reflects on how easy it is to let intimacy drain away, relationships fade, and precious moments die: "You can soon become so engrossed in study, then in professional cares . . . in getting and spending. . . . You may so lay waste your powers that you find too late with hearts given away that there is no place in your habit-stricken souls for those gentler influences that make life worth living."[2]

Are gentler influences that make life worth living a cornerstone of your home? As in Griffin Hospital, is your home lovingly, consciously, deliberately constructed so all who enter it are soothed and protected and nourished?

It strikes me how similar the stories from our dot-com culture are to the poignant stories of families torn apart by World War II in the 1940s. As we try to compress our relationships into less and less time—just as computers crunch masses of data in less and less time—we find ourselves feeling as if we're under fire, fighting the enemy, trying to hold the cultural onslaught at bay. After we fought the "evil demons" of Nazi Germany in WWII, we were supposed to find peace and prosperity. But the demons appear to be coming from within. Since WWII, mental illness, for instance, has steadily risen in all developed countries around the world.

This war, it appears, is often entirely of our making. And like WWII, the full costs may not show up until later.

We are experiencing the most prosperous times in decades. Three-car garages stand on every block. But the emotional bankruptcy runs rampant. Depression is epidemic, the divorce rate is still at 50 percent, and only one in five children with mental illness receives needed medical treatment, according to the National Institute of Mental Health.[3] "Before our lives wither away into dust, we might ponder how much more prosperity human beings can possibly survive," say Drs. Lewis, Amini, and Lannon in *A General Theory of Love.*

SETTING SACRED INTENTION AT HOME

We've consciously or unconsciously allowed many societal influences, from TVs in our kids' bedrooms to late-night Internet surfing, to come into our homes. We've welcomed more technology, interruptions, and machines into our homes without asking whether they are in our best interest. The way we reclaim a compassionate, healthy home is to consciously create it. Just as you did with yourself earlier in the book, state your deliberate, sacred intent for your home. What is your mission? What is your intention for your home? What will your home stand for? What will it offer to those who live there? What will it wrap around those who leave it each day?

What is your intention? "One of the things that's absolutely gotten bumped off the path of life is intentionality," says Sue Patton Thoele, author of *Heart Centered Marriage.* "The busier we are, the more instantaneous we are. We expect instant gratification, but have less mindfulness and thoughtfulness for our intention."

You can create your intention for a loving, compassionate sanctuary in many, many ways. You can, for instance, do rituals, prayers, ceremonies, and blessings to spiritually and energetically create a loving home. Before you even move into a house, you can say prayers as a family to raise the light and love found within. To ask that your new home always strengthen and sustain you and bring out the very best in your family for the highest possible good.

"If your overall conscious and subconscious Intention is to instill an uplifting energy into a home for the betterment of the occupants and the betterment of humankind . . . so it will be," says *Sacred Space* author Denise Linn. "If your overall intention is to create a safe and magical haven for the rearing of children . . . so it will be. Your Intention can be likened to a journey. Your overall Intention is your destination and your specific Intentions can be likened to the signposts along the way. Take time to ask yourself what is your overall goal for the house and the people who dwell within its walls?"

If your overall intention, as Linn says, is to create a safe and magical haven for raising your children—and for growing your own soul—then you consciously allow in your home only the things that serve your purpose. That means you don't allow in violent video or computer games. You don't allow in violent and inappropriate music, TV games, drugs, guns, or other weapons. You don't allow in people who are toxic and harmful to the sacred intention of your home and those who dwell within.

DELIBERATELY ADD BEAUTY AND LIGHT

If your intention is to create a sacred, magical haven, you purposefully and deliberately create a home filled with what amplifies love and light. And these things don't have to come from a designer store or an upscale furniture god. They can include flowers and plants and rocks and tree branches, poems, pets, music, prayers, art, and many objects from the natural world.

Our boys like to collect rocks from favorite mountain streams to remind them of our days playing in the mountains. To hold that playful energy in our home, they scatter the rocks, from the kitchen to their bedrooms. It is their intention to bring some of the rarefied, spiritual mountain energy into our home.

Some families set up an altar with candles and sacred objects at the entrance of their homes. One family I know has a heart hung on the front door to signal that the family members want love to dwell within and for all to enter with loving hearts. Another couple I know places angel statues all over. Some have pictures of birds or doves. What is your intention for your home and how can you outwardly express what you want to reside there?

Create your physical space so it is an outer reflection of your inner heart. Warm the hearts of those who come into your home with your choices. Art is one very powerful way you can wrap your walls with sacred intention. Geraldine Lloyd transformed her early 1900s restored mansion with art. On her dining room walls, she fixed bits of broken mirror into a mosaic, "so all who eat here will see each other in a new way," she says.[4]

The things we put on our walls also can deliberately inspire us, open our hearts, and keep our energy high. In this respect, many of us have been powerfully inspired by Alexandra Stoddard, the wonderful interior designer and philosopher of contemporary living, who has written more than fifty books to help us ritualize every day with ceremonies and celebrations for eating, sleeping, and bathing.

Stoddard loves to have the art of French artist Roger Muhl on her walls. "Living with his paintings is a dream because the walls open up to sun-drenched scenes of Provence. Through color Muhl expresses light and the joie de vivre," she says.

Stoddard first met Muhl in 1961, when he had his first one-man show in America. She felt an "immediate spirit connection" to his work. "The hair stood on the back of my neck. Energy shot through my body. I realized instantly that this was my living Claude Monet."

When she met Muhl, then thirty-one, she saw his positive, life-affirming point of view about his art. "He told me he chose to only paint the joy of life, the beauty, and the light. Each of his paintings—whether intimate interior scenes or rooftops, water or flower gardens, flower bouquets or food—makes you feel alive and more uplifted than before you saw it.

"Roger Muhl expands us, increases our hearts, and shows us how much beauty we have in our common everyday experiences at home."[5]

KEEPING LOVE CONSISTENT

What do you intentionally weave into your home, from your walls to bathrooms, that increases your heart and those of your children? It seems as if we know how to do this whenever a new baby comes into our homes. We painstakingly and lovingly create a nursery with the utmost love and intention, choosing things that will wrap our new angel-come-to-earth with tenderness and affection.

But if you walk from that love-saturated room down to your family room and your baby's sibling is playing Nintendo, shooting people as simulated blood spatters the walls, do you see how that loving intention is shattered? We can't build and maintain our loving intention for our domestic sanctuary if we let violence in. We have to become more deliberate, vigilant, and loving about what we allow to enter our homes.

Become clear about your intention. Whatever you focus on, you will magnify in your home. So, back to Mother Teresa's message: Compassion in the home begins with looking into the eyes of those we live with. How do we do this when we are stressed, exhausted, and consumed with worry about the next mortgage payment?

Begin at the beginning. Again, set the sacred intention that when you enter your home at day's end, your home is waiting for you as a sanctuary, a spiritual haven. It is a place of succor, comfort, and nourishment. Don't allow your work stress to shatter that intention. Again, there are many, many ways to do this. Decide that you will leave work pressures at work. Say it out loud, "I leave you here," as you back away from your desk. As you drive home, imagine tossing your workplace stressors out the window. Leave them at the red light, and when it turns green, visualize them left behind. As you stand at your front door, close your eyes, breathe deeply, and imagine leaving any stress outside for the powers of nature to hold and neutralize. If you work at home, it's equally important to leave your stressors behind as you enter your home sanctuary.

Remember and use the HeartMath tools described in chapter 4. Or better yet, take some HeartMath classes or stress-reduction and centering classes (see the resources section at the back of this book for contact information). Check your local hospital or community education program for additional classes. Get some tapes on relaxation techniques. Learn together as a family so stress doesn't undermine the foundation of your family. Seek family counseling, if needed. Talk out your stress. We need to teach and model good coping skills to our kids, who are increasingly anxious and need tools to help them cope with that anxiety.

These are powerful lessons we can model for our children. When we choose not to make our homes an extension of our work, then we can better focus on and be present enough to see those we love with the eyes of love. A real estate agent recently remarked that for many people, "Home is just a place they crash and get some sleep for the next day's battle." If this is true, how sad. But, on the other hand, I know many, many people whose intention is to lovingly craft a home that nurtures, supports, and brings people together. If your office is home based, set the sacred intention to keep it separate from the peaceful, centered, nurturing atmosphere of the rest of your home.

What is your intention for your home? What is there to support that intention? Do you have family pictures, candles, foods, color, grandparents' photos, flowers, plants, smells, postcards from favorite vacation spots, and poetry that beckon your hearts to relax and expand? We can weave the same elements into our workplaces to make them more loving and grounded.

HOME AS SANCTUARY

We all get buffeted and battered by outside influences when we're away from home, so returning home needs to be healing. One way we can ensure that our homes will be a stronghold, a haven of loving energy, is to ground them in the energy of the earth. We can ask that all the healing energy, strength, power, and equilibrium of the earth come into and balance our homes. We can pray, with our children, that the loving energy of the willow trees, the hawks that circle above, the springwaters below, the blue sky each morning comes into and fills our homes with light and love. We can do this before we move in; we can do this daily. We can do this when our families are being rocked by outside forces.

We can also strengthen that loving bond with nature by expressing our gratitude: feed the birds, avoid using weed killers, practice organic gardening, talk to the trees and flowers lovingly. We find it charming when Saint Francis of Assisi did this, and think of his spiritual, loving power. Why scoff at this in our own lives? Again, as the compassion stories of heart activists throughout this book illustrate, it's time to come home to our hearts. Literally. Powerfully.

This is practical, concrete, real-as-it-gets stuff that can work to make our lives what we wish them to be. Try getting up each morning a few minutes earlier, and find a beautiful tree or the sunrise and speak out loud, "Please help me be a more loving, heart-centered person. Fill me with love to go outward in compassion." Watch the color fill the morning sky at 5:30 A.M. and say, "Please let the light fill me and propel me and guide my every choice to be as loving as I possibly can."

Do this for ten days; the difference will be palpable and powerful. It will be hard to go back to living the old way. When you invoke the power of the natural world, "Your home will become a fortress in times of change. Anyone who enters your home will be subconsciously affected by the earth's energy and will leave your home feeling more grounded and certain of their direction in life," says Denise Linn in *Sacred Space*.

EXCAVATING UNHEALED WOUNDS

Once we have performed these types of rituals to enhance our sanctuary, we are better prepared to enter it with loving eyes, to see those we live with more compassionately. But it goes much deeper than that. Being able to see clearly with love means we have already accepted and look on ourselves with unconditional love. It involves excavating any emotional blocks that prevent us from entering lovingly into a loving relationship with others.

It's hard to gaze on those we love with soft eyes if we've been hurt in the past and have armored our hearts. "For those of us who had to shut down, to 'not see,' to suppress our feelings in order to survive our own childhoods, becoming more mindful can be especially painful and difficult. In those moments when we are ruled by old demons, when harmful beliefs, destructive patterns, and nightmares from our own childhoods rise up and we are plagued by dark feelings and black or white thinking, it is particularly difficult to stop and see freshly," point out Myla and Jon Kabat-Zinn in *Everyday Blessings: The Inner Work of Mindful Parenting*.

Many people, says Stephen Levine, suffer from "relationship senility." We get hurt so many times that "we're unwilling to try anymore, so we close our hearts to each other."[6]

It's almost impossible to fully love our partners or children if we don't fully love and accept ourselves. If you are insecure and "hollow in your center," says Alexandra Stoddard, you may even try to tear others down. We need to nurture ourselves, understand, heal our past wounds or we will not be able to give from a strong, stable, loving core. One of the greatest gifts we can give our families is to heal our emotional and psychological blocks, working with a therapist if needed, so we can strengthen the core of our compassion within ourselves.

There is nothing like being in intimate relationships with other people to bring up all our old unhealed anxieties, fears, and sorrows. And if we refuse to heal those wounds, but instead project them onto another person, we extinguish intimacy. "I call it the poison of projection," Sue Patton Thoele remarked in our interview. "If we project onto others the darkness we carry within, how can we possibly treat them with compassion?"

We need to acknowledge where we've been hurt and wounded, without "waving them over someone else's head like a very blunt instrument," she said.[7] One of the biggest ingredients of a compassionate marriage is the ability to accept and embrace those whom we don't understand and with whom we disagree.

ACCEPTING DIFFERENCES WITH LOVE

Know that love can be counted on to flow and endure, no matter how imperfect and flawed we are. Philosopher Mark Dillof has studied relationship difficulties and conflicts. Over the years he's noticed that older couples with happy relationships have passed through a sort of inferno of the expectation of the perfect partner. "Something seems to have happened over the years. They let go of certain requirements and demands, and it hasn't ended sourly, but something else has occurred. They've stayed together and endured the strangeness of the other partner and something good has emerged."[8] We dam up our flow of love—or keep our "windows of our belovedness clouded over" when we "forget to listen to the melody of the Divine during the day," Sue Patton Thoele writes in *Heart Centered Marriage*.

Listening to the melody of the Divine requires that we not get sidetracked from our heart centers by rushing to do all the things we think we should do or have to do, Thoele points out. It used to be that our jobs tore us away from our families, and now it's a whole multitude of activities we convince ourselves we just have to do, such as endless sports competitions, increasingly held on Mother's Day, Father's Day, and other holidays.

Paring back our lifestyles and career commitments allows us to live more simply so we can live more richly with our loved ones. Take the time it takes to foster deep, satisfying relationships. A bumper sticker I saw the other day said, "Having a good time. Wish I were here."

How about you? Does this strike even a distant chord? Take the time to begin to feel your heart again. For instance, many, many families—some say a huge movement is afoot—are taking back their lives and saying no to endless soccer, volleyball, debate, and hockey road games. "Some kids and parents are saying 'enough,'" the *Denver Post* reported recently in an article headlined "Breaking Point." The article went on to say that families are backing out of time-devouring functions like swim teams to instead spend time together biking, camping, and just relaxing.[9]

I know of families that forgo traditional scheduled outings, like organized baseball, but make their own. One family goes out of state to reconnect with relatives on fishing trips. Another family has a camping night on the living room floor. Each child gets to take turns "camping out" with Mom and Dad. Other families have a lunch-out routine, taking one child at a time, so each child feels focused on and special.

"For fast-acting relief, try slowing down," actress and comedienne Lily Tomlin says.[10] Slow down enough to listen to stirring music together. Children really feel their heart centers with music. Take time to cook together and sample great pasta and hearty soups as the candles burn down. Look into your children's eyes, cup their chins, and tell them, "You know, you are really precious to me." In this world, where notes go home from school regularly about the latest neighborhood predator, children know there are threats to their health. They need to be held in your arms and told that they are safe, that they are loved.

Fall back into love with one another by spending time together. It's hard to keep the oxygen that allows a relationship to breathe and thrive if we connect for only a few minutes each day, which is the average time a child spends in conversation with a parent.

Also freely borrow from other people easy ways to reconnect on a heart level with your kids. Tell stories from your day, for instance, at dinner. Our family likes to share our "highs" and "lows" from the day. We lifted this ritual from the *Story of Us* movie. We hope it builds empathy for what we each experience when we're apart.

We know a family that has "star night" in which members look at the heavens through their telescope. Others like the ritual of going to a Colorado Rockies baseball game together. Some families bake pies together. When I was growing up, one of the things I loved most was when our whole family piled outside on hot, humid summer evenings and played baseball and ate ice cream that Dad made by hand. I can still see him sitting next to the freezer, adding the ice, pouring on the salt, while we watched the paddles going around in the thick, yellow creaminess. I remember my siblings and I coming home from school and immediately racing outside with Mom to rake mountains of leaves for leaf forts and tunnels. I can still remember the pungent scent of palm-sized oak, hickory, and maple leaves. What do you remember? What do you want your kids to remember? It is in these simple moments that compassion takes root.

BEING GRATEFUL FOR COMPANIONSHIP

The Levines have a ritual in which, several times a day, they stop and look deeply into one another's eyes to see what is deep and true and sustaining. How often do we really look that deeply into the eyes of our partners or our children for the purpose of seeing what they hold? Draw strength from that practice. Do this with your children in the morning and again at night.

All children want to be fully seen and appreciated. All children need to feel they are looked upon each day with affection and tenderness. I remember hearing an eight-year-old at my son's summer camp telling all the kids that it was her birthday. "Cool," they said. "Is your family celebrating tonight?" She looked down at the ground, "No, we're getting new carpeting instead. They said we don't have time for a party."

We need to fully see one another and express that we see the preciousness that's right before us. A recent study showed that the average child under age five watches three to four hours of television a day. The Kaiser Family Foundation found that the average child, from ages two to eighteen, takes in five and a half hours of media each day, such as from televisions and computers.[11] Conversing with the Simpsons is a scary substitute for our affection. Bart Simpson will never show up and help your child with his homework. He will never tell your child how awesome or special she is.

One way we can try to connect with our kids is to try to empathize with what they are going through. We can try to remember what it feels like to be a preteen with acne sprouting. We can try to empathize with what it takes to get up and face your peers day after day. Healer, teacher, and writer Robyn Michelle Dolgin, like many of us, finds inspiration from the Dalai Lama. She "wholeheartedly" embraced the Dalai Lama's message of compassion, mindfulness, and nonjudgment after reading his book *Ethics for the New Millennium*. "I wanted to invite the Dalai Lama into my home if he were ever in the area. I consider my home to be sacred space and a respite from the world as it has come to be. I couldn't help but think a weary traveler might appreciate this refuge."

But then it occurred to Dolgin that the correct action was to "invite what the Dalai Lama represents into my home and into my beingness. Numerous events and opportunities teach me to do this on a daily basis," she said. "Yet, it's my own pain that speaks to me the loudest about compassion for others and their plight in life. It keeps me connected in an endearing way."

One day, for instance, Dolgin got a wooden sliver lodged into her finger, which was "excruciatingly painful." But then she realized her pain was nothing compared to the suffering many people have. And she also gained new empathy for her daughter. "Memories of my daughter's painful experience with ingrown toenails following an accident not only diminished my own pain, but let me realize how she might have felt."

Even if she can't recall how difficult it was to be a teenager, having a teenage daughter still gives Dolgin plenty of opportunities to practice compassion. "Children have a way of being our best teachers. If we can't offer the gift of compassion to family and friends who share our sacred spaces, where else might we expect them to receive it? How can we expect them to learn the act of compassion if we don't model it for them in their own centered place of refuge?"

Dolgin's own mother imprinted her with the teaching "Do unto others as you would have them do unto you." This ethic was so instilled in her that "to do otherwise would be unthinkable, if not impossible. I am grateful for this imprint."

STAMPING OUR HOMES WITH LOVE

According to Robyn Dolgin, we can imprint our homes with love and caring in many simple ways. She helps people create sacred space in their homes and offices. Her suggestions are grounded in and inspired by traditional and contemporary Feng Shui principles and her almost twenty-five years of experience in horticulture, landscape design, and work as an energy worker and healing arts practitioner.

"While creating sacred space, people need to first bring nature indoors. Next, they can be mindful of loving, caring, and being grateful for everything they consciously choose to bring into their living or work spaces. The simplest objects, whether it's a pine branch or a garden stone, when imbued with love, radiate an essence of love and Spirit felt by all those who enter your space. It is from that essence that compassion, mindfulness, and non-judgment are born."

The word *sanctuary* means holy or sacred space, author Jennifer Louden reminds us in *The Couple's Comfort Book*. Is your home designed as sacred space? How about your office? If not, how would you make it so? Louden suggests asking yourself what that space would smell like, sound like. "If this refuge could be anywhere, where would I have it?" she says. Then find a space in your home where at least some of these elements can be honored, she suggests. Consult experts and books to get some cues for creating your own sanctuary.

GOING OUTWARD IN SERVICE

Spend the time it takes to build a compassionate bedrock from which your family's love can then extend outward. Many people find that when they do take the time to just relax, be, incubate, and grow their love as a family unit, they eventually reach a point where they feel renewed and want to extend that sense of well-being to others. They want to serve. Some families choose to help build Habitat for Humanity houses together. Others like to shovel walks for the elderly. Others regularly serve meals at the local homeless shelter or volunteer at school as a family.

"Dining together to build family relationships also provides opportunities to discuss current-event examples of generosity or need," said Swanee

Hunt. Among her friends, one family has a ritual of handing a check to their teenagers and having them fill out the name of a nonprofit recipient. Then the teens deliver their check in person, to "follow the gift" to its destination—a real place with real people.

Hunt gives away half of her earnings each year to various organizations and causes. "But of all my endowments, none is more important than giving my children a sense of themselves as connected to the world—to every part of it—slicing across social strata like geological layers, into the complex and molten core."

But be mindful that the core of your family, as with yourself, has to be shored up and deepened before you can connect with that greater core. Too many people run around doing "good deeds" out of a sense of obligation and "shoulding," and they don't really experience that wonderful sense of their hearts swelling and reaching out to another. They never discover that great soulful flush that comes from connecting with someone else's soul. So they get burned out or find no meaning in the "do-gooding." They end up feeling resentful and hollow because they aren't really acting from a full and generous heart base. And their kids never learn the treasure and gift of real service, of loving others as you love yourself.

If your family does service work together, talk about it afterward. Explore how it felt and why you each enjoyed it. Explain why it's good to give back. Help your kids see the full meaning of it all. Help yourself, actually.

Finally, let compassion conversation flow from that base. Especially if we're working in environments where we feel it's not "safe" or "appropriate" to speak from the heart, we have to be able to do so at home. We have to be free to express our anger, our sadness, our fears without feeling as if our families or partners can't handle it or will judge us harshly or love us less.

Being a safe container, a vessel for someone else's feelings, is a very powerful, loving act, says Sue Patton Thoele. "I have a dear friend who noticed a few years ago that her granddaughter hadn't liked her for several weeks. When she visited her granddaughter, she would turn her head away and say, 'Go away, Grammy.'"

One day the little girl was sitting on the couch, coloring, and the woman's daughter, the little girl's mother, was fixing dinner in the kitchen.

The grandmother said to her granddaughter, "Dear, you've been angry at Grammy the past few weeks. Would you be willing to tell me why?"

"Yes," the girl said, "I hate it that you love my mother." Her mother overheard this and protested, "But, hon, my mother loves me, like I love you."

"Yes, I know—but I hate it," the girl said even more strongly. The mother and grandmother looked at one another, and both said respectfully, "Well, thanks for telling us how you feel."

The next week when Grammy went to visit again, her granddaughter jumped off the stairway where she'd been waiting and yelled, "Grammy, I'm so glad you're here!"

If we can accept, hold, acknowledge, and not try to change someone's feelings, that unconditional acceptance and love can, in turn, allow us to freely and naturally express whatever we are feeling and deepen our bonds. As Thoele says heartily and best: "We all have enough shit to work through on our own without having to juggle someone else's lack of acceptance." Love that woman.

MAKING SPACE FOR EMOTIONAL RELEASE

Thoele calls such relationship practices "compassionate detachment." That means our hearts can flow outward toward others or situations, even when they turn difficult, without "having our emotions or egos caught and sucked into the vortex." What a compassionate way to relate to teenagers who are bombarded by pressures all day long, or even small children, who need to know it's safe and *okay* to sound off at home.

The steam valve has to be opened somewhere, sometime, or the toll of keeping our feelings inward will become too great. Therapists' offices are full of people who weren't given that opportunity as children to safely express their true feelings. A lot happens to our kids, from bullying to the pressure of college exams to losing a parent, and if they aren't allowed in our homes to process their feelings, that pain goes inward and resurfaces through anxiety, depression, even suicide.

Healing can occur only when we allow ourselves and our kids to release emotions. Healing occurs when our kids can see that we trust and find comfort in one another, and that we can share anything—even the things we did to betray ourselves or the family. What we did may not have been appropriate. It may not have been okay, yet we are still accepted and loved.

Dr. Christiane Northrup, in her book *Women's Bodies, Women's Wisdom*, likens this emotional release to the treatment of an abscess. She calls it emotional incision and drainage: "Any surgeon knows that the treatment for an abscess is to cut it open, allowing the pus to drain. When this is done, the pain goes away almost immediately, and new healthy tissue can re-form where the abscess once was. It is the same with emotions. They too become walled off, causing pain and absorbing energy, if we do not experience and release them."

Family relationships will always teach us exactly what we have to learn about compassion if we can stay open to the lessons. Maybe it's in those most painful relationships that we really enter the academy of enlightenment. There will always be family members who can "rip out our hearts and leave them lying on the freeway," says Thoele. Maybe it's through those gut-wrenching relationships that we can really advance our education in the art of living.

Thoele's difficult relationship with her sister has allowed her heart to become even lusher. "My only sister was mean, just as I had a grandmother who was a mean and cruel woman," says Thoele. "It seemed as if the cruelty hopped down a generation to my sister, who was a drop-dead alcoholic from her teen years. I went through years of agony asking, 'Why does it have to be this way?' I gave up thousands and thousands of dollars trying to help her."

SEEING PERFECTION

Thoele continues: "Finally, I got it. I was looking at this relationship with my sister from my own judgment. I was viewing her life as a life wasted, and I was the target. What if on a soul level this was a life that was learning more than I could even imagine?"

Thoele happened to be at the ocean, walking on the beach, when she got the word that her sister had died. "As I was walking along, I asked for a sign that her life wasn't wasted and worthless, that it had been *okay*. And then I saw a conch shell lying in the sand. It looked absolutely gross, like old cement." Something compelled her to pick it up.

"It looked like hell on the outside, but when I looked closer, I saw a hole in the outer shell. And when I looked inside, the inner shell was smooth and pink and soft to the touch. That symbolized to me that no matter what our outside shell looks like, at the core we are smooth, and soft, and soulful, and full of goodness," said Thoele.

Recognizing that goodness at the core of our family members, when they are ranting, petty, vengeful, and duplicitous, may be the ultimate heart challenge. That doesn't mean we let people abuse us or walk all over us. Thoele learned not to call her sister or talk with her after she'd been drinking, because she could be abusive.

We have to love ourselves first by setting boundaries, by never tolerating emotional or physical abuse. Seeing others with compassion doesn't mean we let them take advantage of or hurt us. No name-calling, ridiculing, "butt-heading," hitting, or kicking. Accepting that behavior or treatment from others is martyrdom of the worst kind. It's self-destructive and then we cease to be compassionate to ourselves and all others.

It's amazing how many kids are being conditioned to feel that these are *okay* ways to express themselves. Look at any kindergarten in any school in any town in the country. It's common to see biting, hitting, and name-calling when young kids get frustrated. We need to do a better job of teaching kids appropriate ways to channel their emotions and frustrations.

MAKING FAMILY PLEDGES

Teach kids how to see the goodness in all people, in all life around them. Because when we feel that we are surrounded by goodness, we won't be as tempted to react violently. We will be more "impeccable with our word," as Don Miguel Ruiz urges us to be in *Four Agreements*. We can use language with one another to cast a spell, not break it, he says. Make vows in your home; write your pledges down as a family. Here are some pledges Ruiz suggests: "We will not use words with one another that curse, destroy, belittle, blame or heap on guilt. We will use language that conveys love, support, tolerance, acceptance." Again, this is setting our intention that we will sanction only compassionate conversations in our homes.

We need to love ourselves well because it will generate loving words, Ruiz says. "How much you love yourself and how you feel about yourself are directly proportionate to the quality and integrity of your word. When you're impeccable with your word, you feel good; you feel happy and at peace," he says.

We can ease our tension before we come home to our loved ones, so we don't come in the door with stress, strain, and a headache. So when we drag ourselves in and hear our children singing and jumping around, we don't yell, "Shut up! You have an ugly voice. Can't you just shut up?" as a mother did in Ruiz's book. From then on, her daughter couldn't sing because she felt she had an ugly voice. Words are powerful beyond words.

Speak with loving words and tones because they fill up our homes and linger in the air, in our pillows at night, in the wood and curtains by day. We all know that after a horrible argument when things are said that shouldn't have been, a sense of poison lingers in the air. Our words change the energy in our homes and make them magical, or deadly.

Build a compassionate home as a resting place, as loving arms that enfold and comfort and strengthen us. "Our first and last visceral certainty is that we are safe and satisfied only when we are encompassed by loving arms and that we flourish only within the ambiance of adoring eyes and shared joy," says Sam Keen in *To Live and Be Loved*. "We long for tacit knowledge, for soft caresses, lips on lips, skin gliding along skin. In the once-upon-a-time of childhood and in the fullness of our sexual maturity, we find respite from fear and suffering in that sanctuary we create when contoured bodies cuddle quietly or entwine in passionate love."

Too often we idealize this kind of love but fail to practice it, Keen says. "This is the Great Puzzle that confronts us all. Something stops us from laying claim to the heartland, the homeland we have never left. Why do we hide from ourselves? Why don't we apply the knowledge that we have about love and meaning? Why isn't love the cloud that guides us by day and the pillar of fire by night? Why do we own a castle and live in a shack?"

Love, concludes Keen, "is not a spectator sport." We have to get off the bench, into the field, into the dirt, into the grass. It's time we all get messy, sweaty, heated, and lusty with celebration in the spirit and love of this timeless sport.

As you focus on creating a compassionate, sacred home—and workspace—rely on this prayer and invocation by Robyn Michelle Dolgin.

A Prayer for a Sacred Home

Great Spirit, all of Oneness and the Light, Earth Mother, Father Sky, Brother Sun, Sister Moon, Grandmother Water, All Living Things and the Stone People, Each of the Four Directions and All Dimensions in Between, Spirit of this House and All Other Spirit Guides, All of our Human Allies, we give great thanks for all that you are and ask for your presence, participation, assistance and blessing as we establish this home as our own for the time that we have been given. May it be a place of beauty, peace, healing, and growth for all who enter it. Ho. ("Ho" translates to "So be it" in native cultures.)

8

Softheartedness: Nourishing Compassion with Small Acts

THE PREVIOUS CHAPTERS HAVE EXPLORED how we can use our senses, our gifts of sight, hearing, touch, and the ability to communicate to live out of our hearts. They've discussed how when we bring all these gifts together, we each have unimaginable power of compassion to make this earth a more humane place. "At the core of our being lie resources many of us never dream we possess, much less imagine we can draw upon," says Paul Rogat Loeb in *Soul of a Citizen*.

But be a wise steward of those heart resources. Initially, as you rediscover your heart, you might feel so powerful that you feel driven to do something larger than life to save the world. That save-the-world impulse often stems from the ego that wants the visibility and fame—not from the true heart. Don't start running around in a good-deeded froth. It's too easy to do lots of altruistic acts and not have your heart in them. Instead, build the core strength of your heart slowly and deliberately with the smallest possible steps.

GROWING COMPASSION SLOWLY

Take it easy. Slowly nurture your compassion skills, as you would any skill you intend to strengthen. Treat your heart a bit more gingerly. Fortify it with small gestures of affection that make all the difference to someone else. Spend one hour a week volunteering at the homeless shelter, instead of immediately jumping on its board. Spend several hours a week helping one child learn to read instead of overhauling the class curriculum.

"Give your compassion the opportunity to grow," points out Victoria Moran in *Love Yourself Thin*. "Don't push yourself into actions that seem absurd to you. If, however, you find yourself catching an uninvited insect and releasing it outside instead of reaching for the bug spray, don't think that you've lost your mind. You may instead have found your heart."

You can as easily find your heart in the small gestures, maybe even more so than in the grandiose ones. Compassion is not a life of mythic self-denial, says Henri Nouwen in *Here and Now*. Compassion doesn't require "heroic gestures or a sensational turnaround. In fact, the compassionate life is mostly hidden in the ordinariness of everyday living.

"The question that truly counts is not whether we imitate Mother Teresa, but whether we are open to the many little sufferings of those with whom we share our life," adds Nouwen. "Are we willing to share our time with those who do not stimulate our curiosity? Do we listen to those who do not immediately attract us? Can we be compassionate to those whose suffering remains hidden from the eyes of the world?"

SEEING BEYOND THE OBVIOUS

In *Here and Now*, Nouwen wisely points out how much hidden suffering exists in our world of seemingly abundant material joy: "The suffering of the teenager who does not feel secure; the suffering of the husband and wife who feel that there is no love left between them; the suffering of the wealthy executive who thinks that people are more interested in his money than in him; the suffering of the gay man or woman who feels isolated from family and friends . . ."

Once we are willing to peer beneath the surface of life, we can better see the pain of other people and hear the call of compassion right where we are in the smallest gestures, concludes Nouwen. And actually, aren't we just as moved by the small radical acts of love people do on our behalf as we are by the big stuff?

When Pablo Pandolfi goes to dialysis at a Buenos Aires clinic, something he's endured for eleven years, what eases his discomfort and touches his heart the most is that his doctors and nurses treat him and the other patients like family. They know which patients get upset if they're not given the same blanket every session and which ones enjoy hearing tango music as their blood is being cleansed. Pandolfi, a former disc jockey, always brings a small tape player to his thrice-weekly dialysis sessions, and often the nurses sing along with the music. "Thanks to this kind of atmosphere, the hours pass quickly. We talk, we tease each other, we listen to music, we laugh," Pandolfi says.[1]

Compassion begins "in the moment," as Pandolfi's caregivers at the Gambro clinic express simple appreciation and respect in everyday moments. They also show that compassion is never pity, never feeling better-than or condescending about someone's suffering. Compassion is not about feeling sorrow for someone from a detached, righteous place; it is about letting others so affect us that they crack open our vulnerable places. They touch our own pockets of pain, and in that solidarity we can say, "I feel your pain because I have been there too." Reflecting on his life in *Here and Now*, Nouwen says the moments of greatest comfort and consolation were when someone said, "'I cannot take your pain away, I cannot offer you a solution for your problem, but I can promise you that I won't leave you alone and will hold on to you as long and as well as I can.'"

SPARKING CIRCLES OF COMPASSION

Binding our hearts to others in these seemingly small ways seems to trigger the most sweeping repercussions. When Rachel Eyre Hall's brother developed AIDS, she knew she couldn't take his illness away or fix his disease. But she noticed that once he was diagnosed, few people even wanted to touch him. So she trained as a massage therapist so she could soothe him with massage.

The repercussions of Hall's love, however, radiated far beyond her and her brother. Hall eventually convinced the Sacramento, California, AIDS Foundation to set up a massage-therapy program for others with AIDS. Since then thousands of free massages have been offered.

Hall even brought her program to Mother Teresa's leprosy and tuberculosis clinic in Calcutta. In 1996, Hall became one of only eighteen young people to receive the Gold Congressional Award for "volunteer services and personal development." Her brother died in 1998—but what a legacy she created for him.[2]

LOVE IN THE SMALLEST OFFERINGS

Because our hearts are so sensitive, even the smallest amount of compassion causes them to swell and open dramatically. Begin to slowly, deliberately extend the circle of compassion to all you come into contact with. Love surges through the smallest cracks. Following the Columbine High School tragedy, many of the families whose children were shot said the gestures that have helped to heal their wounded hearts were the simple ones.

"On days when we were particularly down, we would come home and find a lasagna waiting for us," said Ann Kechter, who lost her son, Matt. Other times, they received homegrown tomatoes, music, or poems.[3]

Sean Graves, whose spine was nicked with a bullet, leaving him in a wheelchair, said his family has been awed by the continuing gestures of love from the world community. One package arrived from Nova Scotia with only his name and town—no street address. "And it made it all the way to our house," he said. "Inside was a T-shirt and a letter that said, 'Whenever you want, come up, and we'll go lobster hunting.'"[4]

Dawn Anna, who lost her daughter, Laura Townsend, found solace in a package of candies sent by a five-year-old stranger. Think how small but powerful a gesture that is. Columbine has taught her "that people are so good and so caring and so giving."[5]

Small acts of compassion can show us how lovingly connected we all are. Pain is pain whether you live in the shadows of Littleton, Colorado, or Nova Scotia. And when we do take the time to ease that pain, the ripple effects are miraculous. Remember how good, how caring, how giving you naturally are when your heart struggles to express its full beauty. Extend your circle of compassion a little more all the time, to those around you, including the creatures in nature.

Don't neglect the natural world in your small acts. The smallest gestures can bloom into the most amazing things. A man in my community named Elan Shamir took the simple act of planting a few trees on his own. Over ten years, many people, attracted to his mission, have joined and formed the ReLeaf organization and planted thousands of trees. Our environment begs for us to view it with tenderness. "Until he extends the circle of compassion to all living things, man will not himself find peace," wrote scientist Albert Schweitzer.[6]

Compassion begins within our own circles. Sometimes it's the small things, quietly done, that move us most. Fred Edmonds, a Congregational minister, once described how he viewed the circle of love: "Delight comes when we care for someone knowing what it feels like to be cared for—because someone has cared for us. We delight in loving God in gratitude that God has taught us what it is to be loved. We delight in loving our neighbor knowing what it is to be loved by someone else."

Edmonds recalled a time when he was in college, needing to go to the grocery store in the pouring rain. "The store was about two miles away and my only form of transportation was my own two feet," he said. "I put on my raincoat and set out. I had gone only a few blocks when the college chaplain, driving by in her car, happened to notice me, and she stopped."

The chaplain took Edmonds to the store, waited for him to do his shopping, and gave him a ride back to his dorm. "I remember feeling an overwhelming debt of gratitude to her. And I remember her saying, 'Someday, when you have a car, you can give someone a ride to the store in the rain.'"

Love, Edmonds reminds us, is a "joyful response to having been loved."[7] When we love the circle of people who orbit in and out of our lives, we are etching a memory on their hearts they'll remember the rest of their lives. When was the last time you helped someone in from the rain? How did it make you feel? Who might be in the downpour right now?

Whose dream could you support, whose day could you ease, whose potential could you see, whose heart could you stroke? Whose life could you recognize as precious?

SMALL GESTURES KEEP THE FIRE BURNING

It's the small ways we can begin to do that. Think of how, when people tell you about something wonderful that happened—a seemingly insignificant little something—their faces just glow. They are lit from within. Someone has helped keep their inner fire ablaze. You can see how they carry in their hearts a vivid memory of how that felt.

Such stories of simple loving gestures flowed in for this book, like fruit on the vine, over the Internet. Even diluted in this fashion, not being able to see the senders' emotions, eyes, or gestures as they told their stories, I could still sense how much they vibrated with affection.

"I've had the amazing experience of being the receiver lately of many, many amazing acts of love," began Cynthia, a business consultant. She went on to divulge that she'd been dealing with cancer and coming to grips with its financial toll on her life. At a stage in her cancer treatment when she had no time or energy to even think of billing a client for work she'd performed, a note suddenly came from them. "They simply sent me a check for the services I had earned. . . . It was amazing," she said. "But more than that, it reaffirmed that there are loving, caring people that support the corporate towers."

Six of Cynthia's business clients also got together and organized a fundraiser for Cynthia's medical expenses that they called the Harvest Festival. They invited all of Cynthia's clients, friends, and all of their friends. In three hours, the women raised more than $10,000. "If I were writing a book, it would be about all the love and caring behind the Harvest Festival. I wish that everyone could once in their life experience that without the cancer," said Cynthia.

EMPATHY MAKES LIFE RICHER

What a wish to fulfill. Sometimes the simplest act of empathy acknowledges that, in our hearts, we want to help carry someone else's burden. And when someone sees us in this way, in that moment of being seen and fully known by another, our fears and night terrors and all lighten in remarkable ways. When you look back on your life, you'll see that it's often the little acts of kindness that made life worth living.

The littlest things make a huge difference. A passenger on a Southwest Airlines flight wrote his appreciation to the company CEO after witnessing a radical act of love on a flight to New Orleans. "As we were preparing to leave the gate, a little boy sitting in the row in front of me started crying. This was not a small, quiet whimper, but a loud and scared cry. The boy moaned that he missed his dad. He was traveling alone," the man wrote.

Watching this, the passenger knew that a typical response would be for the flight attendant in charge to console the little boy during takeoff and then scurry back to her job. "This attendant, however, went far beyond that. She sat with him, her arm around him, soothing him and keeping him occupied throughout the flight. Only occasionally did she get up to do her regular duties, always returning to this boy's side. She was a calming and protective presence for him, and he soon calmed down and even joked with her on the flight. Once we landed in New Orleans, she escorted him to the main hall where he was united with his mother."

The man went on to write that it was "reassuring" to him to see "such extraordinary care and genuine concern." He was "comforted to know that, with Southwest, my kids will be treated as people and protected as they fly."[8]

Compassionate gestures are extraordinary to witness or be the recipient of. We all need "protection as we fly," literally and figuratively. We all need to know that someone cares about us. The smallest things show we care. The littlest acts can make a huge difference.

One woman e-mailed her story saying that she slowly, carefully lets her spiritual side be known at work. One thing she does is to lay out a book on forgiveness in her cubicle: "When someone asks if they can read it, I tell them to take it and pass it on instead of returning it. Then I put out another copy of the book. On average, I go through two books a month."

When she turned fifty-seven, this woman said she had an awakening. She decided that "not showing human compassion at work was wrong. We spend so much of our life at work, we need to be rejuvenated spiritually. We cannot spend so much of our lives being drained and not be replenished."

She went on to slowly act more from her authentic self. "Now I allow words like 'patience,' 'understanding,' 'kindness,' 'being in tune,' 'looking inward,' 'asking the Big Guy for help' into my conversations when appropriate," she said. "The response has been in kind. The more I allude to spiritual matters, the more others come forth with thoughts of their own. It's almost like they are relieved to know they are not alone."

SHINING LIGHT IN THE DARKNESS

Small gestures of love can go a long way in reassuring us that we're not alone. They can be something we can carry with us into the darkest, loneliest spots of our lives. When Carla Frenzel goes to her eighth-grade class at Grant Middle School in Denver, she knows that part of her job is to acknowledge her students as human beings—many of who have suffering far beyond their years, some of who go to lonely, less-than-compassionate homes every night.

"Once I was having the kids write and read their autobiographies to the class, and this student got really defensive. She just did not want to write or share her autobiography. So we brainstormed all these questions that the kids could ask their parents, but she still was really defiant."

The girl finally shared with Frenzel why she was so opposed to sharing her autobiography—with anyone. "Look," she said, "my dad was only fourteen when I was born. He didn't care what I did." And it turned out she was getting limited love and nurturing from her mother too.

Frenzel's reaction was to acknowledge and empathize with her student's story. "That's really, really tough," she told the girl. Frenzel said that she will never hold back from sharing her heart with her students; it's one thing she loves about her job. "We have to acknowledge their lives, experiences, hurts, and all they've gone through. . . . We have to let them know their lives are important. Education is important, but we have to understand these kids are human beings first. Whatever we're studying, the kids have to know I care about them."

What can you do? Hearing these stories about the power of the smallest gesture, what else can you do to act tenderly? A woman in my community is giving a teddy bear to all breast cancer patients at our local hospital. What more can you do to offer someone comfort?

What final blocks must be removed from your thinking to allow you to commit tender acts? Think of times when a loving act may be the only rational response to an irrational, untenable situation. Consider how coming from a place of love in all your professional dealings may shift them to a higher plane. Sometimes we overanalyze love and spiritual intention, and just need to choose small radical acts of love to feel love again.

LOVE AS A FEELING

Brett Pavel, a minister at the Gathering, a New Thought Church in Fort Collins, Colorado, loves a quote from author Stuart Wilde: "Too much thinking is a terrible disease. It brings on awfully chronic symptoms, such as seriousness."

We can read lots of spiritual books and store them in our intellects and understand how the spiritual laws of the universe work, Pavel commented. "But when we leave this physical realm and go back to pure love energy, we don't go there as an intellectualized piece of academic information or a book. We go as a feeling. We leave here as a feeling."

Many famous, rich people make their fame and fortune by getting on a stage and telling other people that love moves everything, Pavel observed. They teach people how to be their most powerful, loving selves. But then they go backstage and are jerks to those around them.

"Love is not about reading the books. It's not about getting up and talking about it," said Pavel. "It's about living the example. We can't talk about being in love without doing the work. We can't be in joy if we aren't doing the work of loving others."

Pavel, who is also a Realtor, got a chance to practice this recently through his work on a real estate transaction. Clients came to him and said, "Brett, we found the house we want to buy, and we want you to help get it for us."

And then they told Pavel who the agent representing the seller was, and his heart sank. He'd worked with this person before and had had many negative experiences.

"Yet, I knew that my clients were very wonderful, and I could talk to them with truth. I knew we could affirm and pray for what we wanted to create. I knew that this couple chooses to move to love in every possible situation," he said.

So they affirmed and prayed that the real estate agreement would close smoothly and lovingly for all parties involved. Pavel practiced seeing the other Realtor with loving thoughts and intention. And then in the final days, it went sour—and got very emotional.

Intellectually, Pavel knew that he should remain calm and loving, but emotionally he struggled. "One minute I could surrender to my heart and see this other Realtor as perfect, with a little child inside, but the next minute I was mad because this person was doing this to me again."

He and his clients had long conversations about staying in a place of love even though it felt difficult. And finally the deal went through. At the closing his clients brought the other Realtor a birdhouse that the wife had made. The Realtor said, "You know, I've been a Realtor for years and no one has ever given me anything like this before."

Through his tears, Pavel was in awe of the gift of love given by the couple. "It was such a surrender to the heart," he said. "She said that each day as she felt challenged by and irritated with this Realtor, she would go and build the house, frame the roof, put in a nail, paint a flower, screw it all together, and pour loving energy into the house as a gift. No matter what happened, she was going to give a gift from her heart. That was really great work, wasn't it? That commitment to be in love. Their choice to move to a loving place. In my opinion, there is no higher work than what that couple did. And you don't have to believe in any dogma or read any books or go to any church to understand that, though it is wonderful to attract and gather with people."

CHOOSING FOR LOVE

What keeps you from moving to a loving place? Is it habit? Or is it the time involved to make the effort? Again, if you don't have time or energy for these meaningful acts of love, what else can be so important? Or is it possibly fear that holds you back? Are you terrified that unmasking your heart will hurt? Are you afraid, for instance, that if you start showing greater affection to those around you that you will be scoffed at, that you will be misunderstood, or even worse, that you may look, well, foolish? Sometimes it's the most foolish gestures of all that touch someone's soul on a level nothing else ever can.

One Valentine's Day, Kenny Moore, corporate ombudsman for KeySpan Energy, raided his sons' stash of Barney valentine cards. He distributed them to dozens of people at work, from the chairman at the "top" to the unionized people. He wrote messages like "Dear Sue, thank you for bringing your heart to KeySpan" and dropped the valentines on his coworkers' desks. "I thought 90 percent would think I was crazy, but my experience was just the opposite. The chairman and some of the executives said, 'Thank you. No one's ever done this to me.'"

Moore later heard back from another person who said, "I can't tell you all the details, but your card touched me in a special way today." Moore was in a meeting six months later with a KeySpan executive when he noticed his Barney valentine card stuck to the wall. "Now I get valentine cards back with messages like 'Kenny, thanks for your laughter and your friendship.'"

The smallest gestures bring the most expansive, larger-than-life

music hung from the trees." Cameron stayed in England and wrote many moving songs straight from her heart.[5]

We each have internal music that beckons to be expressed. You can't wait for others to acknowledge your gifts. Where are your unsung lyrics? What sings inside you waiting for you to hear it? You can't wait for your family and friends to "get it." The poet Jelaluddin Rumi once said, "I want to sing as birds sing, not worrying who listens or what they think."[6] Johann Sebastian Bach's brother so didn't get Bach's gift that he tortured him, hiding his music so he couldn't practice. He punished him if he practiced, so Bach practiced by candlelight—and permanently damaged his eyesight.

If you've been hearing the music forever but are afraid to let it play out, keep in mind something Julia Cameron shared, "This is what I most want to say to people about their dreams. If you are passionately in love with something that you wish you could do . . . the odds are, perhaps you can. And that like me, you are simply very afraid to try it."[7]

FACING DOUBTS AND INSECURITIES

What is your dream, and has your heart bought into it? If it hasn't, what's keeping you from plunging headlong into life? Have the years of being told you're "not enough"—not musical enough, as Cameron was told, not sexy enough, not smart enough, not successful enough, not courageous enough, not talented enough—thrown cold water on the fire that once burned within? How often are you letting your heart be overruled by the "coulds" and "shoulds" screaming from your left brain? How soon are you ready to stop "shoulding" all over yourself? What is at stake is too high to ignore.

Never stifle your dreams out of fear of what others will think. Out of fear that they may be threatened because they can't follow their own dormant dreams. Never play it small, so others can play it big. I once knew a woman who was the chief assistant to a huge star, a mega household-name diva. Angela, the assistant, was the public relations (PR) person, the troubleshooter, the dry-cleaning runner, the Hollywood television show go-between, the sounding board, the errand person, and the Academy Award gown picker-upper.

And Angela was not entirely happy. She longed to do her own performing of sorts—she wanted to teach alternative health classes. She longed to leave the gypsy life of the road behind and nest and create her own home sanctuary. She wanted a quieter, more nurturing pace. She longed to have a relationship with someone.

Angela had chronic back problems that persisted even with the best conventional and alternative treatments. It wasn't until she followed her own dream, it wasn't until she quit her high-paying, big-visibility job and followed her heart that her back pain eased. She also found a wonderful home and a relationship.

Never play it small so others can play it big. Never. Never be afraid of your own power, as well. Never duck your duty to be conspicuous because you are afraid to shine. "Our deepest fear is not that we are inadequate. Our deepest fear is that we are powerful beyond measure," said Nelson Mandela, former president of the Republic of South Africa, in his 1994 inaugural speech, quoting Marianne Williamson. "It is our light, not our darkness, that most frightens us. We ask ourselves, 'Who am I to be brilliant, gorgeous, talented, and fabulous? Actually, who are you not to be? You are a child of God. Your playing small doesn't serve the world. There's nothing enlightened about shrinking so that other people won't feel insecure around you. We were born to manifest the glory of God within us. It's not just in some; it's in everyone. And as we let our light shine, we unconsciously give other people permission to do the same. As we are liberated from our own fear, our presence automatically liberates others."

LIVING THE DREAM IS NOT ALWAYS EASY

Are you now living your dream, in full blinding color? What does it feel like? Sometimes it does feel less than the fairy tale than we've been conditioned to believe. Our bodies do have limitations, even if our spirits are flying out on the road ahead of us, as people like poet David Whyte know. Whyte knows what it's like to get off the elevator onto the fourteenth floor of a nondescript office tower in yet another city. Dusk falling once again, he finds himself, yet again, entering a steel, chrome, and glass building somewhere in North America, hoping to reintroduce at least one soul to the sheer magic of his or her own existence.

Hours earlier, Whyte was on a plane as it lurched through ominous clouds toward Chicago's O'Hare Airport. Exhausted from an intense speaking schedule, crammed against the window, Whyte wished he were at home with his family.

But now he's at his engagement, one of hundreds he does each year. He talks of love and longing, merging your personal values and creativity with work, of connecting and meaning. He often caresses the fluid words of his and others' poetry—"the language of the heart speaking into the world."

After he's been talking for a while to his Chicago audience, Whyte pauses, drawn to look across the crowded room at a man sitting in the audience, his mouth wide open. The man is sitting beside a window; his face is illuminated by the florescent lights reflected off the glass so you can see nothing of the night outside. "He looks like a three-year-old having a deep experience of memory," Whyte thinks to himself. "Ahhh. This is why I came. This is why I do this work."[8]

EXAMINING PURPOSE

Why do you do your work? Have you discovered the magic of your own existence? Do you feel you belong where you are? Are your professional choices grounded in heart-centered reasons? If not, why not? If we are committed to following our hearts, we must pause and look across the crowded rooms of our lives to make sure our hearts are fully present. Does your work make your heart sing? Is there room for your heart to breathe and expand in your choices each day, the people you associate with, the goals you follow?

When you look across the landscape before you, does your heart sigh, "Ahh. Yes. This is why I do what I do."

We each were born with a unique, indelible signature of who we are and who we are destined to be. In the mystical movie *The Legend of Bagger Vance*, there is much talk of each of us having our "authentic swing," which is our authentic spirit and purpose.

Is your swing uniquely your own? Is it in alignment with your divine purpose? If we choose to be someone other than who we are meant to be, what kind of resignation and hopelessness must that be stirring inside us? There is rampant despair in our world; depression is at epidemic levels. How much of your despair or restlessness is bound up in your heart? How much of your depression comes from that gnawing, uneasy sense that you aren't doing what you came here to do? Your heart can't live with that.

Search your heart. Does the path you're following have heart? In *The Teachings of Don Juan*, Carlos Castenada requests Don Juan's advice on how to know which path to follow. Don Juan suggests he ask himself, "Does this path have heart?" The path with heart makes for a "joyful journey," Don Juan says. "As long as you follow it, you are one with it. The other will make you curse your life. One makes you strong; the other weakens you."

FINDING THE PATH WITH HEART

What path are you on? Does it have heart? If not, what does it contain? Is that what you want to be the signature you leave on the world? What else might you be drawn to? What brings you intense joy, so much so that when you do it, you lose all track of time? What would your life be like if it weren't governed by fear, requirements, expectations, and your own inner restraints? Once I did a workshop about following your soul's desires and a woman whispered to me afterward, "I'm going to do just that—once I pay off my RV."

That lingered in my head forever. So much so, that I started writing a song that began something like, "I'll be as free as I can be—once I pay off my RV." Too much is at stake in our responsibility to be compassionate people, parents, and stewards of the earth to let our RVs and their material equivalents get in the way of our hearts' longings. It's really hard to be compassionate with others if we aren't even loving ourselves enough to follow whatever it is that makes our hearts sing. Do what makes your heart sing. Light that fire. "Generate a strong, burning desire to live and live as fully and as well as you possibly can," says life coach Lloyd Thomas. "That may be your most difficult psychological task. Some old familiar ways of living must be modified or replaced."[9]

TIME-OUTS CAN BE USEFUL

Sometimes, it is necessary to literally step away from our lives to discover what's true and necessary. When Janine Geske accepted an appointment to the Wisconsin Supreme Court, she knew she would miss directly working with people in need in her community. She'd always tried to ground her life in a philosophy that she describes here in a speech to a class of high school graduates: "Regardless of what you do with your life, you ought to spend time with people who do not have the same opportunities you have. If you don't spend time with people who have doors shut in their faces, you won't understand the problems, and you won't be part of the solution."

Five years into her ten-year term, Geske was asking herself those very questions. Was she doing the hands-on work she really liked to do? The answers were pretty obvious. "I was frankly miserable most of that time," she said. "I just didn't like it. It was very isolating. I spent most of my time with six other professional justices, and I basically got along with most of the people on my court. I did speeches around the state each week, but it was no substitute for the hands-on stuff I liked to do. It got to the point that I was weeping as I was driving to court."

But Geske was still struggling with what her heart really wanted to do. What would put her back on her intended path? She felt she needed to remove herself from her usual life to gain those answers, which she knew were spiritual in nature. This is where a strong support network can help. Geske said, "I cooked up this idea to organize a retreat to the Dominican Republic to a center that was run by Jesuits who work with the poor."

On a New Year's Day, she and a group of attorneys, judges, and a law school dean left for a week in the Dominican Republic, living and working with the local people. She slept in a shack without plumbing, electric lights, or water. Her host family used rocks as tools and kerosene in a can for a lamp.

They cooked their meals over an open fire outside. Heartsick, Geske thought of all the stuff in her own life. "The trip was not intended for us to go down there and 'do good,'" she explained. "It was meant to help me reaffirm the importance of relationships in my life and my gifts to interact with and work one-on-one with people. It reaffirmed that that is where I find my energy and joy. I had gifts on the court, too, but that is not where I found my joy."

FINDING JOY AND FULFILLMENT

Six months later, Janine Geske made another retreat to Boston College, where she finally decided to leave the state supreme court to open a private mediation practice—an amazing heart-over-head decision that rocked the legal community in the Midwest. "My decision to leave the court is a very difficult one and a very personal one," she said. "It will be difficult for some lawyers and judges to understand. But prestige and stature and money are not what drive me. I want to do more."

Geske, who was chief staff attorney for the Legal Aid Society of Milwaukee more than twenty years ago, said, "I miss looking into the eyes of people, seeing the hurt, and trying to do something about it."

There is no doubt now where she finds her joy: "When I am working with people, connecting with them, and helping them to make their lives better, and seeing their joy." Pursuing your passion will always make you a kinder, softer, more joyous person. It always makes you more magnanimous toward others and the world around you.

We need a lot more magnanimous hearts to inhabit our world. You can be part of a chain reaction, just as Catherine Ryan Hyde depicted in her book *Pay It Forward*. Favors aren't paid back, but moved forward to others down the line. Sounds like a concept that might have come from an openhearted woman. "I didn't set out to write a 'feel good' book," Hyde said in a news article. "It's important to me to stress that, because I know writers sometimes do that—say, 'I'm going to write a mystery because mystery sells.' But I never do that. I write from the heart and worry about the market later."[10]

Write from your heart—and worry about what to do about it later. Spend twenty minutes each day for the next five days—just five days—journaling from your heart and see what it would write to you. Ask yourself the following question: "Am I aligned with my heart's desires?" If the answer is no, ask your heart what you would need to do to be in perfect alignment with it. What is your own unique path with heart? Can you follow it, knowing, of course, that it won't be easy?

"You have to listen to yourself and do what your muse tells you," writes Alexandra Stoddard's heart in *Making Choices: Discovering the Joy in Living the Life You Want to Lead*. "It's simple advice, but very difficult for many of us to follow. The key to our sense of well-being is to be guided by our heart, which yearns to choose the challenging, original path."

TERROR MIXED WITH EXHILARATION

I always, always remember Dr. Christiane Northrup, author of *Women's Bodies, Women's Wisdom*, saying that when you feel equal amounts of exhilaration and terror, you are exactly where you need to be. Heart work is not for the retiring, for the meek, or for those who cling to the path of least resistance. Following your heart may not always be easy. Nothing worth doing ever is. There are always "strings attached." There are always your own insecurities, panic attacks, failures, exhaustion to overcome. There will always be others' scorn, ridicule, fear, and jealousy. People who pull back from following their own dreams will always try to dilute yours. Follow your dreams anyway.

Go into the fire, says David Whyte in this excerpt from his poem "Self-Portrait":

> I want to know
> if you know
> how to melt into that fierce heat of living
> falling toward
> the center of your longing. I want to know
> if you are willing
> to live, day by day, with the consequence of love
> and the bitter
> unwanted passion of your sure defeat.
>
> I have heard in *that* fierce embrace, even
> the gods speak of God.

As you go into your fire—or even look at the flames flickering from a distance, wondering if it can really consume you, gain inspiration from the stories of others who followed their hearts despite the odds. Mary Cassatt, the brilliant Impressionist painter, knew she was put here on the earth to create beautiful masterpieces. And thank God she did. But when twenty-one-year-old Cassatt told her father she was going to Paris to become an artist, he didn't run out and buy her watercolor brushes. He told her, "I'd rather see you dead." When Elisabeth Kübler-Ross broke new ground in her work to bring more respect and focus on the terminally ill, many of her colleagues told her that her work was a waste of time.

Most of us don't have obstacles that daunting to overcome, but we still hold back from following our hearts. Be prepared. When we go into the fire, or even consider it, our logical minds might try to extinguish it. Sometimes our analytical minds just can't accept our hearts' vision of ourselves.

Sometimes when we try to summon our hearts and follow their guidance, it's hard to even make that connection. We get so caught up in the flow and feel of our days that we lose perspective. Sometimes it helps to step away from the whirl of life and, from afar, look back at what we see.

SEEK THE HEART IN SILENCE

If you're unable to literally leave the landscape of your life, go deep into a meditation to a place that you absolutely love. Maybe it's the woods; maybe it's an ocean beach. Through deep breathing and visualizing, take yourself to that exquisite scene again. See the sun filtering down through the canopy of leaves. Smell the brine and salt of the ocean. Try then to call forth your heart and see what it most desires.

The more time Janine Geske spent in contemplation to unearth her heart's desires, the more opportunities appeared. Among other things, she now serves as a mediator between parents whose children were killed and those they are suing for retribution. "I do mediations with people in pain. . . . I help parents resolve the most devastating losses, and it gives me such joy to help them through that. In three out of four cases, we are able to settle the lawsuit peacefully."

Geske also teaches law students how to be compassionate mediators, how to use compassion to turn adversarial litigation into peaceful resolution. Additionally, she is an advocate for and participant in the restorative justice program in prisons, which brings together offenders and victims and their communities to promote restitution, understanding, forgiveness, and healing. Geske's work will soon be featured in a documentary produced by the Fetzer Institute.

Geske's advice for those trying to reconnect with their hearts' desires? "The best thing to do is to journal, writing down where you really find excitement and joy in life. Be attentive to that. Write down when you think you had a good day."

Then come back in a month or two and take a look at what you've written. Consider going on a retreat, not a vacation, advises Geske, to "have some silent place, simple and quiet, to reflect."

Sometimes it's absolutely necessary to leave the environment that keeps our hearts obscured so we can find our hearts anew.

How else can we begin to really live from our hearts, to craft a more compassionate life for ourselves in which we honor what our hearts are drawn to do? In which we get out of our own way and let our hearts lead us? Don't wait until your life, or plan, or response is perfect. Don't wait until your skills are perfect. Remember Henri Nouwen's point that the people doing the healing with a community aren't those who are whole and have their act together; rather, the people who are more available to heal the woundedness of others are those who are also struggling with their own brokenness and who are ministering to themselves.

HEED THE HEART THAT SPEAKS

And really listen to your heart when it speaks to you. Don't negate it, downplay it, or ridicule it. Our hearts whisper to us and sometimes elevate us to such a startling, heart-stopping level that we can no longer ignore them. We can no longer chalk it up to a midlife restlessness or a funky mood. The next time you feel especially anxious, out of sorts, or depressed, ask whether those feelings might come from a conversation your soul is trying to have with you. Is your soul trying to reach you through that sense of angst, through your fears? "That which oppresses me, is it my soul trying to come out in the open or the soul of the world knocking at my heart for its entrance?" asks Rabindranath Tagore.[11]

When our hearts and souls call to us, they just amplify the refrain until we finally "get it." And sometimes those calls come in the most illogical, inexplicable, mysterious ways. Be open to your heart speaking to you through serendipity and miraculous messages. They usually come too. Even if our rational minds can't justify or explain them, our hearts can.

Ardath Rodale is testament of that. She is chief executive officer of Rodale Press, which publishes *Prevention, Runner's World, New Woman,* and other magazines as well as best-selling books. Rodale found the strength to listen to her heart even as it was being split open by the most painful losses. In 1985, her son David died from complications of AIDS. He'd been sick for only five days and diagnosed only two days before his death.

After David's death, Rodale became one of the first people to share with groups all over the country, from Lutheran church groups to celebrity gatherings, the story of AIDS from a personal viewpoint. But, first, she had to heed the messages in her heart. "The hardest experience to face in life is the death of a child," she said. "But in my heart, I kept hearing David urging me, 'Mom, you have a story to tell. Please help people understand.'"

As Rodale continued to tell David's story around the country, serendipitous messages reinforced the rightness of her work, showed her that she was following her own path with heart. One evening she went to a Lutheran convention where more than one thousand people listened to her message of the need for unconditional love to shine on those with AIDS as children of God. Remember, this was when our society was still coming to grips with AIDS, and hearts were very closed toward those who developed this disease.

"I was hoping that the Lutherans would open their hearts wider and be more understanding of people who have AIDS. It was a tremendous experience and one of the very best speeches I ever gave."

SERENDIPITY BRINGS SUPPORT

As Rodale was driving home from the convention, the sun shining on her face, she happened to glance in her rearview mirror. She saw her husband Bob's face smiling as if he was walking in back of her car. Tears streamed down Rodale's face because she knew Bob was really proud of her. She knew his love surrounded her and strengthened her as she went about her heart work.

Ardath Rodale also knew she'd received a spiritual sign of support because her husband, Robert Rodale, had been recently killed in a traffic accident in Moscow. Long a visionary and proponent of sustainable, organic farming, Bob was in the country to help the Russians modernize their agricultural methods.

The most serendipitous, divine, miraculous events occur to place us on our path. They come as gifts to reaffirm that, even in the midst of great pain, our hearts can still sing. "I do think my greatest gift in life has been my opening myself up to share our lives and help other people," Rodale told me.[12]

Know that when you follow your heart, the doors will open to you, which is what happened to radio talk-show host Ellen Abell. She was doing consulting work for a large corporation when she began to see how much of the corporate world embraces and puts out very aggressive language. "I saw that much of the language they used was focused on attacking and was very dismissive of anything spiritual, compassionate, or humane," Abell said in our interview.

She was tapped to help a department within the company create a new slogan for their product line. "When they surveyed people in their organization, the slogan that became the most popular was 'Kill, kill, dead, dead.'

"The whole time I was listening to this conversation, jotting down notes, and I felt that the language they were using and the climate they were describing had a lot to do with attacking, annihilating the competition. It felt like I was sitting in what I imagine a military setting during wartime to be like, hearing the same language from the generals and majors. I was stunned."

She wondered how women in the organization, who are often especially sensitive to violent language and behavior, felt. Or what talk about killing and destroying and annihilating brought up, even on a subconscious level, for people of color or people who'd been victimized in their lives.

LISTENING TO OUR REACTIONS

"This whole thing went through my mind, and I personally felt very uncomfortable and extremely dismayed about what I was hearing," said Abell. "And I thought, 'I'm not sure this is the right place for me. I don't want to be part of promoting this kind of thinking and behavior.' Frankly, in my opinion, it's not a long step from 'let's kill the competition' to being aggressive and not being able to turn it off. You can't spend twelve hours a day in annihilation, killing, aggressive, massacre mode and then go home and be tender with your wife, husband, and kids."

And Abell realized, "My God, what am I being a party to here? Energy goes into the universe. Just because you want this destructive energy to stop here, it doesn't."

So Abell began to search for something, a purpose, that was more congruent with her values. And one day she was reading a newspaper and came across a list of the northern Colorado radio stations. She started thinking, "I should do a radio show." She didn't even know why she thought that. She had no previous broadcasting experience; she was trained as a psychologist.

"I had flirted with the idea from time to time months before, but it was never anything serious," said Abell. But when she began making phone calls, the universe showed her it was serious about the idea. She called a station, KCOL, and found out that, serendipitously, a spot had just opened up for a new program.

"I went in and pitched my idea for a show for women that would explore our entire natures, spiritually to emotionally. I wanted a show for women because I felt a real dearth of programming for women in our community. I really wanted to come home to my strong passion for working with women, exploring how to make our lives better in the world. The station managers said, 'This sounds good.'"

Abell was amazed. She also was amazed that the show quickly garnered a lot of interest. Pretty soon, women—high-profile women—were calling her to get themselves booked as guests on the show.

"I was very surprised at the momentum that all of a sudden just seemed to happen around me. I thought, 'This feels right because it feels divine, without feeling hard.' Some of the most prominent women in the country and popular from their own work agreed to come on my show, like Suzie Orman and Joan Borysenko. I was like, 'Wow, how great!'"

The moment she went on the air, people gave her feedback that she sounded so comfortable, natural, like a duck to water. Abell remembers it all being "great fun."[13]

PLAYING WITH OUR HEARTS' DESIRES

Whenever you need to keep your heart aligned with your true purpose and desires, even in the midst of your terror, feel the potential for "great fun." We don't do a good job in our culture of embracing the energies of delight and play, and we need to know that doing so is often our highest radical act of love for ourselves.

When you are thinking about, musing on, or following your dream, tuck the following poem into your thoughts. It's offered by heart visionary, corporate ombudsman, poet, and artist Kenny Moore for a sense of heart solidarity with all the people everywhere who are also facing their greatest fears to live their highest dreams.

The Mystery of the Calling

To stand in front of the emptiness week after week.
A desire to create.
A call to sharing.
The tingle of uncertainty is ever present.
The fear of failure looms in an intestinal knot.
The prospect of success bodes even more fearsome.
Why go through the exercise?
Why put pen to ink?
What meanings has the colored brush for the virgin page?
It is the desire to bring forth.
The small belief that I have something new to offer.
The charisma from the gods bestowed with purpose.
The blood flows through my veins unawares.
The synapses pop, making connections unheard of.
The heart sustains a calling larger than myself.
The discomfort can be endured.
The uncertainty can be passed beyond.
What remains is the mystery of the calling.

II

Heart Activism:
Reinventing Institutions with Love

ONE OF THE WISEST, most prophetic voices we have on the need for compassion is, of course, the Dalai Lama. In a world torn apart by divisiveness, eye-for-an-eye vengeance, and religious bigotry, he has forever been urging us to turn the other cheek and practice compassion as "the universal religion." Over and over, as in *Transforming the Mind,* he stresses like a mantra: "My religion is kindness."

His voice is so fiercely prophetic now because he sees clearly that the future of humanity depends on each of us developing our own warm hearts. And, today, we suffer because, as the Dalai Lama says, "It seems as if there is no particular institution that has special responsibility for taking care of the heart."

DEVELOPING THE WARM HEART

Modern education, for instance, while "very good" seems to be focused on solely developing the brain, that is, on intellectual education. "Insufficient attention is given to the development of the person as a whole, in the sense of becoming a good person or developing a warm heart," points out the Dalai Lama in *Transforming the Mind.*

This has to be a grassroots, seed-where-you-are kind of movement. Each of us has to be willing to be a full-fledged, outspoken advocate for shaping our institutions into organizations and gatherings that take care of and nurture our hearts. If they don't already do that, we have to lead them. We can't wait for someone else to do something. We've waited too long as it is. We each have to seed this new radical acts of love movement.

Daunting? Yes. Impossible? Not at all. Upon reading many of the stories in this book so far, you might have found yourself incredulous, saying, "I could never do that. I'm not that powerful." And you might have listed all the other things you lack that prevent you from becoming a heart activist in the truest, hugest sense. You may feel you don't have the spiritual strength, the physical stamina, or the emotional balance, skills, confidence, contacts, hours in the day, and so on to really live out of your heart.

When we start to doubt the breadth and scope of our hearts, this is when we have to avoid our rational minds. By the time you even begin to consider going into your heart, you are already no longer the same person you were before. You have already remade yourself with greater creativity, stamina, soul, and power than before.

If you've done even some of the heart work shared in this book, for instance, you've already so opened yourself up to the power of Spirit—the Divine, God, however you wish to describe the power of the universe—that you are now an immutable force. You are already someone who can accomplish feats you could never have before. Compassion and any true work of the heart allow us to move outside ourselves, beyond the confines of our physical beings, and tap into something both of and greater than ourselves.

Many people, even her detractors, saw this in Princess Diana's life as she immersed herself in compassionate gestures. *Daily Telegraph* columnist Bill Deedes was critical of Diana until he went along on one of her trips to South Africa to heighten global awareness of the suffering caused by land mines. On that mission to Angola, "I formed the impression that if she is given the right mission she almost moves out of herself and becomes a different person altogether," Deedes said.[1]

LOVING PURPOSE ENERGIZES

The right mission—whatever most calls to our hearts—transforms us and fills us with such divine energy that we are capable of things we once only dreamed of. Love is such an uplifting force that we can become heart activists who surmount our fears, our physical fatigue, and our own crippling self-doubts. Nothing is as daunting to overcome as our own doubts.

If you keep telling yourself that you don't "have what it takes" to live out of your heart, start telling yourself a different story. It's true that running around doing volunteering marathons when your heart is never in them to begin with is depleting, draining, dispiriting. You do feel incompetent, to a degree. But true compassion, doing something that feeds you so much you can't possibly imagine ever giving up, is the consummate "antidote to burnout," said Swanee Hunt in our interview.

"The work some of us do, by nature, is overwhelming. Some of us say we won't tolerate suffering in the world and will deal with the problems that affect billions of people," said Hunt, a humanitarian and former ambassador to Austria, who helped broker discussions for peace in Kosovo. Hunt does the jobs that many people say can't be done.

Drawing from innate compassion, that wellspring available to us all, allows her to be the catalyst for change that is causing epic shifts in our world. "What feeds me and keeps me there, doing the jobs many people say can't be done, are the highly personal moments with individuals where I spend a wildly disproportionate amount of time just listening. That's all I do.

"Meeting with a local woman. Holding her hand as she talks, looking into her eyes, not offering any solutions. I get an energy from that. It feeds me so I can go another three months working on policies to affect hundreds of thousands of refugees."

Hunt has reflected on that "energy" we get when we are doing the works of full-blown heart activists. She suspects it comes from those "tremendously powerful" places in our psyches that compassion blows wide open, as healing counterparts to the bombs that split open the Bosnian countryside during the war.

TAPPING THE SOURCE OF OUR STRENGTH

"There are places in our psyche, compartments we don't consciously tap in to, that are tremendously motivating," Hunt told me. "My hunch is that when we are compassionate, we go to a different part of our psyche. When I spend forty-five minutes with a refugee, she becomes a mirror that opens someplace inside of me, and it's a place where I have felt wounded, lost, displaced. It's a place where I have felt bereft."

When that vulnerable, empathetic place in our psyches is illuminated—

if we don't slam it shut and keep "chugging along like a big locomotive, producing, producing, producing"—then we find our greatest source of strength and true power, Hunt said. "I'm talking about a very different moment when all I am doing is connecting with a person. There is a huge power here. Jung would call it the 'collective unconscious.'

"There are lots of theories to try to explain this connection, but compassion unlocks that place in the psyche. We are like a tree in a sense, and the compassion is the roots that seed the structure. If you don't have the root system, then over time, with enough erosion, a windstorm will come along and knock the giant tree to the ground," explained Hunt.

Heart activists know their roots come from something both of and greater than themselves. They know we aren't given the big dream without the Big Help. They know a seemingly infinite force flows through them; grounding, strengthening, and uplifting; transcending their obstacles in ways they couldn't possibly do alone. It's as if when we signal to God that we are willing to take our hearts to the streets, we are met at the intersection and nudged, steered, and sometimes shoved and dragged along the most infinitely amazing routes.

And it's often when we are still seeking the entrance to our path, stumbling and lost, that we most are surrounded with help, I'm convinced. Helen Keller once described this beautifully: "Have you ever been at sea in a dense fog, when it seemed as if a tangible white darkness shut you in and the great ship, tense and anxious, groped her way toward the shore with plummet and sounding-line and you waited with beating heart for something to happen? I was like that ship before my education began, only I was without compass or sounding-line, and no way of knowing how near the harbor was. 'Light! Light!' was the wordless cry of my soul, and the light of love shone on me in that very hour."[2]

CALLING ON SPIRITUAL SUPPORT

If we seek it, if we cry out in the dark for it, if we ask, we will receive more spiritual help than we could possibly imagine, as I wrote in *Embracing Our Essence: Spiritual Conversations with Prominent Women*. The book features the spiritual discoveries, epiphanies, and struggles of twenty-nine high-profile heart activists, such as Jane Goodall, Elisabeth Kübler-Ross, and Joan Borysenko. Their songs were different, but the lyrics were the same. They all said that "from the moment we arrive on earth, we are enfolded, literally bathed in the support of a Higher Power, angels, spiritual guides, and more love and light than we could ever imagine. All we have to do is ask. . . . We are not powerless. Far from it. We are filled with an immense power for beauty and goodness."

All we have to do is ask, and the pathway is paved. Again, we aren't given the big dream without the infinite help. When Dr. Gregory Plotnikoff dreamed of a healing center at the University of Minnesota Medical School that would treat patients and train medical students in an interdisciplinary, humane, spiritual way, he wasn't sure how his dream would be perceived.

In the summer of 1996, Dr. Plotnikoff and University of Minnesota colleague Mary Jo Kreitzer proposed the idea to the vice president for health sciences. They didn't know how the meeting would unfold. "We said, among other things, that we wanted to look at culture, faith, and health care. What does it mean, for instance, to be a Buddhist from southeast Asia as a patient in a Minnesota hospital? We said we wanted to see interdisciplinary teams of doctors, nurses, social workers, and public health workers in the same room with patients. We said we wanted to look at complementary healing practices," Dr. Plotnikoff recalled.

They waited for the vice president's response, and then the golden words slipped from his mouth: "I was hoping someone would come up with a proposal like this." And he didn't stop there. He went on to say, "We need a vision, a statement of how this fits with the mission of the university." He then sent out an e-mail to almost fifteen thousand people at the university announcing the creation of the new Center for Spirituality and Healing and asking that a task force for the project be formed.

BIG DREAMS COME WITH BIG HELP

We aren't given the huge dreams without the huge assistance. We just need to stop being afraid to ask for what we want. We can't just care about how patients are treated, how children are educated, how businesses conduct themselves, how well we treat the environment. Plain sympathy and concern aren't enough. They must be coupled with concrete, grassroots, sweeping heart activism if the flame is to blaze and not be dimmed by fear and hatred. We have to become on fire with that inner fire, both in our hearts and minds—and in our actions.

We have to commit radical acts of love, even when those radical acts involve dissent from the often-brutal status quo we see around us. About 12 million children live in poverty in the United States, and 11.9 million kids have no health insurance. In 1998, 3,761 children and teens in the United States lost their lives from gun violence, according to the Children's Defense Fund. "If we do not speak, lobby, write, picket, protest, and vote for these children, who will?" asks Marian Wright Edelman, defense fund director.[3]

There is much to take us from simple caring to radical action. If we but believe we can make a difference. If we only know with all our hearts that we have a huge stake in restoring the love we need to thrive. It's time to be outspoken, lovingly and purposefully strident. It's time to demand that the status quo be overturned by compassionate, radical acts of love.

Robert Kennedy expressed this eloquently in the 1960s:

> It is not enough to allow dissent. We must demand it. For there is much to dissent from.
>
> We dissent from the fact that millions are trapped in poverty while the nation grows rich.
>
> We dissent from the conditions and hatred which deny a full life to our fellow citizens because of the color of their skin.
>
> We dissent from the monstrous absurdity of a world where nations stand poised to destroy one another, and men must kill their fellow men . . .
>
> We dissent from the willful, heedless destruction of natural pleasure and beauty.
>
> We dissent from all those structures—of technology and of society itself—which strip from the individual the dignity and warmth of sharing in the common tasks of his community and his country.[4]

What are you ready to dissent from? Where are you no longer willing to be sidelined? What do you care so deeply about that you have to take a stand? For what are you willing to call on and activate all your spiritual force and assistance? Your angels are ready to galvanize all their collective strength for the glorious cause of bringing heaven to earth. You just have to ask.

Corinne McLaughlin and Gordon Davidson, who work to reinfuse politics with greater passion and spirit, say we can all "reclaim our power as a people by aligning ourselves with this Divine Purpose as a catalyzing fire within our hearts and within the heart of the body politic." McLaughlin and Davidson also concur that in their work, "We have found an immense amount of help is available from spiritual dimensions if we but ask for it."[5]

The people in this book confirm over and over the same timeless story: Just when they went, even tentatively, out on a limb, just when they decided to walk, or even just look, into the fire, against all odds, miraculous things happened to kindle the fire. Just when they began to dream the dream come true, magic unfolded.

Mariah Mannia had a dream based largely on her own hard-won battle with depression. When she was nineteen, a doctor told her that she had a "brain disorder" and that medication was her only hope. "I was devastated when after three years, I discovered that medication was not a way out but rather a pathway to another kind of imbalance for me," said Mannia. "I sank deeper and deeper into despair until one day I realized that I was going to have to be the one to heal myself. No doctor, no medication was ever going to make me well. I had to do it."

So Mannia sought out alternative healing approaches, including nutrition, exercise, spiritual practices, emotional release work, and other steps. After a few years, she began to better handle her depression when it reappeared, and she experienced times of remission and wellness. And this is when a vision came to her. "In September 1997, I was awakened early one morning by a vision. It was not a dream, but a vision that was so powerful it demanded to be written down. What came to me was the image of a community that provided a holistic treatment approach for depression and surrounded people with a supportive environment in which to heal."

GETTING CLEAR ON THE VISION

In Mannia's vision, she saw a network of professionals offering services for depression and a peer network for those experiencing it. She saw a resource library and monthly workshops that would offer information and solutions. She envisioned weekly support groups that focused on creating wellness rather than merely treating symptoms.

Mannia, who has a background in finance, administration, and social services, said she didn't know the first thing about how to bring her vision into reality. "But it was clear to me that I was being asked to do just that. Amid the fear of the unknown, I said a simple yes, and that's when the miracles began to occur."

A few months later, through her life partner, Mannia met a kind and gentle man. She had lunch with him one day, and he asked her about her aspirations. He listened politely as she re-created her vision for him.

"What happened next has awed me every day since. He turned to me in such a casual manner and asked to see a simple plan of this vision because he said he was interested in funding it. My heart skipped a beat as I slowly realized what he was offering," she recalled.

Mannia went home and drafted a plan; then she brought it back to the man. He immediately gave her a check for ten thousand dollars.

Mannia continued, "That was three years ago, and since then, this angel has continued to support the Depression Wellness Network with thousands of dollars. In turn, in the first eighteen months of offering services, the network has supported more than one thousand people."

Mannia said it's not just the financial support that she finds so phenomenal. It's the way her benefactor gives support, trusting that her vision will help those struggling with the darkness to find their way to light. "And that trust in me, more than anything else, has helped me take huge leaps in my own healing journey, which has not been without its challenges. It's when we begin to listen to our heart and allow it to guide us to the work that we are here to do that we often are forced to face the demons of unworthiness, self-doubt, and lack of faith. But it has been one of the most miraculous paths I have ever traveled and I give thanks for this angel's act of kindness and mercy every day of my life.

"When we get intentional and deliberate in our dreaming, support and guidance can start flowing to and through us in amazing ways," believes Mannia.

UPLIFTED BY SPIRIT

And many people, like full-blown heart activist Peggy Marengo, believe that this divine flow is what gives us the strength, vision, and sheer stamina we need at 2 A.M. if we are going to birth this new world. When all is said and done, the power of Spirit coursing through our veins is often the only force that allows us to rock the baby when we are beyond exhaustion, to make the phone call to our senator when we just want to sink mindlessly into another *Friends* episode, to speak out at a meeting when we really want to stay meek and mute.

Marengo told me that people often look at her children and ask, "How do you do this? How do you get up and do this every day?" Marengo and her partner, Alison Smith, have adopted ten children with physical and emotional challenges. They've also parented six biological children.

When Marengo was still recovering from colon cancer, they adopted a baby girl—the nation's first adoption of a baby who was HIV-positive. The baby, Luci, is Elisabeth Kübler-Ross's godchild.

Marengo said, "When people ask me how I do this, I say, 'This is not my energy. I know what my energy level is, and this is not my energy.' This is coming from the force, or whatever you believe your spiritual energy comes from, and the more we immersed ourselves in Luci, the more it came, the more there was to go around.

"And that sounds like a cliché, but it is really, really true. It still is seventeen years later. This I truly believe: If I stopped doing the work we do, we would cease to be who we are and who we became. But we choose to do this, and we are who we are, which brings energy, which allows us to do more."[6]

That's huge—HUGE! as Oprah Winfrey loves to say on her show. Know, too, that your heart path may not be adopting special children. It may not be sparking a peace movement. It may not be radio work. It's usually something right in front of you that won't let your heart go, that keeps whispering to you at night, and that appears on every street corner or magazine you read or through every person you talk to.

FINDING OUR CALLING

What does your heart feel drawn to love, adore, even unconditionally? What keeps reappearing in your thoughts, dreams, encounters, and intuitive flashes like a rhythmic pattern sent directly from the beat of your own heart? What just won't let you go? And you feel that if you don't do something about it, if you don't respond, you will explode with frustration—or sink into despair?

Think of the great Gnostic quote: "If you bring forth what is within you, what is within you can save you. If you fail to bring forth what is within you, what is within you can destroy you."[7]

What calls you with such force that you can no longer ignore it or it will totally call into question who you are and everything you believe in? What do you have to make a stand for without wavering, no matter the costs? Again, it may be right in your own backyard. Your radical act of love may be delivered right to your doorstep, as Mildred Lee, who was introduced in chapter 6, found.

Lee, sixty-seven, was honored in 1999 as one of the first "Spirit of Women" recipients by *Prevention* magazine. She got that distinction because she followed her anger. Remember Matthew Fox's call, "Follow your anger, it will take you to what you love"? Lee became "angry, totally angry" in 1990 because drug dealers started taking over her neighborhood. Whenever she came home after a long day at work, she saw people selling drugs right in front of her house and at the intersection nearby.

"I live right on the corner of a busy thoroughfare, and these guys had come and set up shop in my whole block. They even had the street blocked off where I had to go into my driveway. I'd see them selling the drugs from their trunks. I'd see the money exchanged."

Lee found out the drug dealers had befriended several women from several homes in the neighborhood, which gave them an "in" to the area. Never doubt the power of your actions, even the misguided ones. Many of the residents weren't speaking out because they were afraid, Lee concluded.

"I wasn't afraid. I was never afraid," she said. "What were they going to do, kill me? I was so angry because I knew they didn't belong here. I was tired of looking at them twenty-four hours a day. I knew that eventually there would be violence; it was just a matter of time."

Lee was so angry and tired that she told a friend, the Reverend Williams, that she'd decided to move out of the home she'd lived in since 1981. But he said, "Don't let those punks run you out of your own neighborhood. I will help you. I had the same problem in my neighborhood, and we ran them out."

So Lee decided to stay and fight back. She tried to mobilize her neighbors, but very few really wanted to get involved. "I told them, 'You are already involved because these people are selling drugs in your neighborhood,'" she said. She talked with the police, and they told her if she could muster support, they would hold a meeting with city, state, and federal law enforcement officials.

But Lee could still get only five neighbors to come. She described the experience: "I suppose my neighbors were afraid. I was never really afraid because when my husband died, I had four children; the youngest was six and the oldest was about fourteen or fifteen. And I had to do things. I kept getting pushed around because I was a woman. When I felt taken advantage of, I learned to say, 'You won't do this to me.'"

The combination of having to raise her children as a single parent and her religious faith brought her courage to restore her neighborhood. When she couldn't rally many of her neighbors, Lee called in the family troops, coaxing relatives who didn't live in the neighborhood to come anyway to swell the audience.

There were more law enforcement officials than citizens at the meeting, but it was enough. "They told us they knew we had a drug problem in our neighborhood, but were just waiting for the residents to come forward," she said. "And we were the first to come forward. The police guaranteed us we would see a difference in thirty days. From then on, things accelerated. More community meetings were held, and the mayor's office, some churches, and the group Mad Dads also got involved."

On the flip side, several of the drug dealers also attempted to intimidate Lee. One morning she was in the street picking up debris, often fast-food and other containers tossed in the street by the dealers. "We homeowners still wanted to keep our neighborhood nice and neat, and someone has to have the initiative to clean it up," she explained. One of the dealers came by on his bicycle. "As he got close to me he started going really fast, and I just looked him in the eye. And he came back and did it again. I guess it was to frighten me, but he didn't," Lee recalled.

This is one formidable woman. Another day when Lee was working in her garden, the same dealer drove his car by and accelerated as he got near her, spitting rocks around her. "It's got to be something really terrible to make me afraid," Lee said.

Finally, those reclaiming their neighborhood decided to act on the

mayor's suggestion that they hold a parade—a very unusual parade. Lee explained, "We put a couple of caskets on the truck bed and made signs and closed off the streets in the immediate area so we could march. Several hundred people marched with us.

"We stopped in front of the known drug houses in the area with the truck carrying caskets. We held signs, chanting 'Down with dope, up with hope' and things like that."

Afterward, a police officer in a vehicle parked right across the street from Lee's house for thirty days. Not long after, on a Wednesday night, Lee came home from work to find people surrounding her street again. She thought, "I am just so tired of these people. Now I don't know what to do." Lee saw a van parked on the side street along her house and concluded it was yet another drug-dealing enterprise right under her nose.

"I went outside to turn on my water hose to water my yard, and I thought, 'I'm going to turn on my hose as fast as I can and wet these cars all down,'" she recalled.

As she turned to spray her interlopers, a man came across the street and said, "Lady, I am a police officer. The van over there is full of FBI agents." She replied, "That's wonderful because I was getting ready to wet up some FBI agents." Lee continued, "That night, through their sting operation, they arrested about forty people coming up right outside my door to buy drugs. Two nights later they arrested a bunch more and caught almost one hundred people in a two-day period."

Immediately after the sting operation, Mildred Lee's neighborhood was restored. The drug dealing was gone. Their Fairfax Neighborhood Association continues to meet and continues to attract and magnify goodwill. Because of their grassroots efforts, the city of Omaha was awarded $6 million in federal community improvement grants.

THE DIFFERENCE ONE PERSON MAKES

Mildred Lee is now retired from her job with the Nebraska Job Service, but she's working harder than ever before. She's helping elderly people receive home-improvement grants for roofing, furnaces, and other projects. Under her direction, a vacant lot once slated to become a dumping site is now a neighborhood garden, and several state agencies have created the Safe

Haven Program, an after-school project that matches latchkey children with senior citizens.

Lee's guiding philosophy? "Someone has to do it. If you want to make your community or your life better, then you have to take a stand."

You have to "be willing to stand inside yourself and say, 'This is who I am' and not back down from it," says Oprah Winfrey.[8]

Where do you yearn to make a stand in your life? What needs your voice for compassion, for radical change? In your heart of hearts, what are your deepest beliefs? Could they be channeled to spark grassroots change in your neighborhood, community, organization, or cultural institutions?

What has kept you from channeling your passion? What obstacle is holding you back? What do you fear will happen if you stand in your truth? Now, ask yourself, Will that really be that terrible? What could really be more difficult than living an unauthentic life in which your deepest beliefs lie dormant?

Philosopher Parker Palmer studied the lives of people like Rosa Parks and Nelson Mandela who have followed their hearts, despite all the fallout. "These people," Palmer writes, "have understood that no punishment could be worse than the one we inflict on ourselves by living a divided life." By choosing to "stop acting differently on the outside from what they knew to be true inside," Rosa Parks, Nelson Mandela, Gandhi, and so many other heart activists lay down a path we can trace with our own compassion as a compass.[9]

Often, as we've explored, many of us have no problem with living from our hearts—except when we hit the workplace floor. Then we are embarrassed, chastised, afraid, and hesitant to show appropriate affection and compassion. That's why some of the most radical heart activists are found now in the workplace. That's often the toughest bastion for sanctioned compassion. But when someone leads the way, as is often the case with visionary ideas, others follow suit.

STARTING RIGHT WHERE YOU ARE

Ardath Rodale, who has transformed her workplace with compassion, often hosts visitors from companies and organizations situated around the world. Her intention to make her company, Rodale, a compassionate workplace attracts like-hearted people who want to see how it's done.

Often it's done by changing the outward appearance of your corporate structure so it mirrors your heartfelt intentions, Rodale shows them. Her company has long signaled its intention for a more humane world by publishing magazines and books that promote holistic lifestyles and environmentalism. But Rodale wasn't content with stopping there.

She wanted to foster a corporate culture where the heart, souls, and passions of her employees were nurtured. She began by making sure all offices were soulfully beautiful. The buildings were surrounded by land so people could walk outside and be still as they walked among the trees. She decorated the walls with art and photography.

If her employees were wrestling with a new challenge or project, she sometimes encouraged them to go into the mountains or to a natural setting where their minds and souls could find greater clarity. She made herself emotionally available to her employees. She was willing to share their thoughts or burdens. She wasn't afraid to hug them, even if other executives frowned at her display of affection in the workplace.

Rodale created quiet rooms where employees could go to be still, meditate, pray, or reflect. She created yoga and massage classes and brought in motivational and inspirational speakers to discuss bringing your passion and inner fire to work.

All of Rodale's efforts, from the art-covered walls to the creativity retreats, reaped fabulous effects. But, still, something was missing. Deep in her heart, she heard the message that there was still more to do to nurture the heart of her company.

BOTTOM LINE BEYOND MONEY

"What we have lost in the age of technology and are now trying to regain is the value of the human spirit in our life and work," said Rodale. "People today have an increased longing for spiritual need, but we so often go after it with literal hardware instead of with sensitivity of the heart. We need to touch—to feel, to care, to love, to hug, to cry—to be aware how our actions affect others. The bottom line is beyond financial survival."

What more could she do to foster a company where each employee is viewed as sacred? she wondered. And then one day the answer came in the form of a contractor. The company was uniting its entire book division in one building and during the architectural discussions, Rodale realized what she wanted: "Because the building will be so large, I want the center to have a heart. We will have a kiva as its center, to symbolize the heart of our organization."

"A what?" they asked, incredulous. "A spiritual, sacred center," she replied.

When they began to design the kiva, the contractors envisioned a well-lit room. "No, no, " Rodale said. "The light will come only from a skylight in the center of the room."

So the design for the kiva unfolded. And when it was built, a shaft of light fell on a concrete birdbath made years ago by David Rodale. In its center, Rodale placed a large crystal to catch the light beams from above. On the first day that she entered the hushed room—the sacred kiva at the heart of her company—Rodale was stunned. Employees had already laid offerings on the birdbath, from coins to poems.

Many come now to the kiva just to sit and be still. Once Rodale walked past and heard beautiful guitar music floating from within.

One day, one of Rodale's employees, Cindy, asked if she could be married in the kiva. And so she was one candlelit night as her friends, family— and Rodale family members—gathered.

As Rodale watched the couple light a candle together, she realized she had found her answer. And she will find more in the future. But for now, this kiva makes her workplace a more heartfelt place.[10]

BRINGING JOY TO OTHERS

How open is the heart of your organization? Do you sense that many people long to make it even richer? How could you become a heart activist right where you are to rekindle a sense of passion and joy within your workplace?

That is what brought Kenny Moore, an executive at KeySpan Energy, into the heart activist role, as he works to light fires in organizations. As he does so, he's rapidly being recognized as a visionary in the spirit-at-work movement. "To go forward successfully, we need to go back," Moore believes. "Companies had their origins as places of passion and shared community. Rekindling that initial spark and creating the environment for it to burn brightly is the responsibility of leadership. It's as much an interior work as an exterior work. Daunting . . . yes; optional . . . no."

Moore is a prime example that there may never be a convenient, perfect, under-our-control moment in time to step into the role of a compassionate leader. He knows more intimately than most that we often serve best when we serve from a wounded heart. Scholar Joseph Campbell once said there are two ways to gain wisdom. One, to be zapped with instant insight. Two, through suffering. It was through a measure of both that Kenny Moore deepened his innate compassion that now transforms the heart of KeySpan Energy.

As was mentioned in chapter 5, long before Moore joined the corporate world, he spent fifteen years in a monastery as a Catholic priest. He eventually left, went back to New York where he was raised, and decided to look for a job. He assumed he'd have to leave his old, spiritual life behind to fit into business.

He was fortunate to meet an Irish Catholic executive with the former Brooklyn Union Gas Co. who hired Moore because of his background, not in spite of it. "I spent the first few years being Joe Corporate," Moore said in our interview. "I designed and implemented the company's first performance appraisal program. And I met the woman who would eventually be my wife."

Life seemed to be golden, and then the glow flickered. Moore was diagnosed with what doctors said was incurable non-Hodgkin's lymphoma in its most advanced stages. "I went into shock and depression. I had just started dating this woman. But it turned out that her uncle just happened to work at the National Institutes of Health doing experimental cancer research and treatment."

When he informed his company that he'd be gone at least a year—if he survived—they told him to do what he had to do; they would cover for him. "That was a testament to this company," said Moore.

But Moore wasn't given much hope. He was told that he might catch leukemia from the treatment. His doctors told him, "Even if you survive, never expect to have children."

Moore not only survived, also he and Cynthia were married—and now have two boys. And since returning to his job, he's carried his "near-death experience" in his heart, knowing that the wounds in him can now better heal the woundedness of people he works with.

"When I went back to work, it was now even more clear to me that I could be dead tomorrow. There was no way then that I was interested in climbing the corporate ladder," explained Moore. But once he stepped down from the rungs, it was as if somehow he ascended within his organization without making a step.

Even though he didn't have a business degree but a master's degree in theology, he was trusted by senior management to implement incentive plans, oversee cost measures, and crystal-ball some long-term projections for the company. "And other odd things began to happen too," recalled Moore. "When I was meeting with people, they began to close their door and say, 'Kenny, I want to talk with you in confidence,' and they would share things."

RADICAL CHANGE BEGINS WITHIN

Kenny Moore realized that many people in the company were very knowledgeable, but no one, including management, ever asked for or listened to their wisdom. "Listening without a rejoinder or judgment or correction— this is so powerful, but nobody does it," Moore told me.

In 1997, when Brooklyn Union was merging with KeySpan Energy, Moore knew many employees were feeling the loss of a one-hundred-year company tradition. He knew some people were feeling angry, disoriented, and confused—and that these reactions were appropriate and normal. But people needed to know they were normal responses to the change.

So Moore gathered about fifty managers together to air their feelings about the merger with the company president, Craig Matthews. As they revealed their concerns, suggestions, fears, and excitement, the company's in-house illustrator captured their feelings in drawings. One drawing was a large banner that said, "We're Not in Kansas Anymore."

Matthews listened to their feelings and thanked them for their honesty and openness. He expressed his regret that rumors and speculation were causing unnecessary anxiety. He assured the employees that the company would retain the best of both cultures in its merger.

Employees' hearts were touched by this exchange. One employee,

Frank, later wrote a thank-you note to Matthews in which he said, "It was your willingness to share in our collective fear and pain that I found so rewarding." He went on to conclude, "You expressed your empathy and compassion for us, yourself, and the larger Brooklyn Union community. Most of all, you were willing to listen to the many thoughts of the group, even those that had to be troublesome to hear."

Most mergers fail, Moore concluded, because companies ignore the hearts and minds of their employees. Brooklyn Union's management team bucked this trend by opening to all the employees' thoughts, ideas, solutions, and wisdom surrounding the merger.

Several years later, Moore was told that he would be promoted. He was overjoyed. "Is this because I'm such a good manager or trainer?" he asked.

"Actually, no," he was told. "You're not that good."

What Moore's management found attractive about him was that he listened to people. He actually cared about the employees, and they trusted him, and his common sense was sound. Moore explained, "They said, 'You know we're going through some rapid change now, so all our executives are going away to conferences and listening to Stephen Covey and Peter Block and all these guys talking about a model of leadership in which management engages the hands and hearts of their employees. And our managers, our engineers, and accountants are coming back and saying, 'These guys sound like Kenny Moore.'"

So they wanted Moore to be corporate ombudsman. He was horrified. "I didn't want that position," he recalled. "I was embarrassed. I didn't think it would help my career. I thought I was dead in the water. It turned out I was devaluing those human skills. I was the last to see it. I didn't understand how rare they are."

But Moore accepted the position as KeySpan's corporate ombudsman, and the organization transformed into one of even more heart than before. He remains in awe of how the company's top leadership is so openly candid and visible in their support of him and his contributions to the company.

"I was with our chairman, Robert Catell, at a Mets game at Shea Stadium last month because we were asked to throw the first pitch out. Now, I have no interest in baseball; I'm a poet. I said, 'Could I read a poem instead?' They said, 'Don't embarrass yourself. Just throw the ball out.' So here we are, on the field with 50,000 people watching, being introduced to the chief marketing officer of the Mets. And our chairman turns to him and says, 'This is Kenny Moore. He left the priesthood because we need him more. He is staying close to our employees and fostering the soul of our organization.'"

Moore's doctors have told him he's in remission and has a 90 percent change of being cancer free. Moore knows, too, that the future is uncertain—for everyone. "Aren't we all temporary employees?" he says.

UNLEASHING THE HEART

Wise, wise, heart-wise man. What holds you back from being a Kenny Moore right where you are, whether it's a convenience store or a medical clinic? Are you afraid your plate is already full? Are you so busy with the business of making a paycheck that you aren't making a living? Are you afraid, as happened to so many people in the sixties, that you will get burnt out, exhausted, sick, disillusioned?

Many of those you've met in this book will tell you that just the opposite happens when you follow your heart. That when you make the commitment to become a heart activist, it's as if you step onto a plane and into a place where greater energy flows through you. And when we are "in flow," say authors Charlene Belitz and Meg Lundstrom, "occurrences line up, events fall into place, and obstacles melt away. Rather than life being a meaningless struggle, it is permeated with a deep sense of purposefulness and order."

As Belitz and Lundstrom describe in their book *The Power of Flow*, following your heart, stepping into the flow, makes us feel "connected to something larger and greater than ourselves. Life is rich with meaning, magic, and purpose. We feel vital, alive, joyful."

And then come those magical moments of synchronicity, "the meaningful coincidences in which outside events, seemingly disconnected in time and space, link up with our internal state and connect us with the greater whole."

Things just fall into place, as they appear meant to be. Even as others scoff or question your sanity, the seemingly impossible is laid in your lap. When you combine your spiritual intention with your heart's intention, it becomes almost like following a prescription, Robin Casarjian, director of the Lionheart Foundation, told me when we spoke.

"I've not struggled with what I should be doing next. I'm just along for the ride," she laughed. "It's that simple. The bus picks me up, it opens the door, I get on, when the bus stops again and the door opens, I get off. My fundamental calling is teaching forgiveness and a path along the road to teaching forgiveness is the whole emotional literacy curriculum in prison."

Each week, said Casarjian, two thousand more people are imprisoned. Does this pierce our hearts even slightly? Does our compassion extend to this population? Is it a measure of our society's unconditional love that we do little or nothing to rehabilitate and heal our prisoners? As mentioned in a previous chapter, eight years ago, Casarjian decided she had to give her heart to this incredibly controversial and tough issue.

SEEING WITH LOVE SPARKS MAGIC

Because she had written a book on forgiveness, Casarjian was invited to speak at a prison. She thought to herself, "What better place is there to process the idea of forgiveness—to see the light instead of the lampshade over someone? What better place to be with people seen only as criminals and instead see them as spiritual beings with the capacity to love and to heal?"

But when only eight men showed up for her talk, her idealism faltered. "Oh, this is terrific—the beginning and the end of my prison career," Casarjian thought.

Then she was invited to speak at another Massachusetts prison. When Casarjian arrived, she was amazed to see more than one hundred prisoners waiting for her. They listened in a thoughtful way. And she sensed their profound hunger to make meaning out of their lives.

Casarjian concentrated on seeing those one hundred men as human beings with the capacity to love. She didn't deny they must have done something horribly wrong. But she went in with an open heart. As she did, she sensed the prisoners' whole beings change. They intuitively received her unspoken message of compassion. They knew she saw something valuable in them that even they themselves couldn't see.

She said to the inmates, "Every human being has a core fundamental goodness. One of the best ways you can use your time here is to get to know who you really are. To really experience the peace, dignity, and positive potential of your own true nature."

As the prisoners leaned forward, it was so quiet you could hear their breath rise and fall. No one had ever addressed them like this before. Casarjian went on, "I know you can make a huge difference in the world if you align with who you really are. But because of life and your own personal history—maybe you were abused as a child—you have gotten separated from your inner goodness.

"The work you must now do is the nature of evolving. It is the nature of being a human being. You have to begin to align with that core part of yourselves so you can truly know what it is to be a peaceful and powerful person in the world."

FEELING ACCEPTANCE AND SUPPORT

And Casarjian saw the prisoners visibly moved by her message. Tears filled their eyes. They sighed with a deep sense of relief, even joy. Casarjian saw them yearn to know themselves as more loving and peaceful human beings. But she also saw the profound level of grief and despair among the prisoners.

Once she met with a group who had life sentences, and every time they gathered, the prisoners would be in tears. "Their grief was not just about being in prison, but the grief of a lifetime, of never having had a childhood, never having grieved the abuse they experienced, never having grieved the loss of a parent," explained Casarjian.

So she began to provide a safe space where they could begin the grieving process. As the prisoners began to grow and heal, emotionally and spiritually, Casarjian also felt something stirring within her. She realized that prison work was a calling. She felt a tremendous degree of aliveness every time she was there.

Well, four years went by, and Casarjian was still loving her work—but it was still done on a volunteer basis. She stepped back, and said, "Okay this is good. But I'm not reaching enough people." And then it dawned on her that maybe she needed to write another book to spread her work to other prisons.

But Casarjian wasn't willing to do that unless she could raise enough money to give her book away. It had to be free, so it could spread quickly on a grassroots level.

And so she started the Lionheart Foundation, which became known as the National Emotional Literacy Project for Prisoners. From the very beginning, grace surrounded the project. Once, Casarjian had very little money to keep the project alive, and she prayed, "'God, I've put all this energy into this effort. I can't start this book without $50,000'—that was just the amount that came to mind—to at least get the book done and go to press."

ATTRACTING FINANCIAL SUPPORT

That summer Casarjian was staying with a friend, and without any discussion of Casarjian's financial situation, her friend said one day, "I'm giving you $50,000."

Another time, another friend and board member, Joan Borysenko, put out an appeal for Lionheart in her newsletter. Soon after, a woman called and said, "Can you tell me more about your foundation?" Casarjian talked with the woman for about fifteen minutes and then forgot about the call. Not long after, a stock management company called and said they wanted to transfer some money from the woman.

The transfer was worth $96,000—enough for Casarjian to print her book, mail it, and pay her staff salaries. The book, *Houses of Healing: A Prisoner's Guide to Inner Power and Freedom*, now has a long waiting list in every prison it reaches.

The foundation has given away 50,000 books, and the program is being taught in 2,500 institutions. "One county jail purchased over 1,600 books for each of their prisoners as a holiday present. The human resources staff at the prison said they wanted to do something meaningful for the prisoners," Casarjian told me.

Through her program, Casarjian sees prisoners going from despair to a place of hope and growth. She watches them advance from acting out in rage to finding a more peaceful place. Prisoners stop fighting and, for the first time, work to become good parents for their children. Prisoners grow up emotionally and leave behind their gangs, their drug and alcohol abuse, their abuse of others.

Every day, Casarjian receives letters of gratitude from prisoners and prison staff from around the country. One prisoner, Ruth, wrote, "I was overwhelmed with a sense that you believe in us . . . in our ability to change our damaged selves into thoughtful, mature, compassionate people. You are a blessing to those of us who struggle with ourselves and try to find a more peaceful existence despite external turmoil."

Another prisoner, Lloyd, wrote, "Your ideas have truly touched my soul. Thank you so much for having the courage to inspire prisoners to address issues such as anger, grief, the inner child, forgiveness, shame, dignity and aura. These are truly the tools that set the self free from bondage."

Today, when Casarjian meets with prisoners, she often shares a passage from William Elliott's book *Tying Rocks to Clouds*. This quote, she says, best captures the essence of her work. It carries a message of hope that only someone who has been in the depths of despair can understand. "I could look at the worst in myself knowing the best."

Remember Troy Bridges, the Alabama inmate who transformed his life by surrendering to meditation and the peace and strength it brought him? By stepping into his own "flow" and serendipity his life intersected with Robin Casarjian's and moved him into a full-fledged heart activist position for those around him.

When Bridges first started teaching meditation, eight men regularly met on Wednesday evenings to meditate together. After one session, Chuck, a sixty-one-year-old prisoner serving twenty years for embezzlement, suggested that they try to get a private place to hold their group. Chuck talked to the prison psychologist, who suggested they approach the chaplain. When he did, the chaplain said if the meditation group could come up with a recognized self-help program that included meditation, then he would be able to justify their use each week of the therapy room.

"When Chuck brought me the news, I said, 'Well, we'll just have to find some type of self-help program,'" recalled Bridges. "I gave the idea no more thought, but then something happened the next day that really started me thinking."

CONNECTIONS ARE MADE

While he was working in the prison library, Bridges was given a box of books to shelve. Reaching inside, he pulled out a bright purple book. Serendipity struck. The book was called *Houses of Healing: A Prisoner's Guide to Inner Power and Freedom*. It was written by Robin Casarjian.

Bridges recalled, "Curiously, I opened one of the books and began read-ing. . . . What really caught my attention was that the course began each class with a period of meditation. I knew immediately that I had found a self-help program that would justify our meditation group meeting weekly in the therapy room. What I couldn't have known, however, was that I had found a program that would not only justify the use of a room for quiet meditation, but a course of study that would help me personally heal pock-ets of pain still inside me, and also give me an opportunity to help teach others how to heal their own pain and begin to change the way they viewed their world."

Through the Houses of Healing program, Bridges finally released much of his inner pain stemming from his abusive childhood. For five years, he has taught more than four hundred other prisoners to meditate and has trained ten men as meditation facilitators. In addition to using the words *peaceful* and *calm* and *positive* to describe himself and his fellow inmates, Bridges uses the words *rich* and *magnanimous* and *grateful* when he speaks of himself and others who went through the program.

"When I discovered Houses of Healing, I still had deep pockets of pain from unresolved childhood trauma that continued to affect my behavior, re-lationships, and overall sense of well-being." The program guided Bridges to use meditation, visualization, and cognitive reframing to bring his emo-tional pain to the surface, to examine it, and finally to understand it. It helped him understand that he felt shame and guilt and had never felt un-conditional love from anyone in his life.

He realized how his childhood conditioned him to see life "through a veil of pain." He painfully recalled his mother, who displayed her pain like a "gaping wound" and "soaked her demons in alcohol." He remembered that after many years, she became "as numb and as hard as a pickled egg in a jar of vinegar." Bridges remembered trying to absorb his mother's pain, and how she would often respond, instead of lovingly, like lightning—shocking him like a live electrical wire.

Bridges recalled often hiding during these times in the laundry closet in the bathroom, where he crawled through the small opening, closed the trap door, and wrapped himself in the dirty clothes there, pulling his knees to his chest, hugging them close. And that's when he'd feel safe enough to cry, hoping that his tears would finally wash away his mother's pain.

At times, going through the Houses of Healing program, Bridges felt his self-discoveries and healing were slow, arduous, agonizing, puzzling, "sometimes even wonderful movement through levels of awareness, one painful step at a time."

FINDING A NEW SENSE OF SELF

He finally saw with new eyes that many of his poor decisions and responses in the past were a result of childhood abuse. This realization allowed him to finally forgive those he felt were responsible for his pain. "And most importantly, forgive myself. This allowed me to meet the world with a renewed sense of self-worth," he wrote.

Before the Houses of Healing program, Bridges said, "I saw myself as a separate entity, alienated and alone in a hostile world. Houses of Healing allowed me to see that I was connected to a universe that is friendly and supportive. This made me realize that all we think, say, and do affect each of us, that when I treat another with compassion, then I'm treating myself with compassion."[11]

What magic. What a magical, loving man at the height of his power, even if he is physically disempowered, by our traditional standards. Troy Bridges is as free as free gets, from a spiritual and emotional level. Are we each ready to be free? Are we at last ready to step into that kind of magical power? Can we allow ourselves to heal our own pain so we can feel that kind of compassion for ourselves and those around us?

All it takes is one humane act to galvanize a movement, to be the conduit for a new way of living and thinking. As Robin Casarjian and Troy Bridges show, all it takes is one single act of heart activism to call into question and create epic change in our institutions. Allow yourself to be moved by just one person you know. That's all it takes. Think of Rachel Eyre Hall, who was motivated by her brother when he developed AIDS. It's often the people closest to us who hold the key to our hearts' work, as Hall shows.

You don't have to totally remake your life, though you may feel called to do so. You don't have to give up everything to act out of your heart. It's often just the opposite—you have everything to gain. It's often in giving up the old way of being that we are born anew.

Each person's expression from the heart will be unique. You may be a spark; someone else might be the tender of the fire who keeps it blazing. You may be the one who keeps the fire stoked whenever the blaze falls back to just a few bright embers. You don't have to give your heart over to an organization or an institution to transform it. But you do have to be willing to unveil your heart and make it vulnerable. You do have to be willing to believe with all your heart that being vulnerable and soft are the strongest positions of all.

"It has to do with changing the male archetype in our culture," concludes Stephen Levine. "To be 'too soft' was once considered too weak. Now we see the male image of strength is actually the image of cowardice. In backing through the door, we turned around. . . . People in medicine often think emotions are a weakening, a lessening, a deferment of power. And now we are starting to realize it's the other way around. And sometimes you have to go through hell to see this—that the stronger you get, if you are really tough, how untough you really are."

Those opportunities to show our "untoughness" and ultimate compassion are always close at hand—in all our work, in all our lives, with our children entering the world, and with those who are leaving the world. All that's usually required is just opening the heart to what is right in front of you, not engaging the mind's logic at all, but activating the impulses of the heart.

BIRTHING THE NEW WORLD

On the other hand, maybe all of us really do have to walk out of the life we now know into a place we've never seen or been in before. To help birth the new world. For something new to be born, something has to die. It's just like the cycles of nature. To advance into the springtime of our civilization, we will need to die to the old ways that don't serve us anymore.

And that will mean giving up the old life that maybe didn't sustain us well anymore anyway. It means finally letting your long-ignored inner voice—maybe it's a hoarse scream by now—finally rise to the surface and be attended to. That was the case for Eleanor, who had finally made partner in a successful law firm—and she was miserable.

She chafed at her daily life and work. Even the thought of putting on panty hose and lipstick to look professional was intolerable. So one day when she was driving to work, she pulled over her car. She yanked off her panty hose, gathered up some driftwood, and shaped it into the shape of a skeleton. She tied it all together with shredded bits from her panty hose, and whipped out her lipstick.

On the driftwood she wrote, "I resign." And she did. She began to stay home and bake bread and cookies that she sold to local stores. She began to excavate her authentic self. She began to commit a radical act of love in nurturing herself.[12]

Sometimes to become the heart activists we've come here to be, we do need to step out of the life we were born into and onto the life we were destined to live. To leave the small, elite, more limited circles to go into the vast spheres where our radical acts of love affect millions of people. The smallest act can transform the globe in sweeping ways.

Swanee Hunt was born into silver-spoon, plush, lucrative comfort; the daughter of Haroldson Lafayette Hunt, who became wealthy during the east Texas oil boom of the twenties, thirties, and forties. Her family's fortune is estimated at least two billion.

But early on, she hewed to a different sensibility. Teaching Bible classes in inner-city neighborhoods in Texas, she developed an interest in what creates class differences. She explored meaning-of-life questions and pestered her teachers with questions such as, "How can you talk about a loving God if that God is sending to hell people in Africa who have never heard of him?"

A SENSE OF A CALLING

Yet she started out to embrace the right-wing, conservative sensibilities of her father. In 1964, she was a Goldwater girl and made conservative speeches with her father. But after earning a bachelor's degree in philosophy, a master's in psychology and religion, and a doctorate in theology, Hunt's consciousness was set on the path to make a difference in the world. "All throughout my upbringing, raised as a Southern Baptist, I had a sense that you give your life for service. I had sense of a calling," she says.

In her twenties, Hunt considered giving her wealth away, like her model Saint Francis of Assisi. Instead she decided to use her money to do good: "There are a lot of ways to change the world without money. Mahatma

Gandhi taught us that. But it's also possible to take money and try to use it to leverage change."[13]

Whatever Hunt has touched with that kind of compassionate sight has been transformed. She commits half her annual income to the Hunt Alternative Fund, which serves as "funder, convener, and friend to over four hundred neighborhoods" to ease poverty and discrimination.

"People still ask me, 'Why do you choose to do work with people in trouble? You could be sitting around, eating bonbons.' But my reaction is always the same. That's not a choice for me. Shall I sit by the pool and eat bonbons today or should I do this work? That's not a choice. This is very much my calling."

Hunt's calling to ease others' suffering has taken her to the most acrimonious places that beg for harmony and healing. As President Clinton's ambassador to Austria, she forged a new path in public diplomacy, reaching out to the Austrian people through a weekly newspaper column and radio address.

As mentioned earlier, while in Vienna, she made hundreds of trips to Bosnia, six hundred miles south, to help broker peace negotiations. From Austria, she also hosted negotiations between the Bosnians and Serbs. Additionally, she organized humanitarian projects, buying books to restore the shelves of the destroyed National Library in Sarajevo, trees for the parks denuded during the siege, and more than six tons of musical instruments for ravaged Bosnian schools.

And, as discussed in the previous chapter on listening with compassion, she became increasingly known as someone who reached out to the women, many of whom were widowed and had lost children and other family members in the war.

Women are a major force for peace in Bosnia and across the world, Hunt recognizes. "Like the women of northern Ireland, they have a spirit of cooperation and courage that is extraordinary," she said in our interview.

In 1996, Hunt brought together five hundred women leaders in Sarajevo. They were Muslim, Croat, and Serb women united in their desire for peace. At great personal risk, they pledged to work together for peace and to rebuild their country.

"In this brave new world, the voices of women are vital to healthy social and political discourse," said Hunt. After the Bosnian women's visible alliances, President Clinton launched the Bosnian Women's Initiative, which bolsters women's business ventures and further gives women an economic, social, and political voice. One of Hunt's final projects before she left Austria was to organize a network of 150 female leaders in the new democracies of Central and Eastern Europe. They are now connected via an Internet listserver to share ideas and hopes for advancing women's issues in their countries.

Where does she draw her strength to stay committed to working compassionately? "I draw strength from my closest relationships, from time alone, say with a book of poetry or sitting in church. Last weekend in upstate New York, I went on a walk and found a place completely surrounded by color. That time is tremendously important to me. I don't need much. I don't need more than one hour a week to reach down into my well to give me what I need for the whole week," she explained.

And her immutable faith that she can make a difference, that she is called to make a difference, is an endless reservoir. "People often look at situations, like the issues in Africa, and say, 'This is hopeless.' That is not an option. It's not so much asking myself the question, 'Do I think everything is getting better?' It's asking ourselves a whole different question: 'Can I keep working on this problem? Am I committed?'"

In the end, she won't judge her life by the results, she told me. "All I can do is judge my life according to the effort. And that's what keeps me going."

THE HEART CAN MANIFEST MIRACLES

Are you afraid, in your heart of hearts, that if you live out of your heart, you will fail? Is it that you can't stomach the prospect of finally, finally following your heart—and then falling miserably on your face? Remember the words of Elizabeth Barrett Browning: "Who so loves believes the impossible."[14] Remember that the heart manifests miracles. Remind yourself that when you harness your full intellectual power with your heart power, like when charged particles are brought together, "the result is incandescence," say Drs. Lewis, Amini, and Lannon in *A General Theory of Love*.

Love has "allowed humans to dream of God. To make it. To imagine golden roads. . . . It may be the element that keeps the stars in the firmament," says Maya Angelou.[15] Love is the force behind all forces, so how can you ever conceive of failure if you are acting out of love? And now, let's ramp this up further. If you can truly, truly believe that love is the most powerful law of the universe, if you can accept with all your heart that love allows enigmatic, illogical, implausible, wondrous things to happen, if you can really know deep in your marrow that against-all-odds amazing things can be born from love, then you are truly and forever a heart activist. You will be incandescent.

As this book goes to press, Hollywood is releasing a movie about the Grinch, the green creature whose heart grows three sizes in one day after he has an epiphany of the heart. It looks as if it will be a huge commercial success with kids and adults alike. Is this because it calls to a need in each of us, to a place where we still want to believe such a larger-than-life, magical epiphany could transform our hearts? We still want to believe in the greatest fable of all: love can heal, can comfort, can make everything all right.

Peggy Marengo believes in the fable. She's been incandescent for decades. This story is only from the last few chapters of her amazing life in service to others. As mentioned, she and her partner have six biological children and ten adopted children. Part of their service has been to love, unconditionally, the children with AIDS who joined their family.

CARING FOR THOSE WITH AIDS

"When we look back on the twentieth century, how well we cared for those with AIDS—whether we responded with unconditional love—will mirror the depth of our humanity," predicted Dr. Elisabeth Kübler-Ross in the 1980s. "AIDS poses its own threat to mankind, but unlike war, it is a battle from within. . . . Are we going to choose hate and discrimination, or will we have the courage to choose love and service?"

When she received heartbreaking letters from mothers dying of AIDS, pleading for homes for their children, many of whom were also suffering from the disease, Kübler-Ross decided to sound the clarion call, knowing full well what the personal cost could be. She'd already had homophobic neighbors shoot bullets in her windows, burn crosses on her lawn, and pierce her tires with nails. But she continued to issue appeals in her newsletter for parents to adopt HIV-positive children.

One of these articles caught the eye of Alison Smith, Marengo's partner.

Logically, the timing seemed totally out of synch. Marengo was still recovering from colon cancer surgeries. She knew how grave this particular form of cancer could be; she saw her aunts and uncles die from it. "I turned down any chemotherapy and radiation because I watched my relatives suffer from the treatments as they were dying. I wanted to be well enough to enjoy my family and not suffer from the illness. . . . If this is what I have, I'll make the most of it."

Even though Marengo and Smith knew the future was tenuous, they still felt drawn to contact Kübler-Ross. And when they did, they learned about a one-year-old baby, Luci, who was especially weighing on the doctor's heart. Kübler-Ross said she had gotten a call from a woman in Boston about Luci, who was born to Haitian immigrants in 1985 after a harrowing boat ride to Florida. Luci was abandoned and later found, covered in feces and vomit, in a shoebox in the streets of Boston. She was also HIV-positive.

Barely alive, Luci had been brought to Children's Hospital. Clinging to life, the little girl became the center of a fierce battle among the hospital, social services, the Haitian community, and Marengo and Smith, who desperately wanted to adopt Luci. They quickly discovered that Luci would likely be the first child with AIDS adopted in the United States. It all seemed destined to be, but the institutions involved were still operating out of fear.

"These were the dark ages in our understanding of AIDS," said Marengo. "Elisabeth wasn't welcomed with open arms by hospitals which didn't understand AIDS. They were operating in a time of great fear. Luci ended up being a political hot rock. A lot of systems were working in opposition because she was the first child with HIV placed. And they didn't know how to deal with it."

As the conflict intensified, Luci spent much time in a crib, in an isolated area of the hospital. She was loved by the staff, even the custodial staff who watched TV on breaks in her room. But it was a bleak substitute for a home and parents.

THE FIGHT TO BRING LUCI HOME

After several agonizing months, Marengo and Smith were finally allowed to meet Luci. "The first night I stayed next to her crib, and Luci woke in the night," Marengo remembered. "She looked down at me with knowing eyes and reached out to touch me." Marengo felt as if Luci were signaling that she wanted to go home. But she and Smith continued to be stonewalled by the system. Even members of the Haitian community demanded that Luci belonged to them.

Finally, on Luci's second birthday, she came home with Marengo and Smith. Even then, doctors expected her to live only a few more months. Most AIDS babies in the 1980s didn't live much beyond age two. Yet Luci not only survived toddlerhood, but is now seventeen—a testament to the fact that love is the most healing force of all. Since her birth, Luci has continued to be watched over by Kübler-Ross, even after she suffered a series of strokes. Kübler-Ross refers to Marengo and Smith as "angels on earth."

Luci is the angel, said Marengo. "She is truly the epitome of an angel. Of all of our children, why did she come to us first? Her adoption was the hardest one. It opened the door. After that we were well trained in how to function with the system. We knew the other kids we adopted were sick, but they were not as sick as Luci. Luci came to teach us the ropes. It's kind of like she was there to open our door."

Marengo continued, "It's been a real spiritual journey. The other children didn't come to us with the same spiritual push Luci did. For instance, the woman who contacted Elisabeth Kübler-Ross originally about Luci was seen only once and we were never able to find her again. Who was that woman? No one knows. Elisabeth was never able to find her."

Luci's adoption also showed the couple the fallout they would have to endure if they were to continue building their family as they wanted. Marengo's parents stopped talking to her and wouldn't visit. Many people they thought were friends backed away. Her piano practice took a 50 percent hit. Smith's co-workers were supportive, but in a very strained way. "But we made this commitment, and we aren't people to take on a child and go back on our commitment," said Marengo.

In fact, after the grace of Luci flowed into their home, it's as if some spiritual stardust also came along. When Luci was five, Marengo and Smith walked in the door with their newest daughter, a little two-year-old African American child. Luci, who still found it difficult to even talk, looked up and said, "Oh! It's my Ida!" Marengo and Smith later found out that in an African dialect *Ida* means "love."

And sheer love she was. Though terribly sick at first, Ida grew into a sweet, affectionate little girl. She was fiercely protective of her sister Lotty, who came to the Marengo and Smith home a week after Ida did. Born just three days apart, the girls were like twins.

Marengo and Smith decided that for Luci, Ida, Lotty, and the other children they adopted with special needs, their goal was to "provide a high-quality life." They didn't want to dwell on their illnesses, but to focus on the creation of a loving, healthy, and warm atmosphere.

THE HEALING POWER OF UNCONDITIONAL LOVE

"Each of these children came to us with a very poor prognosis. So our next goal was to make the best of the years they had left," said Marengo. And those years, amazingly, kept unfolding. Along with unconditional love, Marengo and Smith relied on an inexhaustible blend of conventional and complementary care, including reiki, massage, herbs, and acupuncture. Their children's doctors became like family and gave them high hopes. "These children are so healthy, they will never die," the doctors often said.

The couple started to believe it too. Then for about a year, Ida had chronic sore throats and fatigue, but all the blood tests showed nothing wrong.

On Christmas Eve of 1996, Ida came downstairs and said, "Mommy, I have a boo-boo." Marengo discovered that their little girl had a fierce case of genital herpes. Smith and Marengo rushed Ida to the doctor, who treated her and repeatedly insisted that she would respond quickly to the medication. But she never did. Her herpes only spread more virulently.

Smith and Marengo took Ida to the hospital—her first hospitalization ever. She was hooked up to an IV and when doctors discovered she was anemic, they gave her three transfusions. But she only weakened. Soon, Ida's kidneys and liver began to fail, and pneumonia began to fill her lungs. It was the next night that makes Marengo's voice still resonate with awe.

"I hadn't slept all this time, and at one point, I put my head down on Ida's bed and said, 'Honey, I have to go to sleep.' I knew the next day would be just as tough. I was still in denial. I was convinced, and the doctors were convinced, that she would be fine.

"So I put my head down on Ida's bed, and all of a sudden I saw five golden angels hovering over Ida's bed. I was, 'Whooo. . . . Okay. Too little sleep.'"

She turned to her daughter, "Ida, do you see an angel?"

And Ida responded, "Oh. No, no, no. I see lots and *lots* of angels." So Marengo thought to herself, "Well, well. If anyone deserves to see angels and have angels pray for her that would be Ida."

"I was still clearly in denial about why the angels were there," said Marengo.

Two days later, on January 2, 1997, just short of her tenth birthday, as Marengo and Smith held her in their laps, and Lotty held her hand, Ida died.

Soon, the couple discovered that Ida's spirit was still close at hand. Shattered with grief the night of her death, they got into their car and silently began the drive home. A soft snow was falling; the children were in the backseat. Smith turned on the radio, and a song was playing, "The angels are with you. The angels are rainbows."

Marengo glanced back to see Lotty's expression as she heard the song—and saw Ida's spirit sitting next to her.

One night, still grieving over Ida's death, six-year-old Bea (whom Marengo and Smith had also adopted) fell totally apart. For nights, often until 4 A.M., she'd scream and kick and rage, blaming the doctors for Ida's death. HIV-infected, Bea also was facing the terror of her own possible death.

One day Bea announced she would stop taking her medication so "I can be with Ida." Marengo was terrified, and the next night as they sat at the kitchen table, she placed Bea's medication down in front of her and pleaded, "Honey, please. Let's just take the medicine. On the count of one, two, three."

And then she braced herself for Bea's nightly fit of rage. But all of a sudden the little girl's tortured face changed. Her whole being changed. Her eyes, face, and mouth radiated a light and became peaceful, Marengo remembered. Bea gazed over at the place where Ida normally sat and got the most incredible look of love in her eyes, and then she blew a kiss. "Mom, I just saw Ida," said Bea. "Ida just said, 'I love you' and blew me a kiss."

Even after death, a little bit of Ida's heart still lingers. "It turns out, she never left the people she loved," Marengo smiled as we spoke.

LETTING GO OF FEAR

We each are called to be angels on earth. We each have the enormous power within—and divine power in the wings—that Marengo and Smith have. We each can be divine sparks wherever we are, if we only stop doubting the immutable power of love that can make miracles flow all around us. Never, never doubt the power of love. Never, never let your love be pinched off and diminished by the fear that you aren't big enough, strong enough, courageous enough.

"It's all about letting go of fear. The worst enemy of all is fear and it's all about letting go and letting love transcend the fear," Marengo concluded. "People fear getting burned out. They fear having their hearts touched or hurt. They don't get that you have to function at a spiritual level, and that all underlying evil comes from fear. Even though our lives have been touched by death and loss, and we have more children we are in danger of losing, we see that life is a continuous spiral of letting go of fear."[16]

We've let our fears imprison us, keeping us from our hearts. And now it's time to lay down those fears and break free. When I think of the crossroads our culture finds itself at, I can't help but think of the story of Saint John of the Cross, imprisoned and tortured for his efforts to revitalize his Carmelite religious community. In prison, he gradually realized he was dying in his cell. Yet he was afraid that if he tried to escape and was caught, he would be tortured to death. So Saint John of the Cross faced down his fears, took the greater risk, and, amazingly, he escaped. Later he wrote the following poem:

> There in the lucky dark
> in secret, with all sleepers, heavy-eyed;
> No sign for me to mark
> No other light, no guide
> Except for my heart—the fire, the fire inside![17]

Are you finally ready to release your fear and walk into the fire? Can you finally let your fears be purged and purified by the inferno of compassion? As you stand at the edge of the fire, or are immersed, deeply suffused with its power, find inspiration in the following song by Colorado songwriter and vocalist Rachel Stone. She speaks to both the fear and the exhilaration of using the fire inside as our truest guide.

Can you see the fire burning me alive?
Can you see the water drowning my heart and pride?
Can you see the wind is blowing me off my feet?
Can you see the earth is shaking me to the core?

And I used to be so sure of who I was before
I used to know the answers before the questions even came
Now I'm walking through a dream and I don't know what I'm seeing
I don't know what I should believe anymore

So I'll embrace the fire with open arms
I will swim through the water till I find a beautiful shore
I will ride the wind like an eagle with my wings spread so I can soar
I will rule the earth with my insatiable thirst to explore

Because I used to be so sure of who I was before
I used to know the answers before the questions even came
Now I'm walking through a dream and I don't know what I'm seeing
I don't know what I should believe anymore

Fire give me strength
Water grant me tranquillity
Wind fill me with fury
Earth give me the understanding to go on through this world

Then I can be sure of who I am once more
I can find the answers before the questions even come
No more walking through a dream and I'll know just what I'm seeing
I'll know just what I should believe for sure

Fire burn me
Water bathe me
Wind blow me over and
Earth enrapture me

Every corner every plain I call you out I call your name
Set me free and let me see

12

Conclusion:
A Vision of the New World

As explored throughout this book, the previous decades have been dedicated to the power of our minds and intellects. We've tried to solve our problems, come together as a nation, and heal our most painful issues through our greatest intellects.

One side brings together its greatest minds and slings one accusation; another gathers another stellar group and hurls something else. As this all plays out, like a great passion play for the whole world to watch, I keep remembering the spiritual words of folk singer and award-winning performer Emmy Lou Harris: "The world is not going to change unless it's changed one heart at a time, one person at a time. All these movements . . . you can talk about anything, you can legislate all you want, but nothing is going to change until you change yourself and you change your heart. Because, ultimately everything gets back to the heart, everything."[1]

A RETURN TO THE HEART

I think we are so ready to get back to the heart, to restore the wisdom of the heart to center stage in our conflicts that even the finest renaissance, razor-edged minds cannot resolve. Through awakening our hearts, we will not only heal ourselves of the pains that won't go away in our culture, but will also see, as Mother Teresa said, that we should "not wait for leaders; do it alone, person to person."[2]

We have to take back our power and reclaim the power of our hearts. We have to "open ourselves to a new dimension of love that Zen Buddhism calls Big Mind, the spaciousness of divine love," says Stephen Levine. When we fuse our best minds with our fiercest hearts, we will make an evolutionary, conscious leap into Big Mind in our courtrooms, medical clinics, school playgrounds, hospitals, insurance offices, and embassies, as seen through the stories featured in this book. Are we ready for this leap?

SPIRITUAL SEEKINGS UNPRECEDENTED

From the seismic shiftings and shock waves coming from the epicenter of our culture, it would seem that, at heart, we are ready to make this jump. Countless surveys from Gallup polls to *Ladies Home Journal* questionnaires show, over and over, that we are dramatically seeking greater meaning, richness, fulfillment, and spiritual purpose in our lives. And in that seeking we are triggering fault lines in the foundations of every aspect of our culture.

From 1994 to 1999, for instance, the percentage of American adults reporting the need for spiritual growth in their own lives jumped from 20 percent to 78 percent. "Rarely has any society experienced such a rapid shift in attitudes," says Dr. Gregory Plotnikoff.[3]

"These are vision-birthing times that snap us awake like a life-challenging illness," says Joan Borysenko. "They goad us to ask the big questions like, 'What is the purpose of my life? What is the legacy of a life well lived? How can I best be of service to others?'"[4]

All this seeking, sensing, and wondering is a good sign. It means after years of going numb, we are feeling again. Critical masses of people are awakening to the amazing sense of their heart core searching, throbbing, and pulsing again.

MOVING TO THE NEXT LEVEL OF EVOLUTION

That questing for something more will lead us to our inner fire. It will make us receptive to the firelike translucence trying to be born through us. It has elements of genius, compassion, cooperation, and mystical union on the deepest levels. This new world is about restoration of our hearts so they are no longer viewed as mushy or sentimental or peripheral, but as holding "the promise for the next level of human development and for the survival of our world," say Doc Lew Childre, Howard Martin, and Donna Beech, authors of *The HeartMath Solution*.

And this will not be easy. There will always be great upheavals and chaos as something new is ushered in. Nothing of great worth ever comes without some great struggle. We'll be laid bare, and all our imbalances, problems, and truths will come to light so we can finally build a world that is not based on illusions and deception. So our grand denials that "everything is really *okay*" can finally be exposed and examined and healed.

Our individual and collective skeletons "are falling out of the closet. And on those old bones, the living flesh of compassionate respect and conscious social action is growing," says Borysenko.[5]

We are now getting a fantastic glimpse of how beautiful, satisfying, and meaningful this new life will be. We are seeing the flames of compassion no matter where we live and work. We are seeing a glimpse, sometimes a lasting view, of how beautiful life can be. And from that vista, we love what we can see.

We can't let fear of this new world shut down our hearts. We have to stay in the fire even when it gets difficult. Listen to the words of one of the wisest heart activists in this book, Troy Bridges, imprisoned in Alabama, one of the freest hearts you could ever hope to find.

LOVE IS WHAT WE'RE BORN INTO

"Fear is what we're taught. Love is what we're born into," says Bridges. "As a society, we can't learn to live out of our hearts until we replace fear with love, return to our roots.

"Practically, how do we do that? By changing our perspective. If we continue to view each other face-to-back, we continue to fear each other, but if we begin to view each other face-to-face, we learn to respect and trust each other, the beginning of love.

"If we continue to view each other personality-to-personality, our eyes obscure our perception. Recognizing the same larger self inside each of us, we become as clear and as transparent and as powerful as the wind. And we live from our hearts."

Bridges concludes that it's impossible to change everyone's perspective, especially those taught a narrow, limited belief system based on fear and illusion. Instead, "We must change ourselves, enlarge and expand our own perspective," he says. "Changing ourselves, we become a living example in which others are encouraged to change. We then change society one heart at a time. . . . Then all fear will fade in the face of compassion, just as suddenly as bright sunshine let into a dark room."[6]

Let it shine. Oh, let it shine.

$\mathcal{N}otes$

Introduction

1. Anonymous source, Fort Collins, Colo.

2. News report, "Just Outside Hospital Teen Lay Bleeding to Death," CNN News, 18 May 1998.

3. As told by Dr. John Nagel, Mountain Crest Hospital, Fort Collins, Colo.

4. Nyanaponika Thera, quoted in Sharon Salzberg, *A Heart as Wide as the World* (New York: Random House, 1997), 1.

5. Stephen Levine, interview with author, 5 October 2000.

6. Adapted from Ledyard King, "Our Schools Our Future: Finding Solutions Together Teaching Life's Lessons," *South Florida Sun-Sentinel*, 26 August 1997, p. 1A. Reprinted with permission from the *South Florida Sun-Sentinel*.

7. Punnadhammo Bhikkhu, "Compassion Is a Divine Skill That Can Be Learned," *Toronto Star*, 8 May 1999.

Chapter 1: A Return to Love: The Case for Compassion

1. Story supplied by permission of Southwest Airlines.

2. Kari Thorene, "Listening with Compassion," *Yes: A Journal of Positive Futures* 7 (fall 1998).

3. Carol McDonald, interview with author, 19 November 2000.

4. Dr. Gladys Taylor McGarey, "Contacting the Physician within You" (presentation at the Embracing Our Essence conference, Santa Barbara, Calif., April 1997).

5. Priscilla Huston, interview with author, 9 November 2000.

6. Brian Dumaine, "Executive Life," *Fortune*, 26 December 1994.

7. Tom's of Maine corporate Web site: www.tomsofmaine.com.

8. Robert Davis, "Family Ties Operate on Daughter, Doctor Inside," *USA Today*, 23 May 2000, p. 1D.

9. Jelaluddin Rumi, quoted in Richard Carlson and Benjamin Shield, *Handbook for the Heart* (Boston: Little, Brown and Company, 1996).

10. Christina Puchalski, M.D., "Walking the Last Steps of the Journey Together," *Faith and Medicine Connection* 2 (summer 1998).

11. Jean Callahan, *Body, Mind, Spirit*, October–December 1996, 35.

12. Tony Perez-Giese, "Mind over Medicine," *Westword*, November 1996: 14.

Chapter 2: The Hardened Heart: Extinguishing the Fire

1. John Brady, *Bad Boy: The Life and Politics of Lee Atwater* (New York: Addison Wesley Longman, 1997). Excerpt appeared on washingtonpost.com.books.

2. Dalai Lama, quoted in Brian Luke Seaward, *Stand Like Mountain, Flow Like Water* (Deerfield Beach, Fla.: Health Communications, 1995), 228.

3. Leslie Brooks Suzukamo, "More Physicians Are Saying They Can Better Help Patients by Attending to Their Spirituality as Well as Their Bodies," *St. Paul Pioneer Press*, 15 October 1996, p. 1D.

4. Gregory Plotnikoff, M.D., M.T.S., "In Search of a Good Death," *Minnesota Medicine*, May 2000, 50.

5. Dorsey Griffith, "Ease the Mind, Heal the Body," *Sacramento Bee*, 5 April 1998, p. A1.

6. Ibid.

7. Statistic provided by Tiffany Fields, a staff member at Touch Research Institute.

8. According to Dr. Kim Marvel, psychologist, Family Medicine Center, Fort Collins, Colo., as quoted in "Healthy Living Takes Healthy Relationships," *Fort Collins Coloradoan* 27 (February 2000), p. C5.

9. Ibid.

10. Thomas Aquinas, quoted by Matthew Fox (Omega Institute/New Age Journal, Body and Soul Conference, Boulder, Colo., 12 July 1997).

Chapter 3: Heart Monitor: Examining Your Fullness of Heart

1. Anonymous source, Fort Collins, Colo.

2. Meister Eckhart, quoted in Eric Klein and John B. Izzo, *Awakening Corporate Soul* (Gloucester, Mass.: Fair Winds Press, 1998).

3. Helen Keller quoted on Web site: www.womenshistory.about.com.

4. Mary Alice Kellogg, "My Perky Days Are Over," *McCall's*, December 2000.

5. Story shared by Dr. Martin Rossman and *Ways of the Healer* where the story first appeared as "Imagery," fall, winter 1997, 17–21.

6. Eric Harrison, "A Tale of Faith, Hope and Hate," *L.A.Times*, 30 July 1997, p. A1.

7. Elizabeth Menken, M.D., "I Forgave My Sister's Killer," *Ladies Home Journal*, December 1995, 38.

8. Joan Borysenko Web site: www.joanborysenko.com.

9. Susan Skog, *Depression: What Your Body's Trying to Tell You* (New York: Avon Books, 1999), 137.

10. Priscilla Huston, interview with author, 9 November 2000.

11. Terry Tempest Williams, "The Politics of Place," interview with Scott London: www.scottlondon.com.

12. Thomas Merton, quoted in Richard Carlson and Benjamin Shield, *Handbook for the Heart* (Boston: Little, Brown and Company, 1996).

13. Skog, *Depression*, 114.

14. Mary Winter, "Progress But at What Cost?" *Rocky Mountain News* (Denver, Colo.), 13 December 1998, p. 2F, Homefront column.

15. Mariah Mannia, interviews with author, 9 November 2000 and 20 November 2000.

16. Lao-tzu, quoted in Wayne Dyer, *Your Sacred Self* (New York: HarperCollins, 1995), 141.

17. Robin Casarjian, interviews with author, 29 June 1998 and 8 November 2000.

18. Elana Rosenbaum, interview with author, 9 October 1999.

19. Kathryn Guta, interview with author, 5 December 2000.

20. Troy Bridges, correspondence with author, October–December 2000.

21. Jennifer V. Hughes, "Others See Heart Beneath the Robes," *The Record* (Bergen County, N.J.), 25 July 2000, p. 101.

22. Angeles Arrien, "The Soul's Fire" (presentation at the Embracing Our Essence conference, Santa Barbara, Calif., April 1997).

23. Bruno Cortis, *Heart and Soul* (New York: Pocket Books, 1997).

Chapter 4: A Change of Heart: Seeing with Love

1. Thomas Carlyle, quoted in Doc Lew Childre, Howard Martin, and Donna Beach, *The HeartMath Solution* (New York: Harper San Francisco, 2000), 7.

2. Marcel Proust, quoted in Harold Bloomfield, M.D., and Peter McWilliams, *How to Heal Depression* (Los Angeles: Prelude Press, 1994), 251.

3. Gregory Plotnikoff, M.D., "Healing Body and Spirit," *Minnesota Medicine*, December 1996, 8.

4. Ann Careau, interviews with author, 30 July 2000 and 14 November 2000.

5. Leslie Scrivener, "Making Room for the Soul 9 to 5," *Toronto Star*, 7 July 1998.

6. Story shared by HeartMath Institute, Boulder Creek, Calif.

7. News report, "A Living Miracle," ABC News *20/20*, 22 September 2000.

8. Priscilla Huston, interview with author, 9 November 2000.

9. Dr. Larry Dossey, correspondence with author.

10. Corinne McLaughlin and Gordon Davidson, *Spiritual Politics* (New York: Ballantine, 1994), 27.

11. Wayne Dyer, *Your Sacred Self* (New York: HarperCollins, 1995), 144.

12. Ibid., 151.

13. Frances Thompson poem in Corinne McLaughlin and Gordon Davidson, *Spiritual Politics* (New York: Ballantine, 1994), 13.

14. Meister Eckhart, quoted in Matthew Fox, *A Spirituality Named Compassion* (Rochester, Vt.: Inner Traditions, 1979), 34.

15. Albert Einstein, quoted in Arianna Huffington, *The Fourth Instinct* (New York: Simon and Schuster, 1994), 46.

16. Bill Powanda, interview with author, 21 November 2000.

17. Pablo Neruda, quoted in William J. Bennett, *The Book of Virtues,* on Web site: www.inspirationalstories.com.

18. Thomas Merton, *Conjectures of a Guilty Bystander* (Garden City, N.Y.: Doubleday, 1965).

19. Compassion in Action Web site: www.twilightbrigade.com.

Chapter 5: Compassionate Conversation: Listening from the Heart

1. Deborah Sugerman, "Healing Body, Mind, and Spirit," *Minnesota Medicine,* December 1996, 8.

2. Seneca, quoted on the Death and Dying Web site: www.dying.about.com/health/dying/library/weekly.

3. Anonymous. Poem used at University of Minnesota Clinical Medicine I: Professionalism Tutorial. Supplied by Dr. Gregory Plotnikoff.

4. Tamala Edwards, "The Hidden Power of Listening," *O Magazine,* May–June 2000, 124.

5. Gregory Plotnikoff, M.D., "Should Medicine Reach Out to the Spirit?," *Postgraduate Medicine,* (November 2000), 19.

6. Dr. Gregory Plotnikoff, interview with author, 22 November 2000.

7. Sara Rimer, "The Depression Era," *Rocky Mountain News* (Denver, Colo.), 18 November 2000, p. 10H.

8. Judy Foreman, "Talk about What Really Ails You," *Boston Globe,* 12 October 1998, p. C1.

9. Dr. James Gordon, interview with author, 18 November 1999.

10. News report, "Medical Schools Focus on an Old Skill in the New Millennium," ABC News, 25 September 2000.

11. Ibid.

12. Stephen Levine, interview with author, 5 October 2000.

13. "273 Percent Increase in Number of Children with Autism Who Enter Developmental Services System," *L.A. Times*, 15 April 1999. *L.A. Times* Web site: www.latimes.com.

14. Lynn W. Brallier, Ph.D., M.S.N., "The Spiritual Care of the Caregiver," *Spirituality and Medicine Connection*, summer 1999, 1.

15. Christina Puchalski, M.D., "Listening to One's Spirit: The Source of Compassion," *Spirituality and Medicine Connection*, summer 1999, 3.

16. Wally Lamb, "Unlock a Spiritual Prison," *USA Weekend*, 11–13 August 2000, p. 14.

17. Swanee Hunt, interview with author, 23 October 2000.

18. Ibid.

19. Don Marxhausen, interview with author, 11 October 2000.

20. Kenny Moore, interview with author, 16 October 2000.

21. Ann Careau, interviews with author, 30 July 2000 and 14 November 2000.

22. Adapted from Kenny Moore. Original story first appeared as "Organizational Healing: A Core Competency for Leadership," *Genesis*, no. 5, 8.

23. Kenny Moore, interview with author, 16 October 2000.

24. Mary Beth Sammons, "Lunchtime Retreat: Wellstreams Supplies a Sip of Spirituality," *Chicago Tribune*, 1 June 1997, sec. 13, p. 7.

Chapter 6: The Heart Unleashed: Speaking from the Heart

1. Robert Louis Stevenson, quoted on Quotes for Peace Web site: members.aol.com/pforpeace/quote5.htm.

2. Ed Hays, quoted on Quotes for Peace Web site: members.aol.com/pforpeace/quote5.htm.

3. Penn State University Medical School professor Dr. George Simms, quoted in University of Minnesota School of Medicine curriculum *Culture, Spirituality, and Clinical Care*.

4. Dr. Gregory Plotnikoff, interview with author, 22 November 2000.

5. Bailey Stenson, interview with author, 8 November 2000.

6. Carol Schultz, "Times for Trouble," *Denver Post*, 17 September 2000, p. 96.

7. Stephen Levine, interview with author, 5 October 2000.

8. Katie Couric television interview with Jim Carrey, *Today*, 17 November 2000.

9. *Body, Mind, Spirit*, December 1995–January 1996, 36.

10. Janine Geske, interview with author, 23 October 2000.

11. Sue Patton Thoele, interview with author, 8 November 2000.

12. Richard Barrett, interview with author, 24 May 2000.

13. Jon Wheeler, interviews with author, 2 August 2000, 17 November 2000, and 13 December 2000.

14. Nicole Tembrock, interview with author, 2 April 2000.

15. Carla Frenzel, interview with author, 1 November 2000.

16. From Project Pave, Denver, Colo.

17. Dinah Eng, interview with author, 5 October 2000.

18. Mildred Lee, interview with author, 6 November 2000.

19. Julia C. Martinez, "'Man of Character' Recalled," *Rocky Mountain News* (Denver, Colo.), 26 October 2000, p. 2B.

20. Mother Teresa, quoted on Quotes for Peace Web site: www.members.aol.com/pforpeace/quote5.htm.

Chapter 7: Home Is Where the Heart Is: Creating Sanctuaries with Love

1. John Koch, "Cheating Their Kids," *Rocky Mountain News* (Denver, Colo.), 12 November 2000, p. 14F.

2. Jodi Ohlsen Read, "Learning the Art of Medicine," *Minnesota Medicine*, August 2000, 14.

3. Statistic quoted on National Institute of Mental Health Web site: www.nimh. nih.gov/events/roundtable.htm.

4. Kelee Katillac, "Creating Your Own Personal Style," *New Age Journal: Body and Soul Holistic Living Guide*, 2001, 358.

5. From Alexandra Stoddard Web site: www.alexandrastoddard.com.

6. Jean Callahan, "A Higher Love: Getting to the Deepest Levels of Relationship," *Body, Mind, Spirit*, October–December 1996, 35.

7. Sue Patton Thoele, interview with author, 8 November 2000.

8. Mark Wolf, "Mission Impossible: Trying to End Male-Female Conflict Futile, Author Says," *Rocky Mountain News* (Denver, Colo.), 12 November 2000, p. 3F.

9. Sarah Beurskens, "Breaking Point," *Denver Post*, 12 November 2000, p. 9H.

10. Lily Tomlin, quoted on the Lily Tomlin Web site: www.lilytomlin.com.

11. Statistics quoted on Kaiser Family Foundation Web site: www.kff.org.

Chapter 8: Softheartedness: Nourishing Compassion with Small Acts

1. Elisabeth Love, "A Healing, Helping Family," *Gambro Procedo* (February 2000), 6.

2. Steve Rubenstein, "A Sister's Loving Touch," *Good Housekeeping*, December 1996, 24.

3. Kevin Flynn, "Acts of Kindness Dull the Pain," *Rocky Mountain News* (Denver, Colo.), 16 April 2000, p. 6R.

4. Mike Anton, "The Columbine Family," *Rocky Mountain News* (Denver, Colo.), 16 April 2000, p. 2R.

5. Flynn, "Acts of Kindness Dull the Pain," p. 2R.

6. Albert Schweitzer, quoted in Matthew Fox, *A Spirituality Named Compassion* (Rochester, Vt.: Inner Traditions, 1979).

7. Fred Edmonds sermon, 30 October 1994, Plymouth Congregational Church, Fort Collins, Colo.

8. Story supplied by Southwest Airlines.

Chapter 9: Compassion through Suffering: Allowing the Heart to Break Wide Open

1. Josh Quesenberry, "Woman Homeless as Teen Is Perfect Volunteer for Family Agency," *Fort Collins Coloradoan*, 22 April 1998, p. A5.

2. Terry Tempest Williams, "The Politics of Place," interview with Scott London: www.scottlondon.com.

3. Colorado Institute for a Sustainable Future brochure.

4. Jason Crowe, interview with author, 12 December 2000; Jason Crowe Web site: members.sigecom.net/jdc.

5. Stephen Levine, interview with author, 5 October 2000.

6. Matthew Fox (Omega Institute/New Age Journal, Body and Soul Conference, Boulder, Colo., 12 July 1997).

7. 1998 Nobel Peace Laureates Conference Web site: www.virginia.edu/nobel/laureates.

8. Fred Edmonds sermon, 26 January 1997, Plymouth Congregational Church, Fort Collins, Colo.

9. Rabbi Moshe Leib, quoted in Jewish Peace Fellowship Web site: www.jewishpeacefellowship.org.

10. Dick Foster, "From Tragedy, A Mission: Mother of Young Man Who Killed Priests, Warns of Crisis in Mental Health Care," *Rocky Mountain News* (Denver, Colo.), 4 August 1997, p. 8A.

11. Arianna Huffington, *The Fourth Instinct* (New York: Simon and Schuster, 1994), 99.

12. Judi Neal, interview with author, 31 July 1998.

Chapter 10: *The Hungry Heart: Following Your Heart's Desires*

1. 1998 Nobel Peace Laureates Conference Web site: www.virginia.edu/nobel/laureates.

2. Maya Angelou, quoted on the *Oprah Winfrey Show*.

3. Thomas Aquinas, quoted by Matthew Fox (Omega Institute/New Age Journal, Body and Soul Conference, Boulder, Colo., 12 July 1997).

4. Naomi Judd, interview with author, 13 May 1996.

5. Julia Cameron, keynote address at the NAPRA Gala Authors Breakfast (Book Expo, Chicago, Ill., June 1997).

6. Jelaluddin Rumi, quoted in Jonathan Cott, "Deepak Chopra: God, Man and the Media," *Rolling Stone*, 18 September 2000, 47.

7. Cameron keynote, Book Expo, June 1997.

8. David Whyte, interview with author, 10 July 1998.

9. Lloyd Thomas, "If You Fight for Your Life, Chances Are You'll Succeed," *Coloradoan*, 16 November 2000, p. B7.

10. Kelly Milner Halls, "'Pay It Forward' Comes from Writer's Heart," *Denver Post*, 29 October 2000, p. 3.

11. Rabindranath Tagore, quoted in Tian Dayton, *It's My Life* (Deerfield Beach, Fla.: Health Communications, 2000), 35.

12. Ardath Rodale, interview with author, 2 July 1998.

13. Ellen Abell, interview with author, 9 November 2000.

Chapter 11: *Heart Activism: Reinventing Institutions with Love*

1. Bill Deedes, quoted in Mario Testino, "Diana Reborn," *Vanity Fair*, July 1997, 70.

2. Helen Keller quoted on Web site: www.womenshistory.about.com.

3. Marian Wright Edelman, quoted in Susan Skog *Embracing Our Essence* (Deerfield Beach, Fla.: Health Communications, 1995), 30.

4. Robert Kennedy, quoted in Marianne Williamson, *The Healing of America* (New York: Simon and Schuster, 1997), 124.

5. Corinne McLaughlin and Gordon Davidson, *Spiritual Politics: Changing the World from the Inside Out* (New York: Ballantine, 1994), 27.

6. Peggy Marengo, interviews with author, 15 October 1998, 3 March 1999, and 22 October 2000.

7. From Gospel of Thomas at Web site: www.dhushara.com.

8. *Oprah Winfrey Show*.

9. Parker Palmer, quoted in Paul Rogat Loeb, *Soul of a Citizen* (New York: St. Martin's Griffin, 1999), 24.

10. Ardath Rodale, "Living Lessons from the Pattern That Connects Us All," speech at Embracing Our Essence Conference (Denver, Colo., 7 June 1996).

11. Troy Bridges, correspondence with author, October–December 2000.

12. Anonymous source.

13. David Tarrant, "A Woman of Independent Means Puts Her Diplomatic Skills to Work," *Dallas Morning News*, 15 December 1996, sec. E, p. 1.

14. Elizabeth Barrett Browning, from the poem "Aurora Leigh," Columbia Granger's World of Poetry Web site: www.columbiagrangers.org.

15. Oprah Winfrey, "Oprah Talks to Maya Angelou," *O Magazine*, December 2000, 156.

16. Peggy Marengo, interviews with author, 15 October 1998, 3 March 1999, and 22 October 2000.

17. Saint John of the Cross, quoted in Sophy Burnham, *The Ecstatic Journey* (New York: Ballantine, 1994), 33.

Chapter 12: Conclusion: A Vision of the New World

1. Emmy Lou Harris, quoted in Roger Shriver, "Changing the World One Heart at a Time," *E-Gear*, Spring 2000, 36.

2. Compassion/kindness quotes on Quotes for Peace Web site: members.aol.com/pforpeace/quote5.htm.

3. Gregory Plotnikoff, M.D., "Should Medicine Reach Out to the Spirit?" *Postgraduate Medicine*, November 2000, 19.

4. Joan Borysenko Web site: www.joanborysenko.com.

5. Ibid.

6. Troy Bridges, correspondence with author, October–December 2000.

Interviews

Ellen Abell
Richard Barrett
Troy Bridges
Ann Careau
Robin Casarjian
Jason Crowe
Dinah Eng
Carla Frenzel
Janine Geske
James Gordon, M.D.
Kathryn Guta
Swanee Hunt
Priscilla Huston
Elisabeth Kübler-Ross, M.D.
Mildred Lee
Stephen Levine
Mariah Mannia
Peggy Marengo
Don Marxhausen
Carol McDonald
Kenny Moore
Judi Neal
Gregory Plotnikoff, M.D.
Bill Powanda

Christina Puchalski, M.D.
Ardath Rodale
Elana Rosenbaum
Bailey Stenson
Nicole Tembrock
Sue Patton Thoele
Jon Wheeler
David Whyte

Recommended Reading

Borysenko, Joan. *A Woman's Book of Life: The Biology, Psychology, and Spirituality of the Feminine Life Cycle*. New York: Riverhead Books, 1998.

Casarjian, Robin. *Houses of Healing: A Prisoner's Guide to Inner Power and Freedom*. Boston: Lionheart Press, 1995.

Childre, Doc Lew, Howard Martin, Donna Beech. *The HeartMath Solution: The Institute of HeartMath's Revolutionary Program for Engaging the Power of the Heart's Intelligence*. San Francisco: Harper San Francisco, 2000.

His Holiness the Dalai Lama. *Transforming the Mind: Teachings on Generating Compassion*. London: Thorsons, 2000.

Durban, Robert, ed. *Seeds of Hope: A Henri Nouwen Reader*. New York: Doubleday, 1989.

Fox, Matthew. *A Spirituality Named Compassion*. Rochester, Vt.: Inner Traditions, 1979.

Keen, Sam. *To Love and Be Loved*. New York: Bantam Books, 1999.

Levine, Stephen. *Who Dies: An Investigation of Conscious Living and Conscious Dying*. New York: Anchor Books, 1982.

Lewis, Thomas, Fari Amini, Richard Lannon. *A General Theory of Love*. New York: Random House, 2000.

Loeb, Paul Rogat. *Soul of a Citizen: Living with Conviction in a Cynical Time*. New York: St. Martin's Griffin, 1999.

Pearsall, Paul. *The Heart's Code: Tapping the Wisdom and Power of Our Heart Energy: The New Findings About Cellular Memories and Their Role in the Mind/Body/Spirit*. New York: Broadway Books, 1999.

Pipher, Mary. *In the Shelter of Each Other: Rebuilding Our Families*. New York: Putnam, 1996.

Salzberg, Sharon. *A Heart as Wide as the World: Stories on the Path of Lovingkindness*. New York: Random House, 1999.

Shore, Bill. *Revolution of the Heart*. New York: Riverhead Books, 1995.

Skog, Susan. *Embracing Our Essence: Spiritual Conversations with Prominent Women*. Deerfield Beach, Fla.: Health Communications, 1995.

Stoddard, Alexandra. *Living in Love*. New York: William Morrow, 1997.

Thoele, Sue Patton. *Heart Centered Marriage: Fulfilling Our Natural Desire for Sacred Partnership*. Berkeley, Calif.: Conari Press, 1996.

Williamson, Marianne. *Enchanted Love: The Mystical Power of Intimate Relationships*. New York: Simon and Schuster, 1999.

———. *The Healing of America*. New York: Simon and Schuster, 1997.

Resources

Joan Borysenko
Mind-Body Health Sciences, Inc.
393 Dixon Road
Boulder, CO 80302
(303) 440-8460
www.joanborysenko.com

Robyn Michelle Dolgin
Essential EnerCh'I
Feng Shui for Home, Body,
    and Garden
116 N. Washington Ave.
Fort Collins, CO 80521
(970) 498-4074

Dr. Gregory Plotnikoff
Center for Spirituality and Healing
University of Minnesota
C593 Mayo Memorial Building
420 Delaware Street SE
Minneapolis, MN 55455
(612) 624-9459

David Whyte
Many Rivers Co.
P.O. Box 868
Langley, WA 98260
(360) 221-1324
www.davidwhyte.com

National Institute for Healthcare
    Research
Dr. Christina Puchalski, Editor
Faith and Medicine Connection
6110 Executive Blvd., Suite 908
Rockville, MD 20852
(301) 231-7711
www.nihr.org

Dr. Martin Rossman
Academy for Guided Imagery
P.O. Box 2070
Mill Valley, CA 94941
(415) 389-9325

Judi Neal
Center for Spirit at Work
36 Sylvan Hills Road
East Haven, CT 06513
(203) 467-9084
www.spiritatwork.com

Institute of HeartMath
14700 West Park Avenue
Boulder Creek, CA 95006
(831) 338-8500
www.heartmath.org

Dr. James Gordon
Center for Mind-Body Medicine
5225 Connecticut Avenue NW
   Suite 414
Washington, D.C. 20015
(202) 966-7338
www.cmbm.org

Ardath Rodale
Rodale Press
33 East Minor Street
Emmaus, PA 18098-0099
(610) 967-5171
www.rodalepress.com

Project Pave
2051 York Street
Denver, CO 80205
(303) 322-2382

Robin Casarjian
Lionheart Foundation
P.O. Box 194
Back Bay Boston, MA 02117
(617) 267-3121
www.lionheart.org

Mariah Mannia
Depression Wellness Network
9500 Roosevelt Way NE #302
Seattle, WA 98115
(206) 528-9975
www.depressionwellness.net

Jason Crowe, CEO
The Cello Cries On, Inc.
P.O. Box 441
Newburgh, IN 47629-0441

Richard Barrett
Richard Barrett & Associates LLC
1104 Oxner Cove Road
Waynesville, NC 28786
(828) 452-5050
www.corptools.com

About the Author

Susan Skog is the author of *Embracing Our Essence: Spiritual Conversations with Prominent Women*, *ABCs for Living*, and *Depression: What Your Body's Trying to Tell You*.

Trained as a journalist, her science and health writing has appeared in numerous national magazines, ranging from *Science* to *Newsweek* to *Healthy Living*. She has interviewed and profiled many of today's prominent spiritual authors and teachers. She lives in Fort Collins, Colorado, with her husband and two sons.

Have you been touched by a radical act of love? Are you working to transform your part of the culture with compassion and kindness? Susan Skog continues to gather stories of heart activists working to bring compassion to medicine, business, education, science, and public policy. If you have a story you'd like to share, please send it to Susan Skog's e-mail address: sjskog@hotmail.com.

Hazelden Transitions is an initiative between Hazelden Foundation's Information and Educational Services division and Transitions Bookplace, Inc.

Hazelden Information and Educational Services helps individuals, families, and communities prevent and/or recover from alcoholism, drug addiction, and other related diseases and conditions. We do this by partnering with authors and other experts to deliver information and educational products and services that customers use to aid their personal growth and change, leading along a wholistic pathway of hope, health, and abundant living. We are fortunate to be recognized by both professionals and consumers as the leading international center of resources in these areas.

Transitions Bookplace, Inc., founded in Chicago, Illinois, in 1989, has become the nation's leading independent bookseller dedicated to customers seeking personal growth and development. Customers can choose from more than thirty thousand books, videos, pamphlets, and musical selections. Authors appear frequently for special events or workshops in the Transitions Learning Center. Also available in the store is a legendary collection of exquisite international gifts celebrating body, mind, and spirit.

This Hazelden Transitions Bookplace initiative is dedicated to all brave souls who seek to change courses in their lives, their families, and their communities in order to achieve hope, health, and abundant living.

Transitions Bookplace
1000 West North Avenue
Chicago, IL 60622
312-951-READ
800-979-READ
www.transitionsbookplace.com

Hazelden Information and Educational Services
15251 Pleasant Valley Road
Center City, MN 55012-0176
800-328-9000
www.hazelden.org